International Handbook of Chlamydia
2nd Edition

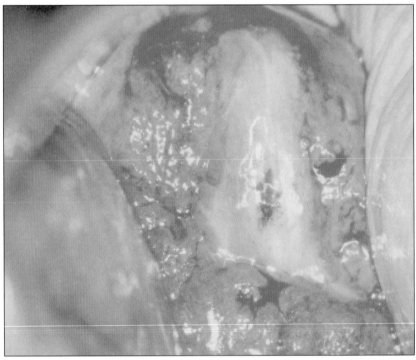

Colposcopic photograph of cervix cleaned with cotton wool demonstrating acute haemorrhagic chlamydial cervicitis. Presenting symptoms:- post coital/intermenstrual bleeding.

International Handbook of *Chlamydia*

2nd Edition

Edited by

Dr TR Moss

*Doncaster and Bassetlaw Hospitals
NHS Foundation Trust,
Doncaster, England*

Acknowledgement
The editor would like to thank Mrs Joan Pleasance
for her continued patience and professionalism.

Printed in the United Kingdom by Alden Press, UK

Contents

Foreword

In recent years bacterial sexually transmitted diseases (STDs) have been overshadowed by the growing epidemic of viral STDs, in particular HIV. In addition, the declining prevalence of some bacterial infections in the last 20 years may have suggested that these agents were diseases of the past, of diminishing importance and of limited interest outside specialist care. This has never been the case with chlamydial genital infections and it is timely that we should review their importance, particularly in the light of recent developments.

Following the isolation of *Chlamydia trachomatis* from genital secretions in the late 1950s the importance of particular serovars has been increasingly recognised. Early work identified *C. trachomatis* as the cause of much symptomatic genital disease and as the putative cause of fallopian tube disease through both direct and indirect mechanisms. Key work in the seventies identified genital *C. trachomatis* as the likely cause of most secondary infertility in the developed world – emphasising the importance of establishing its control as a public health goal. Making the arguments for this and demonstrating the benefits of a major screening and treatment programme for this agent has not been easy.

Epidemiological work, initially within Sexually Transmitted Disease Clinics, has shown that most *C. trachomatis* infection is silent in both females and males. Work outside these settings in the community has confirmed this finding showing high levels of prevalence of silent infection in women, particularly in higher risk groups. Interventions targeted at identifying and treating infection in some of these groups alone has led to a limited level of success in the prevention of early complications of missed infection. However, the prevalence of chlamydia within the community has shown no decline. It would therefore appear that genital *C. trachomatis* infection is hyperendic in the developed world, and that limited interventions within high-risk groups will not lead to its control. The challenge in recent years has been to show that a comprehensive screening programme is practical, acceptable to patients and cost-effective.

A number of health providers had already acted before such data were available and their experience has helped alert us to decisions we may now be faced with. Mass opportunistic testing and treatment programmes in Northern Europe have demonstrated that regular investigation of sexually active women was indeed followed initially by a reduction in chlamydial prevalence. Such early programmes utilised sample collection and processing methodologies that were far from perfect but despite these weaknesses considerable progress has been made in controlling chlamydial disease. This reduction was accompanied by a much larger decline in tubal disease within these countries. Such indirect evidence offered support to the concept that intervention programmes are cost effective. However, these ecological studies have recently come under considerable scrutiny and criticism. The longer term re-emergence of high rates of chlamydial infection within these countries despite sustained levels of testing has led some to question the evidence for control strategies based on opportunistic testing.

Randomised control trials of short term screening programmes have provided clear evidence of benefit in small populations. Healthcare providers in North America and Europe have instigated controlled intervention studies of screening and treatment for chlamydial infections. These projects have looked in detail at the differing expenses of managing chlamydial disease. The majority of the expenses within screening programmes are the costs in clinical time in gathering specimens and initiating contact tracing. Even so, cost benefit-analyses have clearly shown that screening and effective treatment are cost effective within managed healthcare systems.

Modelling of different screening strategies demonstrates that the final set point for chlamydial prevalence after a number of years of implementation is a function of the sensitivity of a screening test, its take up and the chosen re-screening interval. The recent development of new, non-invasive, highly sensitive, molecular technology-based methods for chlamydial identification have been extensively piloted. These tests can use patient gathered samples such as urine. The exact place of these tests and the feasibility of their usage is yet to be clearly established. However, preliminary results from pilot community-based screening projects are highly encouraging showing that these methods are practical, acceptable to patients and yield levels of chlamydial infection similar to those in STD clinic attendees. Follow-up studies showing high re-infection rates have generated debate as to the appropriate screening interval for those at high risk, the role of screening men and the place of active contact tracing. Current investment in screening for *C. trachomatis* genital tract infection has resulted in two chapters on this subject in the second edition of this book.

Contact tracing of partners has always been a central pillar of STD management and control. A debate is currently taking place as to whether a traditional approach of contact tracing is possible if extensive screening programmes are initiated. The international experience suggests that some of the responsibility may be passed to primary care – however this may not be appropriate in all settings and the results of different strategies of contact tracing, having been trialled within pilot programmes in the UK suggest that levels of success are closely linked to operational structures.

A number of infectious agents have recently been identified as key to the development and maintenance of chronic medical conditions. There has been considerable interest in the role of both *Chlamydia pneumoniae* and CMV in the development of atherosclerosis. Although early antibiotic intervention studies have been disappointing, interest in *C. pneumoniae* as a cofactor for cardiovascular disease is still being actively researched and debated.

Great progress was made during the late 20th century in decreasing the tragedy of avoidable blindness following trachoma. Whilst the International Handbook has concentrated on human genital infection with *C. trachomatis* the exciting developments in morbidity due to, or possibly resulting from other chlamydial agents has clearly justified specific chapters relating to non-genital chlamydial disease.

The severe scarring and fibrosis of blinding trachoma clearly demonstrate the end stage of chronic recurrent chlamydial pathology. The immunopathological processes involved are analogous to chlamydial destruction of the female genital tract. Perhaps in the future we may aspire to the 'global elimination' of genital chlamydial infection?

The objective of this text has been to increase knowledge, awareness and understanding of disease due to chlamydial pathogens. It has also been intended to promote a wider debate and to provoke argument when incomplete understanding clearly exists. As in 2001, hypothesis, future speculation and controversy have been encouraged rather than avoided. After a further four years of successful research, we still have much to learn.

Dr Raj Patel
Department of Genito Urinary Medicine,
Royal South Hants Hospital, Southampton, UK

Preface

It is now six years since discussion of new diagnostic techniques in the identification and management of human genital chlamydial infections took place with colleagues in microbiology at Doncaster Royal Infirmary. A wholly unexpected outcome of this meeting was the preparation of a monograph covering clinical and diagnostic aspects of chlamydial infection.

The first edition of the International Handbook of Chlamydia was published in 2001. Interest, demand and distribution exceeded all expectation.

I had been appointed to the Department of Genito Urinary Medicine in 1980 with the primary objective of developing a clinical diagnostic service to identify genital chlamydial infections. Due to the skill, expertise and dedication of the late Stephen Riddington, not only did we rapidly establish a highly effective culture-based chlamydia diagnostic facility, but the number and increase in diagnoses led to the inescapable conclusion that twenty five years ago we were dealing with a Public Health problem of enormous size and significance.

Since that time we have applied the diagnostic technology of three generations of chlamydia testing systems and our ability to detect early cases of chlamydial disease has been greatly enhanced by the introduction of nucleic acid amplification technology.

Genito urinary physicians have long been outspoken in their advocacy for improved chlamydia diagnostic and management facilities.

The scientific progress, advances in understanding of chlamydial pathophysiology and awareness of very worrying changes in epidemiology, together with a far greater awareness of chlamydial infection in the UK population has been enhanced by a willingness amongst our patients to discuss issues of sexually transmitted infection openly in the media. Such discussion is courageous and altruistic, as it is evidently intended to try to prevent or limit the increasing numbers of those women whose reproductive function is avoidably lost.

In the United Kingdom cases of chlamydia have trebled during the last ten years. Each year at least three quarters of a million people are presenting to Genito Urinary Medicine Departments in England alone. This clinical demand will continue to increase. The forthcoming Sexual Health Awareness campaign (the first for some twenty years), is applauded, but will challenge the availability of clinical services to meet patient needs.

During twenty five years of "Clinical Chlamydiology" we have moved from an ill-advised suggestion that chlamydia was "a harmless commensal" to the National Chlamydia Screening Programme.

For all of these reasons I was pleased to be offered the opportunity to edit this second edition of the International Handbook, which has been extensively revised and expanded.

The advent of the Chlamydia Screening Programme merits two chapters. The emergence of lymphogranuloma venereum in the UK could not be ignored. Chapters on non-genital tract chlamydial infection are included to widen the readers' awareness of the complexity, chronicity and long-term implications of other human chlamydial diseases. A revised chapter on pelvic pain is intended to help clinicians with the difficulties of differential diagnosis.

The increasing awareness of subacute, chronic and latent disease is further considered. It is an uncomfortable concept that in 2006 we have no reliable, reproducible, scientifically valid and clinically accurate means of differentiating between complicated and uncomplicated genital chlamydia infections.

At the time of completion of this edition the tragedy of chlamydial infertility and some of the reasons for the continued chlamydia epidemic have been highlighted by a respected UK television documentary. There can be few who watched this programme that would not empathise with the suffering caused by pelvic chlamydial dissemination, and feel a sense of futility regarding our limitations in avoiding this preventable situation.

It merits re-stating that women still die from the complications of genital chlamydial disease via ruptured ectopic pregnancy, and that such deaths occur in all developed healthcare systems. The cost (in terms of individual suffering to women) of a lifetime of pelvic pain, infertility and sexual debility is profound; as is the suffering of their partners. The enormous avoidable financial costs to health service provision have led to further and welcome investment in clinical services in the United Kingdom. Scientifically progress has exceeded expectation. Clinically we can and must do better in the twenty first century to contain the expanding chlamydial epidemic, and prevent its mutilating complications.

Dr T R Moss
Consultant Physician/Clinical Director
Genito Urinary Medicine, Doncaster and Bassetlaw Hospitals NHS
Foundation Trust, Doncaster, UK

CHAPTER 1

Epidemiology of Chlamydia trachomatis

Ian Simms
Health Protection Agency Centre for Infections, London, UK

INTRODUCTION

Chlamydia trachomatis is a bacterial infection of global public health significance. It is associated with trachoma (serovars A, B, B_1 and C), genital infection (serovars D to K), and lymphogranuloma venereum (LGV) (serovars L_1, L_2 and L_3). Trachoma, LGV and genital *C. trachomatis* infection pose contrasting public health challenges. Trachoma, a fomite, was a leading cause of blindness in Europe but disappeared during the early twentieth century, eliminated as much by improved personal hygiene, sanitation and reduced housing occupancy as improved intervention. Worldwide trachoma is the third commonest cause of blindness after cataract and glaucoma, and affects 150 million people, of whom 6 million are blind. *C. trachomatis* is easily treated and the World Health Organisation (WHO) aims to eliminate trachoma blindness by 2020 although, since it is a disease of poverty, this is dependent on economic growth as well as improved healthcare. Chlamydial ophthalmia neonatorum and adult chlamydial eye infections, resulting from autoinoculation with genital secretions, still occur in Europe but are self-limiting and never progress to trachoma. In contrast, genital *C. trachomatis* infection and LGV will not be eliminated in the foreseeable future since both are sexually transmitted infections (STI) with complex epidemiologies. The WHO estimates that 89 million new cases of genital *C. trachomatis* infection occur each year (**Table 1**)[1]. Genital *C. trachomatis* infection can cause pelvic inflammatory disease (PID) and represents a major public health problem to the reproductive health of women in developed and developing countries. This

Table 1. Estimated number of new cases, prevalence and incidence of genital *C. trachomatis* infection between ages 15 and 49, by sex and United Nation global region: 1995[1]

Region	New cases (million)		Prevalence (%)		Incidence (per 1000)	
	Males	Females	Males	Females	Males	Females
North America	1.64	2.34	0.8	2.7	21.46	30.73
Western Europe	2.30	3.20	0.8	2.7	21.46	30.73
Australasia	0.12	0.17	0.8	2.7	21.46	30.73
Latin America & Caribbean	5.01	5.12	2.5	4.0	40.03	40.77
Sub-Saharan Africa	6.96	8.44	4.8	7.1	55.04	65.95
North Africa & Middle East	1.67	1.28	1.2	1.7	19.93	16.29
Eastern Europe & Central Asia	2.15	2.92	1.7	3.7	27.29	37.09
East Asia & Pacific	2.70	2.63	0.4	0.7	6.53	6.75
South & South East Asia	20.20	20.28	3.7	4.9	41.65	44.32
Overall	42.75	46.38	–	–	–	–

chapter focuses on the epidemiology of genital *C. trachomatis* infection and recent developments in the epidemiology of LGV.

Chlamydial research has been guided by advances in diagnostic techniques. Cheap diagnostic tests with good specificity and sensitivity became available in the mid-1980s, and clinical and epidemiological studies quickly established the importance of genital *C. trachomatis* infection and associated sequelae. Chlamydial research continues to be guided by developments in diagnostic methods. Molecular techniques have been applied to chlamydial diagnostic tests that combine ease of collection and transport, with high sensitivity and specificity. Self obtained vaginal and vulval swabs or non-invasive specimens, such as urine, can be collected in non-clinical settings and this has increased patient acceptability and flexibility in study design. Multiplex testing, the simultaneous amplification of several pathogens offers low cost testing, and the ability to investigate concurrent infections. Behavioural research has also evolved. Computer assisted data capture offers increased response rates and improved disclosure of sensitive sexual behaviours.

PREVALENCE, INCIDENCE AND DISEASE BURDEN

Geographically, the majority of genital *C. trachomatis* infections are found in the developing world reflecting provision and access to healthcare, health seeking behaviour and the global population distribution (**Table 1**). Highest prevalences are in sub-Saharan Africa, lowest in East Asia and the Pacific. Although these estimates illustrate the global importance of genital *C. trachomatis* infection, they are biased due to the quality and quantity of the available surveillance data. Many countries do not have national surveillance data and, where prevalence studies have been undertaken, these have generally been derived from high risk groups, such as sexually transmitted disease (STD) clinic attenders. A further source of bias is the high level of asymptomatic infection: up to 70% of infections in women and 50% of infections in men are asymptomatic; a pool of asymptomatic infection that is unlikely to be represented in surveillance datasets.

Genital *C. trachomatis* infection is of public health importance because it can lead to PID. PID can be caused by genital mycoplasmas, such as *Mycoplasma genitalium*, endogenous vaginal flora (anaerobic and aerobic bacteria), aerobic streptococci, and STIs such as *C. trachomatis* or *Neisseria gonorrhoeae*. The dominant cause of PID in developed countries is considered to be genital *C. trachomatis* infection. Between 10% and 40% of *C. trachomatis* cases develop PID[2]. Sequelae of PID include ectopic pregnancy, tubal factor infertility (TFI) and chronic pelvic pain, PID has also been associated with increased risk of ovarian cancer[3,4]. The risk of developing sequelae is dependent on the number of PID episodes: the risk of ectopic pregnancy and infertility increases after one PID episode (odds ratio=6) and again after two episodes (OR=17)[5]. Infertility related to genital *C. trachomatis* infection is of public health importance in sub-Saharan Africa and the treatment of infection and associated sequelae absorb a sizeable part of healthcare resources in developing countries. In developed countries costs have increased substantially since the development of assisted reproduction techniques, such as *in vitro* fertilisation. In 1992, the cost of a subfertility service in one health district in England and Wales with a population of 46,000 women aged 20 to 44 years were estimated to be £0.88 million, a national total of £75 million[6]. Of this cost, 20% (£14 million) was likely to be associated with genital *C. trachomatis* infection and could have been prevented. PID accounts for 94% of morbidity in women associated with STIs (including HIV) in established market economies. Indeed, the burden of PID among women, measured in terms of disability adjusted life years, was higher than the burden of disease associated with HIV among men. In terms of economic cost, both PID and its sequelae are expensive to individuals, healthcare services and economies. In the USA, direct and indirect costs associated with

PID and its sequelae were projected to exceed $10 billion by the year 2000[7]. However, these studies may be inaccurate as the incidence and prevalence of PID are unknown.

Surveillance information is now available for countries in Europe, North America and the developing world, data that have been used as an evidence base for clinical practice, public health action, and control and intervention strategies. However, few have collected data for more than a decade and, where available these data are usually restricted to laboratory reports or attendances at STD clinics. Trends should be interpreted with caution as they are influenced by changes in testing policy, clinical practice, the accuracy of diagnostic tests, access to healthcare, and the prevalence of asymptomatic infection. In addition, the limited number of parameters collected restricts interpretation. For example, in England and Wales episodes of *C. trachomatis* seen in STD clinics have been collected since 1988, but the dataset only includes aggregate information on gender, age group and geographic location. Consequently the data can only be used to show broad trends (**Figure 1**). The increases seen over the past decade probably reflect increased public and professional awareness of genital *C. trachomatis* infection and increased testing. Systems need to be developed to meet the need for detailed, timely surveillance data. It is necessary to collect data on sexual behaviour, demography, microbiology and sexual ill-health.

Studies in various clinical settings have been undertaken to investigate the prevalence of infection, evaluate testing methodologies and assess service delivery. In England and Wales, studies carried out in selected population groups indicate prevalences of 2% to 12%: high prevalences were seen in attenders at STD and termination of pregnancy (TOP) clinics, lower prevalences in primary care. Studies have generally been based on small numbers, confined to healthcare attender populations and have included a wide range of sampling and testing methodologies. The National Survey of Sexual Attitudes and Lifestyles (NATSSAL) 2000/01, a stratified probability sample survey of 11,161 men and women aged 16 to 44 years in the UK, included an assessment of the prevalence of *C. trachomatis* infection as well as associated demographic and behavioural risk factors[8]. *C. trachomatis* was found in 2.2% (95% CI 1.5-3.2) of men and 1.5% (95% CI 1.11-2.14) of women. Suggested rates for incidence and re-infection range from 3 to 34 per 100 person years for incidence and 4 to 51/100 person years for re-infection, rates being highest in those aged under 25 years[9-12]. However, limitations in study design, make the measurement and comparison of incidence and re-infection rates difficult.

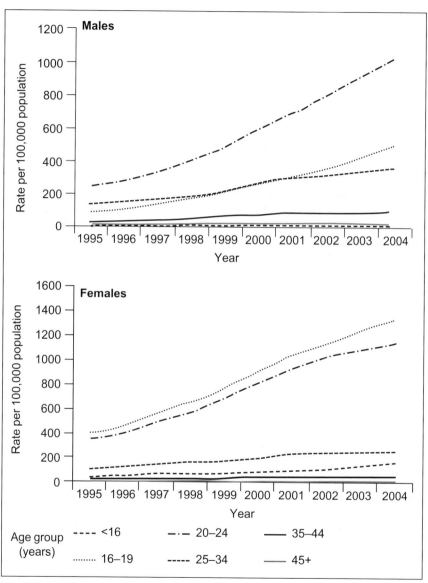

Figure 1. Rate of uncomplicated genital chlamydial infection by sex and age group, United Kingdom: 1995 to 2004

WHO IS AT RISK?

Risk factor studies can identify population subgroups at increased risk of genital *C. trachomatis* infection, and used to initiate timely, effective, intervention and help formulate health education strategies. Aspects of sexual behaviour, such as age at first sexual intercourse, number of lifetime sexual partners, frequency of partner change and unprotected sex, are key determinants of transmission. Age at first sexual intercourse and the number of lifetime sexual partners are known to vary with marital status, cohabitation and socio-economic group. Young people are vulnerable to STI acquisition as they generally have higher numbers of sexual partners and a higher frequency of partner change than older age groups. In addition, young people may be at particular risk of re-infection as they may not have the skills and confidence to negotiate safer sex[13]. These factors are reflected in the high chlamydial incidence seen in the 16 to 24 year age group (**Figure 1**). Studies on specific populations have shown that factors such as being unmarried, the use of non-barrier contraception (or no contraception), a higher frequency of partner change, having concurrent partners and lower socio-economic status are associated with higher chlamydial incidence.

A large number of risk factor studies have been published from various countries, but invariably these have been undertaken in specific clinical settings and are insufficient to allow detailed analyses. The relationship between sexual behaviour and STI prevalence has been little studied in general population samples. Sexual behaviour varies between societies, individuals and during an individuals lifetime. The interaction between the core group (people who have large numbers of sexual partners, concurrent partners and frequent partner change) and the rest of the population is important to STI transmission. The investigation of sexual networks, the basis of interactions between the core and the rest of the population is a key area of research. Behavioural, demographic and morbidity surveillance at the individual level provides more precise estimates of risk factors associated with genital *C. trachomatis* infection. The NATSSAL 2000/01 survey included an extensive range of data on partnerships, sexual practice, condom use, sexuality and risk reduction practices[8]. Results from the survey showed that non-married status, age, and reporting partner concurrency or two or more sexual partners in the past year were independently associated with infection with *C. trachomatis*. Age-specific prevalence was highest among men aged 25-34 (3.1%) and women aged 16-24 years (3.0%).

EPIDEMIOLOGY OF PELVIC INFLAMMATORY DISEASE (PID)

Little is known of PID epidemiology: the burden of disease and associated risk factors are poorly understood. Although a substantial burden of PID is thought to exist in many countries, an estimated prevalence of 1.7% is seen in reproductive age women in England and Wales, surveillance data are only available for a few European countries[14]. Epidemics of *C. trachomatis* and *N. gonorrhoeae* are followed by secondary PID epidemics and tertiary epidemics of ectopic pregnancy and tubal infertility, a pattern that has been seen in European countries[15,16].

Risk factors for PID development are closely associated with those of STI acquisition. High rates seen in women aged 16 to 24 years may reflect longer duration of chlamydial infection or reduced clearance of chlamydial infection in younger women. This could be due to increased host susceptibility, such as a lower concentration of protective chlamydial antibodies, larger cervical ectopy, and greater permeability of cervical mucus than in older age groups. IUD insertion and TOP have been associated with iatrogenic PID, which occurs when instrumentation facilitates the introduction of vaginal and cervical micro-organisms into the endometrial cavity. Factors that influence PID epidemiology, such as healthcare provision, health seeking behaviour, sexual behaviour, contraceptive practice and disease ætiology, vary between countries and over time. For example, douching which has been associated with PID in the USA is only reported by 0.25% of women in the UK. The increased risk of PID associated with TOP described previously has not been seen in recent studies, probably because of the widespread use of antibiotic prophylaxis in the management of TOP.

THE RE-EMERGENCE OF LYMPHOGRANULOMA VENEREUM (LGV)

LGV is endemic to areas of Africa, Asia, South America and the Caribbean, and has been rare in Western Europe for many years. However, a series of outbreaks (that is a greater than expected number of cases over a defined time period) of LGV in western Europe were reported during 2003/4. A cluster of cases was reported in men who have sex with men (MSM) in Rotterdam was identified in 2004[17,18]. By 1st September 2004, 92 cases had been confirmed, many of whom had had multiple sexual contacts (**Figure 2**). Outbreaks in

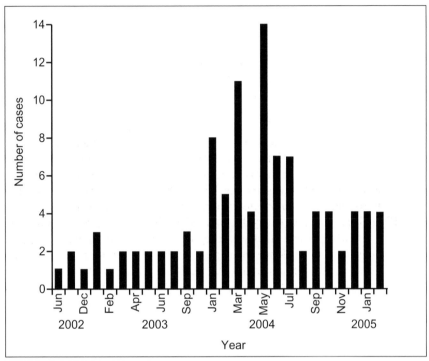

Figure 2. Cases of lymphogranuloma venereum, Netherlands: June 2002 to February 2005.

Antwerp, Paris and London were then reported together with cases in Stockholm and Hamburg[19-23]. The outbreaks have been concentrated in sexual networks of MSM in large cities. High levels of concurrent infection with HIV, gonorrhoea, syphilis, hepatitis B (HBV), genital herpes, and hepatitis C (HCV) were also reported. Cases have been of the L_2 serovar and reported multiple anonymous sexual contacts.

CONTROL AND INTERVENTION

Knowledge of disease epidemiology is central to effective, efficient and sustainable intervention. Primary prevention, based on education and behavioural change, is fundamental to disease control. Behavioural change, such as the increased use of barrier contraception and delayed sexual debut, in response to HIV and STI health campaigns has been documented in European countries and some have been associated with reduced incidence of symptomatic PID[24,25]. However, the major obstacle to primary prevention is a low awareness of PID amongst healthcare professionals and the public. Secondary prevention, or the diagnosis and treatment of asymptomatic infection, has been successful in reducing both the prevalence of genital *C. trachomatis* infection and PID. The two randomised controlled trials that have looked at the effectiveness of genital chlamydial screening amongst asymptomatic women indicated that decreases in the prevalence of genital *C. trachomatis* infection were associated with a 50% reduction in the incidence of PID after 12 months of screening[26,27]. In the USA, intervention based on screening for genital *C. trachomatis* infection has also reduced the incidence of PID and ectopic pregnancy by more than 50% and 20% respectively[28]. Swedish data also indicate that screening for genital *C. trachomatis* infection rapidly reduces the incidence of ectopic pregnancy amongst 20 to 24 year olds[29]. No study has demonstrated that genital *C. trachomatis* screening can reduce the prevalence of tubal factor infertility. Economic analyses have demonstrated the cost-benefits and cost-effectiveness of screening for genital chlamydial infection[30].

CONCLUSIONS

Genital *C. trachomatis* infection is a key global issue facing reproductive health. This is a rapidly expanding area of research but for many countries the available data do not provide an accurate view of the epidemiology of either genital *C. trachomatis* infection or sequelae. This prevents a true realisation of the burden of reproductive morbidity and represents a gap in our knowledge of STI epidemiology. Epidemiological research is a continuous process that requires the routine collection of behavioural, demographic and laboratory data tailored to the public health needs and priorities. However, despite developments in research, we are only just beginning to comprehend the public health impact of this important infection.

Acknowledgements
I would like to thank Dr Marita van de Laar for permission to reproduce the Dutch LGV data, and Mr Neil Macdonald for commenting on the text.

REFERENCES

1. Gerbase A, Rowley J, Heymann D, *et al.* Global prevalence and incidence estimates of selected curable STDs. *Sex Transm Inf* 1998; **74:** S12–4.
2. Stamm W, Guinan M, Johnson C, *et al.* Effect of treatment regimens for *Neisseria gonorrhoeae* on simultaneous infection with *Chlamydia trachomatis*. *N Engl J Med* 1984; **310:** 545–9.
3. Buchan H, Vessey M, Goldacre M, Fairweather J. Morbidity following pelvic inflammatory disease. *Br J Obstet Gynaecol* 1993; **100:** 558–562.
4. Risch H, Howe G. Pelvic inflammatory disease and the risk of epithelial ovarian cancer. *Cancer Epidemiol Biomarkers Prev* 1995; **4:** 447–451.
5. Weström L. Sexually Transmitted Diseases and Infertility. *Sex Transm Dis* 1994; **21:** S32–7.
6. School of Public Health UoL. Effective healthcare: The Management of Subfertility. Leeds University of Leeds 1992.
7. Washington A, Katz P. Cost of and payment source for pelvic inflammatory disease. *JAMA* 1991; **226:** 2565–9.
8. Fenton KA, Korovessis C, Johnson AM, *et al.* Sexual behaviour in Britain: reported sexually transmitted infections and prevalent genital *Chlamydia trachomatis* infection. *Lancet* 2001; **358:** 1851–4.
9. Orr P, Sherman E, Blanchard J, *et al.* Epidemiology of infection due to *Chlamydia trachomatis* in Manitoba, Canada. *Clin Infect Dis* 1994; **19:** 876–83.
10. Burstein GR, Gaydos CA, Diener-West M, *et al.* Incident *Chlamydia trachomatis* infection among inner-city adolescent females. *JAMA* 1998; **280:** 521–6.
11. Hillis SD, Nakashima A, Marchbanks PA, *et al.* Risk factors for recurrent *Chlamydia trachomatis* infections in women. *Am J Obstet Gynecol* 1994; **170**(3): 801–6.
12. Richey CM, Macaluso M, Hook EW. Determinants of reinfection with *Chlamydia trachomatis*. *Sex Transm Dis* 1999; **26:** 4–11.
13. Lear D. Sexual communication in the age of AIDS: the construction of risk and trust among young adults. *Soc Sci Med* 1995; **41:** 1311–23.
14. Simms I, Rogers PA, Charlett A. The rate of diagnosis of Pelvic Inflammatory Disease in general practice: England and Wales. *Int J STD AIDS* 1999; **10:** 448–51.
15. Bjartling C, Osser S, Persson K. The frequency of salpingitis and ectopic pregnancy as epidemiologic markers of *Chlamydia trachomatis*. *Acta Obstet Gynaecol Scand* 2000; **79:** 123–8.
16. Simms I, Stephenson JM. Epidemiology of pelvic inflammatory disease: what do we know and what do we need to know? *Sex Transm Inf* 2000; **76:** 80–7.
17. Götz H, Ossewaarde T, Bing Thio H, *et al.* Preliminary report of an outbreak of lymphogranuloma venereum in homosexual men in the Netherlands, with implications for other countries in western Europe. Eurosurveillance Weekly 2004; **8**(4): (http://www.eurosurveillance.org/ew/2004/040122.asp#1)
18. Nieuwenhuis RF, Ossewaarde JM, Götz HM *et al.* Resurgence of Lymphogranuloma venereum in western Europe: an outbreak of *Chlamydia trachomatis* serovar L2 proctitis in the Netherlands among men who have sex with men. *Clin Infect Dis* 2004; **39:** 996–1003, (http://www.journals. uchicago.edu/CID/journal/issues/v39n7/33690/brief/33690.abstract.html)
19. Ant Vandenbruaene M. Uitbraak van lymphogranuloma venereum in Antwerpen en Rotterdam. *Epidemiologisch Bulletin van de Vlaamse Gemeenschap* 2004; **47**(1): 4–6. http://www.wvc.vlaanderen.be/epibul/47/lymphogranuloma.htm
20. Institut de Veille Sanitaire. Emergence de la Lymphogranulomatose vénérienne rectale en France: cas estimés au 31 mars 2004. Synthèse réalisée le 1er Juin 2004. http://www.invs.sante.fr/ presse/2004/le_point_sur/lgv_160604/
21. Simms I, Macdonald N, Ison C, *et al.* Enhanced surveillance of LGV starts in England. *Eurosurveillance Weekly* 2004: **8**(41): 8/10/2004 Available at http://www.eurosurveillance. org/ew/2004/041007.asp#4

22. Berglund T, Herrmann B. Utbrott av Lymfogranuloma venereum (LGV) i Europa. *EPI-aktuellt* 2004: **3**(25): 17/06/2004. (http://www.smittskyddsinstitutet.se/SMItemplates/BigArticle____3942. aspx#LGV)

23. Plettenberg A, von Krosigk A, Stoehr A, Meyer T. Four cases of lymphogranuloma venereum in Hamburg, 2003. *Eurosurveillance Weekly* 2004: **8**(30). (http://www.eurosurveillance. org/ew/2004/040722.asp#4)

24. Weström L. Decrease in incidence of women treated in hospital for acute salpingitis in Sweden. *Genitourin Med* 1988; **64:** 59–63.

25. Coutinho R, Rijsdijk A, van den Hoek J, Leentvaar-Kuijpers A. Decreasing incidence of PID in Amsterdam. *Genitourin Med* 1992; **68:** 353–5.

26. Scholes D, Stergachis A, Heidrich F, *et al.* Prevention of pelvic inflammatory disease by screening for cervical chlamydial infection. *N Engl J Med* 1996; **334:** 1362–6.

27. Ostergaard L, Andersen B, Moeller JK, Olesen F. Home sampling verses conventional swab samples for screening for *Chlamydia trachomatis* in women: a cluster-randomised 1-year follow-up study. *Clin Infect Dis* 2000; **31**(4): 951–7.

28. Hillis S, Nakashima A, Amsterdam L, et al. The impact of a comprehensive chlamydia prevention program in Wisconsin. *Fam Plan Perspect* 1995; **27:** 108–111.

29. Egger M, Low N, Smith G, *et al.* Screening for chlamydia infections and the risk of ectopic pregnancy in a county in Sweden:ecological analysis. *BMJ* 1998; **316:** 1776–80.

30. Honey E, Augood C, Templeton A, *et al.* Cost effectiveness of screening for *Chlamydia trachomatis*: a review of published studies. *Sex Transm Infect* 2002; **78**(6): 406–12.

CHAPTER 2

Chlamydia trachomatis
– the case for screening

Angela Robinson
Mortimer Market Centre, London, UK

Chlamydia trachomatis is the commonest bacterial sexually transmitted infection in the UK today. Although infections can be asymptomatic, the sequelae can cause severe morbidity which include pelvic inflammatory disease, ectopic pregnancy and infertility, neonatal infections, epididymitis and joint inflammation in men. The direct healthcare costs of management of the complications are high and the human costs, although difficult to quantify, are considerable. Chlamydia screening as a method of secondary prevention for the control of this prevalent sexually transmitted infection has been suggested.

Before embarking on an intervention such as screening, evidence for the effectiveness of this proposed intervention in reducing complications, decreasing overall chlamydia prevalence and cost savings is advisable. The randomised controlled trial published by Scholes[1] was the first "proof" that selective screening for *C. trachomatis* reduced complications. The incidence of pelvic infection was reduced by more than half in the screened population. With a separate methodology, these findings have been replicated in a randomised controlled trial of screening methods by Ostergaard[2]. Other evidence has been obtained from case studies. In Uppsala, Sweden the number of positive specimens fell annually to reach 40% of 1985 level by 1991, after widespread screening became available in healthcare settings which attracted young people[3]. Pelvic infection rates and number of ectopic pregnancies have subsequently fallen in Sweden which suggests that widespread screening for *C. trachomatis* does reduce these expensive complications. In Wisconsin, a programme of selective screening in family planning clinics was set up in 1985. Selective screening was undertaken on the basis of risk factor analysis. The prevalence fell overall by 53%[4].

SCREENING FOR *CHLAMYDIA TRACHOMATIS* AND THE WILSON JUNGER CRITERIA

Wilson and Junger described eight guidelines to consider when deciding whether screening was an appropriate strategy for disease prevention[5]. The evidence to support the case of screening for *C. trachomatis* is discussed below for each of these guidelines.

The condition should be an important problem

There is no doubt that genital chlamydial infection is of public health importance. Pelvic inflammatory disease (PID) is an important sequela which can result in tubal infertility. Cates cites early research from Sweden that first suggested the link between chlamydial infection and infertility, via PID, and encapsulates the evidence to date to assert the causal pathway of infertility[6]. Women with salpingitis and/or PID have a 3–7 fold risk of involuntary infertility[6,7]. Subsequent studies from 1985–1987 confirmed these early findings [8-10]. The proportion of infertility due to tubal damage ranges from 14-20% and chlamydial infection is implicated in 90% of tubal infertility[11,12]. Asymptomatic pelvic infection may result in subsequent tubal infertility with no known clinical episode of PID.

Pelvic infection may lead to other severe morbidity. The most recent UK study suggested that chlamydial infection is implicated in approximately 50% of cases of PID[13]. Compared to controls with no evidence of pelvic infection, women with a previous history of pelvic infection have ten times the risk of non-specific abdominal pain, four times the risk of "gynaecological" pain, an eight fold risk of having a subsequent hysterectomy and ten times the risk of having an ectopic pregnancy[14].

The role of chlamydial infection in ectopic pregnancy has also been documented in several studies[15-18]. Recent evidence has come to light to suggest that *Chlamydia trachomatis* infection is related to ovarian cancer, cervical cancer, and male infertility[19, 20].

The risk of developing sequelae is a function of the burden of infection in various populations and natural history of infection. Prevalence varies depending on the sampling frame. Population based methods select different populations to clinic based sampling. Prevalence data in UK have been reported from various healthcare settings. The two pilot studies of opportunistic screening across a number of healthcare settings in the Wirral and Portsmouth showed higher than expected prevalence rates compared with previous reports from various healthcare settings in the United Kingdom[21]. The highest rates were in 16-19 year old women and range from 9-14%. A meta-analysis of prevalence studies from the United Kingdom[22] found a consistent 9% prevalence among women attending family planning clinics.

Population based screening undertaken in the United Kingdom National Survey of Sexual Attitudes and Lifestyle found 3% among adult women[23]. A postal screening initiative recently published showed an overall prevalence of 2.8% in men and 3.6% in women[24]. The prevalence in men confirms findings from other studies[22]. High prevalence of infection exists in young men, with one American study showing the peak age for all groups of men both asymptomatic and symptomatic as 18–19 years[25]. A Scottish study showed that higher prevalence in teenagers was noted using novel screening approaches than would be suggested by routine surveillance data where 20–24 year old men have the highest prevalence[26].

Data collected through UK Genito Urinary Medicine clinics (GUM) indicate a considerable rise in diagnostic rates over the past few years. This may be influenced by improved laboratory technology and increased sensitivity but a true increase in incidence is a likely explanation.

The natural history of the condition should be adequately understood
Animal models and quasi-natural history studies of infertility have facilitated our understanding of the natural history of genital chlamydial infection[6, 15, 27-29]. DeMuylder[28] *et al.* showed that untreated lower genital tract infection in women leads to upper genital tract infection, which manifests itself as PID. The proportion of women who develop PID is crucial in assessing value of screening but various estimates have been used with an assumed proportion of 10-20% used in modelling. Why some people develop lower genital tract symptoms whilst others do not is poorly understood. Similarly some women develop symptomatic pelvic infection whereas others have 'silent' tubal infection. This is related to host response. Advances have been made in the immunology of genital chlamydial infection. High titres of heat shock protein have been shown to be associated with pelvic inflammatory disease, tubal infertility and a lower take-home baby rate following *in vitro* fertilisation[30].

In men, the consequences of infection seem to be less severe, but can include urethritis, epididymitis, and Reiter's syndrome [31]; infection has been implicated in male infertility through damage to viable semen[20].

Clearance of the infection without treatment does occur, but the exact proportion is unknown. The assumptions used in testing screening models varies but was 20% in the model developed by DoH Expert Advisory Group[32]. The infection is likely to be transmitted to a sexual partner in up to 80% of cases.

The precise understanding of the exact pathogensis of genital chlamydial infection in both men and women is not fully known; however, the knowledge base is sufficient enough for our adequate understanding of the natural history[33].

There must be a recognisable latent or early symptomatic stage

Asymptomatic chlamydial infection is very common; the quoted data of 50% in men and 70% in women derived predominantly from information obtained through GUM clinics may be an underestimate. It may be as high as 90% in men[34]. Symptoms may be transient and therefore infected individuals are less likely to come forward for testing in appropriate healthcare settings. The goal of screening is to detect unrecognised disease in a population of apparently healthy people and sort those with disease from those without[35]. Thus chlamydia is a good candidate for screening if the majority of the infected population is "apparently well," through having no symptoms, or transient or non specific symptoms for which they do not seek healthcare.

There should be an accepted and effective treatment for people with recognised disease.

Wilson and Jungner[5](1968, p27-8) argue that this is the most important criterion to be met prior to initiating screening. "It is clearly vital to determine…whether a better prognosis is given by treating conditions found at an earlier stage…Unless this is so, there can be no advantage to the patient." Studies exploring the pathogenesis and sequelae of chlamydial infection in women have shown that the earlier an infection is treated the less likely that infection is to ascend or cause further complications[36]. Other studies have additionally found that a woman's chance of developing PID increase exponentially with repeated untreated infections, providing additional evidence that the earlier the treatment, the better[37]. However, the treatment should not cause harm. Therefore, toxicity of therapeutic regimens for chlamydial infection needs to be minimal. Choice of therapy is influenced by compliance and by other factors such as pregnancy and type of contraception used. Studies of doxycycline and azithromycin, the two most commonly prescribed antibiotics for chlamydial infection[38,39] have shown high tolerance among infected persons[40]. Treatment of chlamydial infections is safe and effective with appropriate antibiotics.

Facilities for diagnosis and treatment should be available

Facilities for diagnosis and treatment are readily available in hospitals and primary healthcare settings although not used optimally at present. Tests for *C. trachomatis* are routinely undertaken on all patients attending genito urinary medicine services. Testing for *C. trachomatis* is recommended before instrumentation of the cervix. Strong evidence exists for testing all attendees at termination of pregnancy clinics[41]; the evidence for screening before procedures requiring other instrumentation are not so strong apart from pre-IUD fitting[42].

With appropriate professional and public education, other healthcare settings such as community contraceptive clinics and primary care can be developed to provide access for screening sexually active women and men for genital chlamydial infection. Other non healthcare settings such as clubs, pubs, youth venues, and pharmacies are also options now that non invasive samples can be used.

Enhancing present diagnostic testing for *C. trachomatis* in other hospital specialities such as Urology, Accident and Emergency, Obstetrics and Gynaecology (including antenatal and colposcopy) clinics is feasible. The offering of a test as part of the diagnostic process for patients who may have symptoms attributable to *C. trachomatis* should be encouraged irrespective of any additional initiatives to screen asymptomatic patients.

There are obvious logistical difficulties to overcome with regard to offering widespread chlamydial testing in a number of healthcare settings. Antibiotic treatment can be made readily available in most of settings through use of Patient Group Directives. With appropriate links and collaboration, management of *C. trachomatis* can be undertaken in these other settings with specialist services supporting activities of partner notification and follow up as necessary according to defined patient care pathways within a clinical governance framework. Training of clinicians and provision of resources are essential forerunners to screening.

There should be a suitable test or examination available
The Scandinavian experience suggests that even using lower sensitivity tests such as culture and enzyme immuno-assay, together with other measures, screening for chlamydial infection was an effective intervention to decrease prevalence and complications[43]. However prevalence of chlamydial infection has increased in recent years.

The development of sensitive nucleic acid amplification tests (NAATs) has meant that infection can be detected in samples obtained non-invasively. This has revolutionised diagnosis of chlamydial infection and made the introduction of screening even more feasible. There is a choice of non-invasive samples that can be collected from women; urine samples and self taken swabs. Handling time by laboratory staff for urine specimens is longer which makes them more costly to test. A self-taken vaginal swab has proved to be as sensitive as doctor-taken cervical specimens and affords better sensitivity than urine specimens. This is more fully discussed in chapter 4. A urine sample is easily obtained for men.

The test or examination should be acceptable to both public and professionals
In healthcare settings such as GUM, intimate examinations for both men and women are standard. A number of tests are performed, requiring multiple clinical samples to be collected[39]. Thus, in the context of a routine diagnostic work-up, taking of cervical or urethral specimens has not been controversial. However, this can be uncomfortable. Screening must reach those who are apparently well so the acceptability of the test becomes more important. The newer diagnostic methods have been welcomed by populations being screened[44-47]. Lane *et al.* found that 76% of women preferred to collect their own sample via a vulvo-vaginal swab[46], and Gotz showed that home-testing for chlamydia was acceptable – 84% of responders to a survey of home-testing agreed to send a urine sample from home[47]. Studies investigating the potential psychological or emotional 'harm' from chlamydia screening have not demonstrated severe consequences of providing a urine or vaginal specimen.

As *C. trachomatis* is a sexually transmitted infection, management involves at least one other person. To avoid re-infection it is vital that the partner or partners of identified positives are tested and treated as part of the overall strategy. Partner notification for testing and treatment of sexually transmitted infections has proved highly acceptable within GUM clinics. Work undertaken in primary care and in the roll out of the English screening programme through chlamydia screening offices has demonstrated that this activity can be done successfully outside GUM clinics[48]. It is possible that in some settings where discussion of sexual partnerships may come unexpectedly, some patients may find this unacceptable. Appropriate public education to highlight the importance of chlamydial infections is needed to counterbalance the potential problems of identifying a sexually transmitted infection. Clinicians need to be aware of the difficulties that can ensue and have the necessary skills to deal with difficulties that may arise.

There should be an agreed policy on whom to treat as patients, including management of cases with equivocal results
An appropriate infrastructure for follow-up of patients, partner notification and management of partners is needed. Within GUM clinics, there are agreed standards but this package of care can be delivered in other healthcare settings in collaboration with specialist services. Several options exist including the following; devolving some aspects of management within healthcare settings where screening is undertaken; developing appropriate referral mechanisms through care pathways. Local arrangements need to be in place before embarking on screening including a policy on management of patients with equivocal results.

Measuring the success of any screening strategy relies upon appropriate data collection. Genito urinary medicine departments presently play a key role together with public health departments in gathering information about the epidemiology of sexually transmitted infections. Other sexual healthcare providers need to collect a standard data set so that the impact of a screening intervention can be measured. This has been achieved in the roll out of the English national screening programme[48].

In addition to the Wilson and Jungner criteria there are two other components of a chlamydia screening programme to consider – interval and costs.

Screening interval and reinfection
Firstly screening should be a continuous process. Risks for being re-infected with *C. trachomatis* depend on sexual behaviour with regard to both number of partners and unprotected sexual intercourse particularly with an untreated partner following initial diagnosis. Work undertaken in the USA suggests that a significant proportion of patients identified with chlamydial infection become re-infected within 6 months[49] and adolescents who at initial screening

have a negative result are at high risk of becoming infected. In a postal follow-up survey undertaken in Denmark, the re-infection rate for genital chlamydial infection was 30%[50].

A recently completed study of chlamydia incidence and re-infection among 16-24 year old women in England has found a rate of re-infection similar to studies from the US, 24.0 per 100 person-years (95%CI: 19.2-29.9)[51]. Three quarters of re-infections occurred within 7.8 months of follow-up and the key independent predictors of re-infection were recent acquisition of a new sex partner (indicating new exposure) and inadequate treatment of all reported partners from the initial positive test (indicating re-exposure by an untreated partner). These results suggest more frequent screening for women testing positive for chlamydia.

The screening interval will have an impact on the cost of screening as an intervention. With recent data suggesting high re-infection rates in adolescents and high re-acquisition rates in patients known to have had chlamydial infection, people identified with chlamydial infection appear to be an important target group for re-screening. Awareness of the high re-infection risk is mandatory for any educational initiative. Efforts must be directed at accessing partners, who have a high prevalence of chlamydial infection and are the most likely source of re-infection. Centers for Disease Control and Prevention (CDC) have highlighted that rescreening of positives should be considered at 6 months[38]. Mathematical modelling is currently underway to assess whether this recommended screening strategy, or others currently in use, can be used to achieve effective chlamydia control by reducing prevalence in the target population.

Costs of chlamydial infection
Estimating the economic benefits of chlamydia screening is difficult. Initially, programmes in the US were not established based on their cost-effectiveness. Only after several years of screening was a rigorous cost-effectiveness study performed; Marrazzo[52] *et al.* confirmed that indeed the costs of the sequelae were greater than the costs of the screening intervention, given the prevalence of infection and population selected for screening.

There have been additional cost-effectiveness and cost-benefit analyses of chlamydia screening performed. These have concluded that the benefits outweigh the costs and cost-effectiveness can be reached in a few years[53-57]. In assessing the cost-effectiveness of an opportunistic screening programme in England using a dynamic model, targeting annual screening for women 16–20 years of age and biennial screening for women 21–24 years of age, Townsend and Turner concluded that cost-effectiveness would be achieved after four years of high volume screening[32].

The conditions for which screening becomes cost-effective have recently been scrutinised. Exact figures of how much the screening programme costs will be imprecise. A major drawback in all models is the need to make assumptions (probability estimates) about likelihood of development of complications, re-infection rates, uptake of screening in women and whether male screening is included. Baseline prevalence of the target population, defining the target population and uptake and coverage of screening by the target population are crucial. Economic costs of immediate and future sequelae, and the social costs (psychological and emotional impact) of this public health intervention are required. Many of these conditions are either ill-defined or difficult to measure[58,59], thus complicating the accuracy of the cost-effectiveness evaluation and the mathematical methods employed in such an evaluation. The cost of healthcare provision will vary from country to country. Further work on cost effectiveness is required. As more is understood about natural history and more data are available from recent research projects, the probability estimates will need to be modified appropriately.

How should screening be undertaken?

The CMO Expert Advisory Group on *C. trachomatis* concluded that screening and effective management of chlamydial infection would result in considerable health benefits. However evidence for the most cost effective approach to screening is lacking.

The choice of opportunistic screening offered to known "high risk" groups was suggested as more appropriate than a register-based universal screening programme, with call and recall, principally because of the lack of complete registers available from which to invite participants and the inability of such registers to determine who in the age range was sexually active. The National Screening Committee in the UK supported piloting opportunistic screening in the Wirral and Portsmouth[60] and following this there has been a roll out of national screening in UK (See chapter 3). The Health Technology Assessment Programme funded a large research project to address some of the outstanding questions with regard to mechanics of a screening programme some of which has been reported[24]. The importance of including men in screening programmes has been highlighted rather than relying on partner notification but the cost benefit of this approach needs to be evaluated.

Professional and public educational initiatives are taking place. Sex and relationship education in schools is important so that the general knowledge base of the 'at risk' as well as the general population improves. It is also important that healthcare professionals have the necessary skills to support a screening programme. With the high Chlamydia prevalence in many countries, offering widespread screening for *C. trachomatis* is attractive but resource implications and process require further evaluation.

Acknowledgements

I would like to thank Dr Scott LaMontagne for his contribution to this chapter.

REFERENCES

1. Scholes D, Stergachis A, Heidrich FE, *et al*. Prevention of pelvic inflammatory disease by screening for cervical chlamydial infection. *NEJM* 1996; **334:** 1362–1366
2. Ostergaard L, Andersen B, Moeller JK and Olesen F. Home sampling versus conventional swab samples for screening of *Chlamydia trachomatis* in women: a cluster-randomized 1-year follow-up study. *Clinical Infectious Diseases.* 2000; **31**(4): 951–957.
3. Herrmann BF, Egger M. Genital *Chlamydia trachomatis* infections in Uppsala County, Sweden, 1985-1993: declining rates for how much longer? *Sex Trans Dis* 1995; **22**(4): 253–260.
4. Addiss DG, Vaughn ML, Ludka D, *et al*. Decreased prevalence in *Chlamydia trachomatis* infection associated with a selective screening program of family planning clinics in Wisconsin. *Sexually Transmitted Diseases.* 1993; **20**(1): 28–35.
5. Wilson JMG, Junger G. Principles and practice of screening for disease. 1968; Geneva: World Health Organization.
6. Cates W Jr. Sexually transmitted organisms and infertility: the proof of the pudding. *Sexually Transmitted Diseases.* 1984; **11**(2): 113–116.
7. Mardh P-A, Ripa T, Svensson, L and Westrom, L. *Chlamydia trachomatis* infection in patients with acute salpingitis. *NEJM* 1977; **296**(24): 1377-1379.
8. Mabey DCW, Ogbaselassie G, Robertson *JN, et al*. Tubal infertility in the Gambia: chlamydial and gonococcal serology in women with tubal occlusion compared with pregnant controls. *Bulletin of the World Health Organization.* 1985; **63**(6): 1107–1113.
9. Tjiam KH, Zeilmaker GH, Alberda AT *et al*.Prevalence of antibodies to *Chlamydia trachomatis*, *Neisseria gonorrhoeae*, and *Mycoplasma hominis* in infertile women. *Genitourinary Medicine* 1985; **61**(3): 175–178.
10. Robertson JN, Ward ME, Conway D, Caul EO. Chlamydial and gonococcal antibodies in sera of infertile women with tubal obstruction. *Journal of Clinical Pathology.* 1987; **40**(4): 377–383.
11. Page H. Estimation of the prevalence and incidence of infertility in a population: a pilot study. *Fertil-Steril* 1989 Apr; **51**(4): 571–7.
12. Hull MG, Glazener CM, Kelly NJ, *et al*. Population study of causes, treatment and outcome of infertility. *Br Med J Clin Res Ed* 1985; Dec 14: **291**(6150): 1693–7.
13. Bevan CD, Johal BJ, Mumtaz G, *et al*. Clinical, laparoscopic and microbiological findings in acute salpingitis: report on a United Kingdom cohort. *Br J Obstet Gynaecol* 1995; **102:** 407–14.
14. Buchan H, Vessey M, Goldacre M, Fairweather JTI. Morbidity following pelvic inflammatory disease. *Br J Obstet Gynaecol. Jun* 1993; **100**(6): 558–62.

15. Miettinen A, Heinonen PK, Teisala K *et al.* Serologic evidence for the role of *Chlamydia trachomatis, Neisseria gonorrhoeae,* and *Mycoplasma hominis* in the etiology of tubal factor infertility and ectopic pregnancy. *Sexually Transmitted Diseases.* 1990; **17**(1): 10–14.

16. Chow JM, Yonekura ML, Richwald GA *et al.* The association between *Chlamydia trachomatis* and ectopic pregnancy: a matched-pair, case-control study. *Journal of the American Medical Association.* 1990; **263**(23): 3164–3167.

17. Egger M, Low N, Smith G *et al.* Screening for chlamydia infections and the risk of ectopic pregnancy in a county in Sweden: ecological analysis. *British Medical Journal* 1998; **316**(7147): 1776–1780.

18. Cates W Jr. Chlamydial infections and the risk of ectopic pregnancy. *Journal of the American Medical Association* 1999; **281**(2): 117–118.

19. Ness RB, Goodman MT, Shen C, Brunham RC. Serologic evidence of past infection with *Chlamydia trachomatis,* in relation to ovarian cancer. *Journal of Infectious Diseases* 2003; **187**(7): 1147–1152.

20. Idahl A, Boman J, Kumlin U, Olofsson JI. Demonstration of *Chlamydia trachomatis* IgG antibodies in the male partner of the infertile couple is correlated with a reduced likelihood of achieving pregnancy'. *Human Reproduction* 2004; **19**(5): 1121–1126.

21. Pimenta JM, Catchpole M, Rogers PA, *et al.* Opportunistic screening for genital chlamydial infection I: acceptability of urine testing in primary and secondary healthcare settings. *Sexually Transmitted Infections.* 2003; **79**(1): 16–21.

22. Adams EJ, Charlett A, Edmunds WJ, Hughes G. *Chlamydia trachomatis* in the United Kingdom: a systematic review and analysis of prevalence studies. *Sexually Transmitted Infections* 2004; **80**(5): 354–362.

23. Fenton KA, Korovessis C, Johnson AM, *et al.* Sexual behaviour in Britain: reported sexually transmitted infections and prevalence genital *Chlamydia trachomatis* infection. *Lancet* 2001; **358**(9296): 1851–1854.

24. Macleod J, Salisbury C, Low N, *et al.* Coverage and uptake of systematic postal screening for gential *Chlamydia trachomatis* and prevalence of infection in the United Kingdom general population: cross sectional study. *BMJ* 2005; **330**: 940–942.

25. LaMontagne DS, Fine DN, Marrazzo JM. *Chlamydia trachomatis* infection in asymptomatic men. *American Journal of Preventive Medicine* 2003; **24**(1): 36–42.

26. Young H, Allison K, Carrick-Anderson K, *et al.* Chlamydia in heterosexual men: could peak prevalence be in teenagers? *STI* 2005; **81**: 94.

27. Patton DL, Wolner-Hanssen P, Cosgrove SJ, Holmes KK. The effects of *Chlamydia trachomatis* on the female reproductive tract of the Macaca nemestrina after a single tubal challenge following repeated cervical inoculations. *Obstetrics and Gynecology* 1990; **76**(4): 643–650.

28. DeMuylder X, Laga M, Tennstedt C, *et al.* The role of *Neisseria gonorrhoeae* and Chlamydia trachomatis in pelvic inflammatory disease and its sequelae in Zimbabwe. *Journal of Infectious Diseases* 1990; **162**(2): 501–505.

29. Westrom L, Joesoef R, Reynolds G, *et al.* Pelvic inflammatory disease and fertility: a cohort study of 1844 women with laparoscopically verified disease and 657 control women with normal laparoscopic results. *Sexually Transmitted Diseases* 1992; **19**(4): 185–192.

30. Neuer A, Spandorfer SD, Giraldo P, *et al.* The Role of Heat Shock Proteins in Reproduction, *Human Reproduction Update* 2000; **6**: 149–159.

31. Cates W Jr and Wasserheit JN. Genital chlamydial infections: epidemiology and reproductive sequelae. *American Journal of Obstetrics and Gynecology* 1991; **164**(6): 1771–1781.

32. Townsend JRP and Turner HS. Analysing the effectiveness of chlamydia screening. *Journal of the Operational Research Society* 2000; **51**(7): 812–824.

33. Stamm WE. *Chlamydia trachomatis* infections of the adult. in Holmes KK, Sparling PF, Mardh PA, Lemon SM, Stamm WE, Piot P, *et al.* (eds). 1999; New York, NY: McGraw-Hill Health Professions Division, p.407-422.

34. McKay L, Clery H, Carrick-Anderson K, *et al.* Genital *Chlamydia trachomatis* infection in a subgroup of young men in the UK. *Lancet* 2003; **361:** 1792.

35. Mausner JS, Kramer S. Epidemiology – an introductory text. (2nd ed). Philadelphia, PA: WB Saunders Company. 1985.

36. Honey E, Templeton A. 'Prevention of pelvic inflammatory disease by the control of *C. trachomatis* infection. *International Journal of Gynecology and Obstetrics* **78**(3): 257–261.

37. Hillis SD, Owens LM, Marchbanks PA, *et al.* 'Recurrent chlamydial infections increase the risks of hospitalization for ectopic pregnancy and pelvic inflammatory disease'. *American Journal of Obstetrics and Gynecology* 1997; **176**(1 Pt 1): 103–107.

38. Centers for Disease Control and Prevention. Sexually transmitted diseases treatment guidelines 2002. *Morbidity and Mortality Weekly Report* 2002; **51**(RR-6): 1–78.

39. Clinical Effectiveness Workgroup (MSSVD and AGUM). Management of *Chlamydia trachomatis* genital tract infection. 2002; London: British Association for Sexual Health and HIV.

40. Lau CY, Qureshi AK. Azithromycin versus doxycycline for genital chlamydial infections: a meta-analysis of randomized clinical trials. *Sexually Transmitted Diseases* 2002; **29**(9): 497–502.

41. Blackwell Al, Thomas PD, Wareham K, Emery SJ. Health gains from screening for infection of the lower genital tract in women attending for termination of pregnancy. *Lancet* 1993; **342:** 206–209.

42. Farley TM, Rowe PJ, Rosenberg MJ, *et al.* Intrauterine devices and pelvic inflammatory disease: an international perspective. *Lancet* 1992; **339:** 785–788.

43. Ripa T. Epidemiologic control of genital *Chlamydia trachomatis* infections. 1990; *Scan J Infect Dis* (Suppl) **16:** 157–167.

44. Serlin M, Shafer MA, Tebb K, *et al.* What sexually transmitted disease screening method does the adolescent prefer? Adolescents' attitudes toward first-void urine, self-collected vaginal swab, and pelvic examination. *Archives of Pediatric Adolescent Medicine* 2002; **156**(6): 588–591.

45. Hsieh YH, Howell MR, Gaydos JC, *et al.* Preference among female Army recruits for use of self-administrated vaginal swabs or urine to screen for *Chlamydia trachomatis* genital infections. Sexually Transmitted Diseases. 2003; **30**(10): 769–773.

46. Lane JR, Chernesky M, Martin DH, *et al.* Women prefer collection of their own vaginal swabs to cervical swabs or urine to investigate sexually transmitted infections. [poster]. 2003; *Ottawa, Canada: 15th Biennial Congress of the International Society for Sexually Transmitted Disease Research,* 27–30 July.

47. Gotz H, Veldhuijzen I, de Zwart O, *et al.* Acceptability of screening for *Chlamydia trachomatis* by home based urine testing. [poster]. 2003; *Ottawa, Canada: 15th Biennial Congress of the International Society of Sexually Transmitted Disease Research,* 27-30 July.

48. LaMontagne DS, Fenton KA, Randall S, *et al.* Establishing the national chlamydia screening programme in England: results from the first full year of screening. *Sexually Transmitted Infections* 2004; **80**(5): 335–341.

49. Burstein GR, Gaydos CA, Diener-West M, *et al.* Incident *Chlamydia trachomatis* infections among inner-city adolescent females. *JAMA* 1998; **280:** 521–526.

50. Kjar HO, Dimcevski G, Hoff G, *et al.* Recurrence of Urogenital *Chlamydia trachomatis* Infection Evaluated by Mailed Samples Obtained at Home; 24 weeks prospective follow-up study. *Sex Transm Infect.* 2000 Jun; **76**(3): 169–72.

51. LaMontagne DS, Emmett L, Baster K, on behalf of the Chlamydia Recall Study Advisory Group. (2004d). 'Incidence and re-infection rates of genital chlamydial infection in young women in England: results from the Chlamydia Recall Study'. [oral presentation]. Mykonos, Greece: Conference on Sexually Transmitted Infections, European branch of the International Union Against Sexually Transmitted Infections, 7-9 October.

52. Marrazzo JM, Celum CL, Hillis SD, *et al.* Performance and cost-effectiveness of selective screening criteria for *Chlamydia trachomatis* infection in women: implications for a national chlamydia control strategy. *Sexually Transmitted Diseases* 1997; **24**(3): 131–141.
53. Kretzschmar M, van Duynhoven YTHP and Severijnen AJ. 'Modeling prevention strategies for gonorrhea and chlamydia using stochastic network simulations'. *American Journal of Epidemiology* 1996; **144**(3): 306–317.
54. Paavonen J, Puolakkainen M, Paukku M and Sintonen H. 'Cost-benefit analysis of first-void urine *Chlamydia trachomatis* screening program'. *Obstetrics and Gynecology* 1998; **92**(2): 292–298.
55. Howell MR, Quinn TC, Brathwaite W, Gaydos CA. Screening women for *Chlamydia trachomatis* in family planning clinics – the cost-effectiveness of DNA amplification assays. *Sexually Transmitted Diseases* 1998; **25**(2): 108–117.
56. Welte R, Kretzschmar M, Leidl R, *et al.* Cost-effectiveness of screening programs for *Chlamydia trachomatis* – a population-based dynamic approach. *Sexually Transmitted Diseases* 2000; **27**(9): 518–529.
57. Honey E, Augood C, Templeton A, *et al.* Cost effectiveness of screening for *Chlamydia trachomatis*: a review of published studies. *Sexually Transmitted Infections* 2002; **78**(6): 406–412.
58. Washington AE, Arno PS, Brooks MA. The economic cost of pelvic inflammatory disease. *Journal of the American Medical Association.* 1986;. **255**(13): 1735–1738.
59. van Valkengoed IG, Morre SA, van den Brule AJ *et al.* Overestimation of complication rates in evaluations of *Chlamydia trachomatis* screening programmes – implications for cost-effectiveness analyses. *International Journal of Epidemiology.* 2004; **33**(2): 416–425.
60. Pimenta J, Catchpole M, Grey M, *et al.* Screening for Genital Chlamydial Infection, *BMJ* 2000; **321**: 629–631.

CHAPTER 3

Screening programmes for Chlamydia trachomatis

D Scott LaMontagne
Health Protection Agency Centre for Infections, London, UK

INTRODUCTION

The first chapter of this handbook described in detail the epidemiology of genital chlamydial infection. The high levels of morbidity and severe complications of untreated infection confirm the importance of this public health problem. According to criteria established by the World Health Organisation,[1] it has been argued that screening is the appropriate intervention to control this infection.[2] The case for screening was re-examined in the previous chapter; however, "How to screen?" is still a matter of contentious debate. This question is addressed in the text following, which reviews the goal of screening, brief descriptions of select local or national programmes currently operating in several countries, reviews other screening strategies piloted, examines evaluations of screening programmes for either short or long-term success, and concludes with challenges remaining for the field.

GOAL OF SCREENING

Screening targets healthy individuals to detect persons who might be infected.[3] Critical to sorting out potentially diseased persons (true positives) from those without disease (true negatives) is the selection procedure for categorizing the healthy population for whom the screening intervention is designed.[4] This selection process operates on two levels: the population and the screening test. At the population level, the selection process must be sensitive enough to capture persons most likely to be infected, while not overscreening those who are not. And once the screening population is selected, then the screening test should be sufficiently sensitive to detect infections. In both cases, the ideal is to have a high positive predictive value with both the selection of the population to be screened, and the determination of the infected population within those screened.[3]

Determining the appropriate selection procedure for the most likely population for chlamydia screening has been the subject of a vast array of research. Handsfield *et al.* researched this aspect of chlamydia screening in the early 1980s and concluded that using age, clinical symptoms and signs, and sexual risk behaviour for women undergoing pelvic examinations in family planning clinics was a sensitive method to detect infections.[5] Other studies have demonstrated the consistent performance of selection criteria in screening programmes targeting women.[6-9] The inclusion of men as direct screening targets, rather than only through partner follow-up for positive women, is still a matter of debate. Prevalence studies in asymptomatic men are limited. Research has questioned the ability to screen men in clinical settings due to their lower attending rates. It remains unclear how screening men may impact prevalence among women.

The microbiological aspects of determining chlamydia-infected persons from non-infected persons has undergone the most remarkable transformation over the last decade with the development of highly sensitive and specific laboratory methods using new techniques targeting chlamydial antigen DNA.[10] These new nucleic acid amplification (NAA) methods also allow for non-invasive specimens, such as urine or self-taken vulvo-vaginal swabs, to be used, thus improving the possibility of test acceptance to the population targeted for chlamydia screening.[11-13] Improved ability in both selecting the appropriate population for screening and detecting the infection within that screened population, has made developing an organised screening programme possible.

LOGISTICS OF SCREENING

Where and how to screen

Ensuring the infrastructure and resources for a chlamydia screening programme are critical for implementation. The target population must be clearly defined and accessible. Variations in locations for screening and the method by which screening is offered to the target population can facilitate uptake. To access the target population, sites for screening should include clinical facilities with high numbers of young people. Schools, colleges and universities, youth centres, bars and clubs, places of employment, using a local or national census or population registry, pharmacies and other commercial settings, test kits requested over the Internet, or registries in primary care or general practice surgeries offer other opportunities for increasing screening coverage. Uptake by the target population can also be enhanced by collecting non-invasive specimens, such as urine or self-taken vaginal swabs, that are easy to use and do not require expensive equipment. How the offer of screening is made can also be helpful and reduce costs, such as by peer educators, primary care nurses, through the post, or by self-selection. The way in which the population is accessed, screening is offered, and the samples are collected should be considered based on the available physical infrastructure in the area, such as facility capacity, staffing, laboratory preparedness, supplies, computer networks, information support, and communication links.

Samples and test methodology
Ideally only highly sensitive nucleic acid amplification tests should be used, given the proven superior sensitivity, specificity and positive-predictive value of the test. Rapid turnaround of test results in the laboratory will also assure the population tested receives results quickly to allow for timely administration of treatment, if needed.

Management of positives
Protocols for how positive patients will be followed for treatment compliance and partner follow-up are key. Only approved efficacious therapies should be administered according to guidelines from reputable clinical governance bodies. Finally, the transmission loop must be closed to ensure patients are not re-infected from current partners or newly infected from new partners. Contact tracing for chlamydia should be completed for at least the most recent partner(s), and guidelines exist for this. Creative methods for ensuring partners of positives are treated have included expedited partner therapy and patient-delivered partner therapy.

Outcome measures
Screening programmes should have solid financial support and monitoring goals for both the short and long-term, as well as ways to assess fiscal performance and progress towards these goals. Screening is a continual process,[1] requiring funding to be continual as well. Assessment of costs and

cost-benefit analysis should be done as a matter of fiscal prudence. Other performance measures could be structural, process, output or outcome based. Structural measures would assess the capacity of a screening programme to deliver the service. Process measures may include laboratory turnaround time or benchmarks for length of time between notification to and treatment of patients. Number of screening tests performed and contact follow-up ratios are two examples of outputs that have been noted in some existing screening programmes. Cost-effectiveness models of screening have illustrated the key role that screening uptake – the proportion of the eligible, at-risk population who is actually tested – has in fostering reductions in chlamydia prevalence and achieving savings by reducing costs associated with long-term sequelae. Finally, screening programmes should strive to achieve positive outcomes, such as measured reductions in prevalence in the target population, decreases in incident PID cases at least after one-year and further reductions in rates over time, longer term reductions in ectopic pregnancy rates in the target population, and ultimately prevention of infertility.

After screening has been established for several years, with continual assessment of the performance goals, more detailed evaluations of the programme should be completed. This allows for refinements and adjustments in programme components to keep pace with new developments or recent research evidence. A formal cost-effectiveness evaluation may also be needed to understand whether the programme is achieving value for money. As always, the cost of operating a screening programme should be weighed against the cost if the screening intervention did not exist.

Sustainability
Given the continual nature of any screening programme, a new cohort of eligibles will enter the at-risk population. Clinical and non-clinical personnel engaged in the screening programme may also change over time. It is necessary that solid training programmes exist to assist in the learning for new programme staff. Lead sexual health bodies, such as the British Association for Sexual Health and HIV, have standardized trainings on offer that could be of use to local screening programmes. Booster courses may also be needed to keep long-term staff invigorated with the screening programme and to ensure that screening fatigue does not become problematic to local efforts.

CURRENT SCREENING PROGRAMMES

Sweden

Sweden was the first country to use targeted chlamydia screening as a disease control strategy at a national level. The programme provides chlamydia testing to women and men of all ages in conjunction with routine genital examinations already performed at a variety of health clinics. This approach was expanded nationally based on the early success observed in Uppsala county:[14,15] chlamydia detection rates among women decreased from 107.2 per 1,000 examinations in 1985 to 32.3 in 1993, and among young women (ages 15-19) specifically the rates decreased from 198.0 to 45.4 per 1,000 examinations.[15] The national expansion occurred in 1993, with an increase in total chlamydia test positivity noted from 4.1% in 1994 to 5.4% in 1999.[16] Increased testing overall, increased testing of men and young people, and the use of more sensitive tests have been suggested as partial explanations for the increase,[16] but the reason for testing, presence of symptoms, type of clinic, and repeat testing were not assessed.

United States of America

In the US, initial screening programmes were locally or regionally organised, and targeted women attending family planning clinics (focusing on 'infertility prevention') through selective screening criteria, such as aged 24 years or less, new sex partner in the last two months, mucopurlent cervicitis, easily induced endocervical bleeding, and use of no contraception or a non-barrier method.[5] A three-year demonstration project that used age-based for under 25 year old women and risk-based criteria for those 25 years and older in Region X (the states of Washington, Idaho, Oregon and Alaska) was established in 1988 and reported decreases in chlamydia positivity from 10.9% in January 1988 to 6.8% at the end of 1990,[17] with a continued decrease to 4.9% in 1997.[18] Other programmes in the States have also demonstrated success in reducing female chlamydia positivity, including the state of Wisconsin;[19] Indianapolis, Indiana;[20] Birmingham, Alabama;[21] and Columbus, Ohio.[22]

The success of the Region X programme became the model for subsequent expansion of chlamydia screening throughout the rest of the country from 1993-1995 after programme administration transferred to the Centers for Disease Control and Prevention.[18] The National Infertility Prevention Programme screens women to age- (for those under 25 years) and risk-based (for those 25 years and older) selective screening criteria attending a wide variety of clinical settings (not just family planning clinics) and has begun to include testing of men and non-clinic based screening.[18] As with Sweden, the US is observing increases in chlamydia prevalence across many geographic areas,[18] and the switch to more sensitive laboratory tests has been implicated as only partial explanation.[23]

England, United Kingdom
England has the only other nationally organised programme for chlamydia screening. The phased implementation of the National Chlamydia Screening Programme (NCSP) in ten geographic areas began in September 2002, based on a review of the available evidence by the Chief Medical Officer (England)[2] and the conclusion of a feasibility and acceptability pilot of screening.[24] The programme expanded to an additional sixteen geographic areas in 2004, with further financial allocations for screening to be provided to the rest of the primary care trusts (PCTs) in April 2006.[25] The NCSP offers chlamydia screening to men and women under 25 years of age attending a variety of clinical and non-clinical settings. Non-invasive specimens (urine and self-taken vulvo-vaginal swabs) are tested using NAATs.[26] Data are only available for one year of limited screening, so assessment of programme effectiveness at reducing prevalence cannot be made.[26] However, preliminary results from effectiveness modelling of the impact of the screening approach used by the NCSP in reducing prevalence are encouraging, and should be available shortly in the peer-reviewed literature (Dr. John Edmunds, Health Protection Agency, personal communication).

Manitoba, Canada
Researchers from Canada have reported on the impact of introducing chlamydia screening, as a part of a wider control programme, on the incidence of hospitalizations and outpatients visits for PID as well as ectopic pregnancies.[27] Since 1987, the programme in Manitoba, Canada has consisted of testing women (using selection criteria), treatment of positives, partner follow-up and public education to reduce incidence of disease and reproductive sequelae. They reported a decrease in chlamydia incidence from over 40 per 100,000 persons in 1981 to about 12 per 100,000 persons in 1990.[27]

OTHER SCREENING STRATEGIES STUDIED

Delivery of chlamydia screening varies: some have been national efforts and others more local. There are differences in the selection procedures, targeted population, the method of testing, sample type collected, and the evaluation of these efforts. Although not an exhaustive review of all screening strategies tried, a few are described further to illustrate the research exploring 'how to screen.'

Two large pilots of chlamydia screening using registers (one from the total population and one from clinical practices) have just been completed.[28-31] In the Netherlands, a urine sample kit, behavioural questionnaire and invitation to screen was mailed ("postal testing") to a national probability sample of 15-29 year old men and women from civil registries.[30] With an overall response rate of 47% for women and 33% among men, prevalence was estimated to be 2.0% among women and 1.5% among men. However, peak prevalence was noted at 4.3% among 15-19 year old women and 4.1% in 25-29 year old men.[30] Suggestions for using a predictive rule, which is a form of selective screening, have been made from this study.[31]

In England, a similar postal testing pilot was administered to a random sample of 16-39 year old registrants from 27 randomly selected general practices,[28] and reported a prevalence of 3.6% in women and 2.8% in men.[29] Higher prevalence was found among those younger than 25 years (5.1% for men; 6.2% for women), and sexual risk taking was the strongest predictor of infection. Uptake of screening in this initiative was slightly lower than the Dutch pilot (34.5%). The authors suggest chlamydia screening should be offered to all men and women under 25 years of age, and postal screening could augment existing opportunistic approaches.[29] Further studies are needed to assess whether this approach will reduce prevalence or sequelae in the short or long-term.

Postal invitations to screen have also been trialled in Aarhus, Denmark, where a randomised control trial of screening strategies was completed among 21-23 year olds randomly selected from a population registry.[13] This study, also with low participation rate (36% of women; 27% of men), found 6.5% chlamydia positivity in women who submitted samples taken at home and 5.9% among men tested in the same manner.[13] Uptake differed for men and women depending upon the postal invitation method (test kit sent directly in the first instance versus reply card returned to request a test kit).[13]

Postal kits for chlamydia tests have also been tried in San Francisco,[32]

Scotland,[33] and London.[11] Additional studies of screening approaches include general practices,[34] accident and emergency departments,[35] pharmacies,[36] and locations outside traditional medical clinics.[18,37] Finally, in keeping with technologic developments, the Internet has been used for chlamydia screening in Baltimore, USA (www.iwantthekit.org) and Umea, Sweden.[38]

SCREENING PROGRAMME EVALUATIONS

There is little doubt that genital chlamydial infection is a significant contributor to sexual ill-health and most people agree that screening is a viable option for addressing this public health epidemic. Many screening strategies have been implemented, and the evaluation of these programmes has been just as varied. The 'success' of the screening programme hinges upon the definition of 'success.' The use of outputs and outcomes in programme evaluation is common. These can be considered in the short or long-term.

For example, testing uptake might be a marker of how well the programme can engage the target population.[18,29,30] Additionally, the ability of selection procedures for the at-risk population within the programme can be used to assess criteria sensitivity.[8] In the US, Sweden and Copenhagen, reductions in chlamydia positivity among the target population have been used to evaluate programme success.[15,16,17-22,39] Studies have also demonstrated success through measuring reductions in sequelae, such as PID[27,40,41] and ectopic pregnancy.[27] Lastly, effectiveness and cost-effectiveness studies have been used to not only assess the impact of various screening strategies on reducing prevalence[19,22,42-45] and sequelae,[46,47] but to estimate whether a screening programme costs more than the healthcare savings achieved through the intervention.[43,44,48]

There are advantages and disadvantages with all the evaluation techniques used. There may not be any one evaluation that will be able to conclude definitively that a particular chlamydia screening programme is the best or only one that is beneficial. How the programme is organised, implemented and operated as well as the varying definitions of what makes a programme successful shapes the technique used to evaluate that success. This variation continues to make assessment of chlamydia screening programmes difficult.

CHALLENGES FACING CHLAMYDIA SCREENING PROGRAMMES

There is no doubt that *Chlamydia trachomatis* is a significant public health problem. The large number of screening strategies currently in operation or that have been tried suggest that there is a consensus for screening as an appropriate intervention. However, the question of 'how to screen' remains under critical debate, as there is no consensus of what defines the success of the screening programme.

Because 'how to screen' touches upon all the complex and interdependent components of chlamydia screening, limited understanding of one or more areas makes us question the strategy itself. Questions under debate include:

- What is the role of screening asymptomatic men in the success of a chlamydia screening programme? Will it assist in reducing prevalence among women?
- What is the role of treating partners of chlamydia-positive women? How many of the partners need to be treated to reduce re-infection and onward transmission in the population? Is there a herd-immunity gained at the population-level with high coverage of partner treatment?
- If we are going to screen, who should be screened, how often, by what method? How do we ensure sufficient uptake to reduce the consequences of untreated infections?
- Is there only one approach that will work or is a combination of methods needed?
- How do you define a successful chlamydia screening programme? Is it reducing prevalence, preventing sequelae, being cost-effective, or all of these? What is the role of screening coverage and uptake in achieving these goals?

Research will continue to grapple with these issues and over time provide the additional insight required to be effective at tackling this prevalent, preventable, devastating infection.

REFERENCES

1. Wilson JMG and Jungner G. Principles and practice of screening for disease. Geneva: World Health Organization, 1968. Public Health Paper No. 34.
2. Chief Medical Officer. Main report of the CMO's Expert Advisory Group on *Chlamydia trachomatis*. London: Department of Health, 1998.
3. Mausner JS and Kramer S. Epidemiology – an introductory text. 2nd ed. Philadelphia: W.B. Saunders Company, 1985.
4. Hennekens CH and Buring JE. Screening. in Mayrent SL (ed). Epidemiology in Medicine. Philadelphia: Lippincott, Williams and Wilkins, 1987.
5. Handsfield HH, Jasman LL, Roberts PL, *et al.* Criteria for selective screening for *Chlamydia trachomatis* infection in women attending family planning clinics. *JAMA* 1986; **255**(13): 1730–1734.
6. Marrazzo JM, Fine D, Celum CL, *et al.* Selective screening for chlamydial infection in women: a comparison of three sets of criteria. *Fam Plann Perspect* 1997; **29**(4): 158–162.
7. Howell MR, Quinn TC, Brathwaite W, *et al.* Screening women for *Chlamydia trachomatis* in family planning clinics—the cost-effectiveness of DNA amplification assays. *Sex Transm Dis* 1998; **25**(2): 108–117.
8. LaMontagne DS, Patrick LE, Fine DN, *et al.* Re-evaluating selective screening criteria for chlamydial infection among women in the U.S. Pacific Northwest. *Sex Transm Dis* 2004; **31**(5): 283–289.
9. Paukku M, Kilpikari R, Puolakkainen M, *et al.* Criteria for selective screening for *Chlamydia trachomatis*. *Sex Transm Dis* 2003; **30**(2): 120–123.
10. Centers for Disease Control and Prevention. Screening tests to detect *Chlamydia trachomatis* and *Neisseria gonorrhoeae* infections—2002. *MMWR* 2003; **51**(RR-15): 1–38.
11. Stephenson J, Carder C, Copas A, *et al.* Home screening for chlamydial infection: is it acceptable to young men and women? *Sex Transm Infect* 2000; **76**(1): 25–27.
12. Andersen B, Ostergaard L, Moller JK, *et al.* Effectiveness of a mass media campaign to recruit young adults for testing of *Chlamydia trachomatis* by use of home obtained and mailed samples. *Sex Transm Infect* 2001; **77**(6): 416–418.
13. Andersen B, Olesen F, Moller JK, *et al.* Population-based strategies for outreach screening of urogenital *Chlamydia trachomatis* infections: a randomized, controlled trial. *JID* 2002; **185**(2): 252–258.
14. Herrmann BF, Johansson AB and Mardh PA. A retrospective study of efforts to diagnose infections by *Chlamydia trachomatis* in a Swedish county. *Sex Transm Dis* 1991; **18**(4): 233–237.
15. Herrmann B and Egger M. Genital *Chlamydia trachomatis* infections in Uppsala County, Sweden, 1985-1993: declining rates for how much longer? *Sex Transm Dis* 1995; **22**(4): 253–260.
16. Gotz H, Lindback J, Ripa T, *et al.* Is the increase in notifications of *Chlamydia trachomatis* infections in Sweden the result of changes in prevalence, sampling frequency or diagnostic methods? *Scand J Infect Dis* 2002; **34**: 28–34.
17. Britton TF, DeLisle S and Fine D. STDs and family planning clinics: a regional program for chlamydia control that works. *Am J Gynecol Health* 1992; **6**(3): 80–87.
18. Centers for Disease Control and Prevention. Sexually Transmitted Disease Surveillance 2003 Supplement: Chlamydia Prevalence Monitoring Project Annual Report 2003. Atlanta: CDC, Division of STD Prevention, 2004.
19. Addiss DG, Vaughn ML, Ludka D, *et al.* Decreased prevalence in *Chlamydia trachomatis* infection associated with a selective screening program of family planning clinics in Wisconsin. *Sex Transm Dis* 1993; **20**(1): 28–35.
20. Katz BP, Blythe MJ, van der Pol B, *et al.* Declining prevalence of chlamydial infection among adolescent girls. *Sex Transm Dis* 1996; **23**(3): 226–229.

21. Bachmann LH, MacAluso M and Hook EW 3rd. Demonstration of declining community prevalence of *Chlamydia trachomatis* infection using sentinel surveillance. *Sex Transm Dis* 2003; **30**(1): 20–24.

22. Mertz KJ, Levine WC, Mosure DJ, *et al.* Trends in the prevalence of chlamydial infections – the impact of community-wide testing. *Sex Transm Dis* 1997; **24**(3): 169–175.

23. Dicker LW, Mosure DJ, Levine WC, *et al.* Impact of switching laboratory tests on reported trends in *Chlamydia trachomatis* infections. *Am J Epidemiol* 2000; **151**(4); 430–435.

24. Pimenta JM, Catchpole M, Rogers PA, *et al.* Opportunistic screening for genital chlamydial infection I: acceptability of urine testing in primary and secondary healthcare settings. *Sex Transm Infect* 2003; **79**(1): 16–21.

25. Department of Health. Choosing health: making healthier choices easier. London: Department of Health, 2004.

26. LaMontagne DS, Fenton KA, Randall S, *et al.* Establishing the national chlamydia screening programme in England: results from the first full year of screening. *Sex Transm Infect* 2004; **80**(5): 335–341.

27. Orr P, Sherman E, Blanchard J, *et al.* Epidemiology of infection due to *Chlamydia trachomatis* in Manitoba, Canada. *CID* 1994; **19**(5): 876–883.

28. Low N, McCarthy A, Macleod J, *et al.* The chlamydia screening studies: rationale and design. *Sex Transm Infect* 2004; **80:** 342–348.

29. Macleod J, Salisbury C, Low N, *et al.* Coverage and uptake of systematic postal screening for gential *Chlamydia trachomatis* and prevalence of infection in the United Kingdom general population: cross sectional study. *BMJ*, April 2005; **330:** 940.

30. van Bergen J, Gotz HH, Richardus JH, *et al.* Prevalence of urogenital *Chlamydia trachomatis* increases significantly with level of urbaninsation and suggests targeted screening approaches: results from the first national population based study in the Netherlands. *Sex Transm Infect* 2005; **81**(1): 17–23.

31. Gotz H, van Bergen JEAM, Veldhuijzen IK, *et al.* A prediction rule for selective screening of *Chlamydia trachomatis* infection. *Sex Transm Infect* 2005; **81:** 24–30.

32. Bloomfield PJ, Steiner KC, Kent CK, *et al.* Repeat chlamydia screening by mail, San Francisco. *Sex Transm Infect* 2003; **79:** 28–30.

33. Young H, Allison K, Carrick-Anderson K, *et al.* Chlamydia in heterosexual men: could peak prevalence be in teenagers? *Sex Transm Infect* 2005; **81:** 94.

34. Verhoeven V, Avonts D, Meheus A, *et al.* Chlamydial infection: an accurate model for opportunistic screening in general practice. *Sex Transm Infect* 2003; **79**(5): 313–317.

35. Aldeen T, Haghdoost A and Hay P. Urine based screening for asymptomatic/undiagnosed genital chlamydial infection in young people visiting the accident and emergency department is feasible, acceptable, and can be epidemiologically helpful. *Sex Transm Infect* 2003; **79:** 229–233.

36. van Bergen JE, Postma MJ, Peerbooms PG, *et al.* Effectiveness and cost-effectiveness of a pharmacy-based screening programme for *Chlamydia trachomatis* in a high-risk health centre population in Amsterdam using mailed home-collected urine samples. *Intl J STD AIDS* 2004; **15**(12): 797–802.

37. Ford CA, Viadro CI and Miller WC. Testing for chlamydial and gonorrheal infections outside of clinic settings – a summary of the literature. *Sex Transm Dis* 2004; **31**(1): 38–51.

38. Novak DP, Edman A-C, Jonsson M, *et al.* The internet, a simple and convenient tool in *Chlamydia trachomatis* screening of young people. *Eurosurveillance* 2003; **8**(9): 171–176.

39. Westh H and Kolmos HJ. Large-scale testing of women in Copenhagen has not reduced the prevalence of *Chlamydia trachomatis* infections. *Clin Microbiol Infect* 2003; **9**(7): 619–624.

40. Scholes D, Stergachis A, Heidrich FE, *et al.* Prevention of pelvic inflammatory disease by screening for cervical chlamydial infections. *NEJM* 1996; **334**(21): 1362–1366.

41. Ostergaard L, Andersen B, Moeller JK, *et al.* H ome sampling versus conventional swab samples for screening of *Chlamydia trachomatis* in women: a cluster-randomized 1-year follow-up study. *CID* 2000; **31**(4): 951–957.
42. Welte R, Kretzschmar M, Leidl R, *et al.* Cost-effectiveness of screening programs for *Chlamydia trachomatis* – a population-based dynamic approach. *Sex Transm Dis* 2000; **27**(9): 518–529.
43. Marrazzo JM, Celum CL, Hillis SD, *et al.* Performance and cost-effectiveness of selective screening criteria for *Chlamydia trachomatis* infection in women: implications for a national chlamydia control strategy. *Sex Transm Dis* 1997; **24**(3): 131–141.
44. Kretzschmar M, Welte R, van den Hoek A, *et al.* Comparative model-based analysis of screening programs for *Chlamydia trachomatis* infections. *Am J Epidemiol* 2001; **153**(1): 90–101.
45. Townsend JRP and Turner HS. Analysing the effectiveness of chlamydia screening. *J Oper Res Soc* 2000; **51**(7): 812–824.
46. Honey E, Templeton A. Prevention of pelvic inflammatory disease by the control of *C. trachomatis* infection. *Intl J Gynecol Obstet* 2002; **78**(3): 257–261.
47. Kamwendo F, Forslin L, Bodin L, *et al.* Programmes to reduce pelvic inflammatory disease—the Swedish experience. *Lancet* 1998; **351** (suppl III): 25–28.
48. Honey E, Augood C, Templeton A, *et al.* Cost effectiveness of screening for *Chlamydia trachomatis*: a review of published studies. *Sex Transm Infect* 2002; **78**(6): 406–412.

CHAPTER 4

The Diagnosis of
Chlamydia trachomatis *Genital Infection*

Barbara Van Der Pol
Indiana University School of Medicine Chlamydia Laboratory,
Indianapolis, Indiana, USA

DEVELOPMENT OF CHLAMYDIA DIAGNOSTICS

Although chlamydial infections are highly prevalent, this sexually transmitted infection was little known in public health settings prior to the 1980s due to limitations with diagnostic methods. Serology was used to distinguish between acute and chronic infection and to obtain population-based estimates of lifetime exposure. However, serology required specialized reagents, highly skilled microscopists and multiple samples per patient. Culture was standardized in the 1970s making isolation of the organism a useful diagnostic tool. The restrictive specimen collection, transport and storage conditions limited the availability of this test to clinics working with a reference or research laboratory with an interest in *C. trachomatis*.

The first two antigen detection assays developed were the MicroTrak® (Trinity Biotech, Ireland) direct immunofluorescence assay (DFA) and the Chlamydiazyme® (Abbott Laboratories, USA) solid phase enzyme-linked immunosorbent assay (EIA). DFA utilized a fluorescein-tagged monoclonal antibody to allow *C. trachomatis* elementary bodies to be microscopically visualized in cellular smears collected from conjunctiva or the endocervix. Adequate collection and fixation of cellular material onto slides is critical for obtaining a valid test result. This remains the only type of test that has the capacity to directly assess specimen quality. DFA requires an expert microscopist and cannot be done in large batches. EIA used polyclonal anti-chlamydial antibodies to capture chlamydia antigen onto beads. Secondary antibodies were used to elicit a chemical reaction that was detected by a luminometer. An advantage of both assays was rapid completion (2-3 hours) compared to culture, which required 3-7 days for isolation of the organism.

As additional EIA assays were being developed, several point-of-care (POC) rapid assays became available. Both lab-based EIA and POC suffered from low sensitivity (65-85%) relative to culture and questions regarding specificity. However, the rapid turn-around time and the less restrictive requirements for specimen transport made them an attractive option, particularly in high prevalence settings such as STD clinics. In these populations, decreases in sensitivity may be acceptable in exchange for the ability to test for non-viable organisms with rapid turn-around time. In a decision analysis study by Gift *et al.*[1], when the patient return rate was 65% or lower, rapid POC diagnostics provided an increase in the number of patients treated even though fewer infections were identified. This highlights the importance of choosing a diagnostic assay that meets the need of the setting in which it will be used.

The next major advance in chlamydia diagnostics was the utilization of nucleic acid sequences rather than antigens as detection targets. The Pace2® CT assay (Gen-Probe, USA) was based on detection of rRNA sequences specific to *C. trachomatis* and was the first commercial assay with the ability to test for both chlamydia and *Neisseria gonorrhoeae* from a single patient sample. The sensitivity was similar to that of culture, but again there were questions regarding specificity. A confirmatory assay was soon developed to address this issue. The addition of gonorrhea to the test menu made this assay extremely attractive to public health clinics in the United States. Nucleic acid amplification tests (NAATs) followed soon after the rRNA based assay. NAATs use a variety of enzymatic methods to exponentially amplify target DNA or RNA. Amplified product is detected by a variety of means giving the assays unique performance characteristics. Similar to the DNA-probe assay, the NAATs combined chlamydia and gonorrhea testing from a single sample. These assays all provide both improved sensitivity and increased sample flexibility compared to tissue culture, antigen detection and DNA-probe assays.

Antigen-based and DNA probe assays were initially evaluated for regulatory clearance by comparison with culture as this was the existing gold standard for chlamydia diagnosis. DNA amplification tests are more sensitive than culture, thus, the actual sensitivity estimates of early non-culture assays were inflated[2]. Estimation of the performance characteristics of the NAATs proved to be equally problematic due to a gold standard (culture) with less sensitivity than the methods under evaluation. This raised the question of the best method for confirming positive results when the assay under evaluation is superior to the comparator assays[3, 4]. An excellent evaluation of the impact of choosing a revised gold standard is discussed by Martin *et al.*[5] The issues associated with assay evaluation and performance variability underscore the need for validation of assays within each laboratory, not only prior to adoption of a method, but also on a recurring basis.

COMMERCIALLY AVAILABLE ASSAYS

This section will provide brief descriptions of the most commonly used assays currently available. This is not intended to be an exhaustive listing or an endorsement, but rather an overview of those tests that clinicians are most likely to encounter. **Table 1** provides a brief summary of the advantages and disadvantages of various laboratory based assays. DFA tests are not included in the table as they fill a discreet niche and would not be advisable for large-scale screening and diagnostics. Similarly, POC tests are not included as they currently lack the necessary sensitivity to be useful for most chlamydia control programs although they remain useful in certain settings.

Isolation in Tissue Culture
Culture has gone full circle and is now available predominately in laboratories with a research interest in *C. trachomatis*. Culture is no longer an appropriate diagnostic test under most conditions since it is less sensitive than the NAATs, has a significantly longer turn-around time and more restrictive handling conditions. Culture is now requested predominately for use in medico-legal cases, due to the assumption of 100% specificity, and for test-of-cure testing that is requested less than 14 days following treatment. In fact, the specificity of NAATs is such that these should be acceptable for medico-legal cases and reliance on culture reflects the slow pace of change in legal standards. Test-of-cure is rarely performed given the efficacy of single dose treatments now available and is most often performed more than 14 days post-treatment at which point the NAAT assays are appropriate since DNA shedding from the initial infection should be complete by this time. Therefore, unless isolates of organisms are desirable for research purposes, there is no longer a valid justification for culture as a routine diagnostic method.

Table 1. Relative Merits of Commercial Assays

Assay (Type)	Sample Types	Transport Stability	Cost	Throughput	Environmental Contamination Control	Reproducibility	Sensitivity
MicroTrak (EIA)	Good (No liquid cytology)	Good	Low	Very good	Excellent (Washers may become contaminated)	Moderate (Positives should be confirmed)	Moderate
IDEIA PCE (EIA)	Good (No liquid cytology)	Good	Low	Very good	Excellent (Washers may become contaminated)	Moderate (Positives should be confirmed)	Very good
Pace 2 (DNA Probe)	Moderate (No urine or liquid cytology)	Good	Moderate	Good	Excellent	Moderate (Positives should be confirmed)	Very good
Hybrid Capture 2 (DNA Probe)	Moderate (No vaginal swab)	Good	Moderate	Excellent	Excellent	Very Good	Very good
COBAS Amplicor (NAAT)	Excellent	Moderate (Cold chain required)	High	Good	Very Good	Very Good	Excellent
ProbeTec (NAAT)	Excellent	Good	High	Very Good	Poor	Moderate	Excellent
Aptima (NAAT)	Excellent	Excellent	High	Excellent	Good (No carry over control mechanism)	Very Good	Excellent

Antigen-based Detection Methods

Two direct fluorescent antibody assays, MicroTrak direct stain and Pathfinder® direct stain (BioRad Laboratories, USA) are available for staining of smears for visualization of chlamydial elementary bodies. The MicroTrak assay uses a monoclonal antibody specific for *C. trachomatis* major outer membrane protein (MOMP) and does not cross react with *C. pneumoniae.* In contrast, the Pathfinder reagent uses a polyclonal antibody specific for lipopolysaccharide (LPS) that is more broadly reactive and will stain *C. pneumoniae* as well as *C. trachomatis.* The most common use for DFA is staining of conjunctiva smears, predominately in neonates in developed countries. The stains offer the advantage of rapid turn-around time and high specificity. In addition, no other commercial assay has a regulatory claim for conjunctival samples.

The two most commonly used EIA assays are the MicroTrak EIA® (Trinity Biotech, Ireland) and the IDEIA® (Dako Diagnostics, UK). The most commonly used version of the latter is the IDEIA PCE®. Both assays are cleared for use with endocervical, urethral and urine samples, can be completed in one day, and allow batch processing of numerous samples. The only advantage of the MicroTrak is low cost as it has lower sensitivity than other available methods. The IDEIA PCE uses a polymer conjugate containing multiple copies of LPS-specific antibodies and enzymes that results in amplification of the colorimetric output. As a result of this modification, IDEIA PCE reports sensitivities similar to that of DNA probe assays[6]. In settings where the cost of NAAT may be prohibitive, this may be the best antigen based alternative available.

The three POC assays most commonly used are the Clearview® (Unipath, UK), BioStar® (Thermo Electron Corp., USA) and QuickVue® (Quidel, USA). Results are available within 30-40 minutes ensuring that patients can receive results, and treatment if necessary, before leaving the clinic. Processed samples are applied, usually via a dropper, onto a test matrix followed by a chase buffer and/or additional reagents. A visual readout similar to a pregnancy or HIV rapid test is obtained. These tests have excellent specificity but only moderate sensitivity. The main utility of these tests is in applications where return for treatment is unlikely. In settings such as correctional intake, field screening or developing country STD control programs, the trade-off between rapid results coupled with immediate treatment and use of a test with moderate sensitivity may be acceptable.

DNA Probes

Two assays in this class are the Pace2 and the Hybrid Capture® 2 CT/GC assay (Digene Corp., USA)[7, 8]. Both assays can be used to test for chlamydia alone or chlamydia and gonorrhea in combination. Pace2 uses a labeled DNA probe that binds to chlamydial rRNA. Due to the large number of rRNA copies naturally present in each cell, no amplification is required for this assay. A chemiluminescent reaction detects DNA/RNA hybrids. The assay is isothermal and complete in approximately 2 hours. In response to concerns about specificity, a probe competition assay was developed to rule out cross-reactive binding. It is strongly recommended that weakly positive samples be re-tested using the competition assay in order to maximize specificity. This test is being phased out by the availability of reasonable pricing on more sensitive assays.

The Hybrid Capture 2 CT/GC assay differs from the Pace2 assay in that the target sequence is DNA and the labeled probe is RNA. Even though the target is DNA, this test does not result in amplification of the target sequence. Instead, the signal is amplified by use of multiple labeled antibodies specific for DNA/RNA hybrids. This test is similar to the Hybrid Capture 2 HPV assay allowing chlamydia, gonorrhea and HPV testing from the same processed sample. This test has been cleared for use with an automated instrument that allows testing of more than 300 samples per run with results available in 6-7 hours. The assay compares well with NAATs although the sensitivity is somewhat lower. The possibility for carry-over contamination and inhibition of amplification is reduced since the DNA target is not amplified.

Nucleic Acid Amplification Tests

NAATs are currently the best diagnostic tool available in resource unlimited settings[9-14]. Since few settings meet this ideal, it is important to weigh the advantages and disadvantages of other diagnostic tools before making a final selection. NAATs do have several advantages that are independent of manufacturer. NAATs are clearly the most sensitive assays available; all commercially available assays can test for both chlamydia and gonorrhea; and these assays have a broader range of useful sample types that include less invasively collected samples than endocervical and urethral swabs. However, the NAAT assays also share some common difficulties. Amplified technologies are inherently subject to false positive results due to the exponential amplification of target sequences. Any action that involves an open amplified sample is a potential source for aerosol formation and environmental contamination. Once laboratory facilities and equipment (e.g. pipettors) become contaminated, recovering from carry-over contamination may be extremely difficult. A second issue involves the potential for false negative results. Amplification assays require precise salt, nucleotide and enzyme concentrations in order to proceed efficiently. The enzyme that promotes amplification may also be sensitive to heme or other components of blood, mucous and urine. Therefore, a negative result may actually reflect a lack of amplification rather than a lack of target sequence. The proportion of samples that are inhibitory can vary by test method and may be as high as 7.5% in certain populations[15]. However, the meaning of a negative result may be misleading for any test and should always be reported to a patient with a cautionary warning regarding the risk of infection depending on sexual behaviors.

The COBAS Amplicor® CT/NG assay (Roche Diagnostics Corp., USA) uses polymerase chain reaction (PCR) technology to amplify target DNA sequences using organism-specific biotinylated primer pairs. The chlamydial target is located on the cryptic plasmid and is therefore available in 7-10 copies per organism. Following a 3-temperature amplification process, products are hybridized to magnetic beads coated with species-specific probe sequences located interior to the primer sequences. The detection process is based on biotin-avidin interactions. Approximately 96 samples, including specimens and controls, can be tested in one shift with one COBAS instrument. Swabs are collected in a commercially available transport medium. Urine and swabs are stable at 4°C for up to 7 days. Approved specimen types include endocervical swabs, urethral swabs, liquid cytology medium and first-catch urine. Additional samples for which there is evidence of acceptability include vaginal, rectal and conjunctival swabs[16-18]. The Amplicor assay is used by approximately one third of diagnostic laboratories in the US that perform nucleic acid based testing.

This assay includes a measure of inhibition that is based on a dummy DNA sequence in every reaction tube. If the probe specific for this sequence does not give a positive reaction, the sample is considered inhibitory to amplification. This is intended to give the diagnostician evidence that a negative result is truly negative and not merely affected by contents of the sample. Since tests are ordered on a per-tube basis, laboratories have the flexibility to order chlamydia only or any combination of chlamydia, gonorrhea and internal control. In samples for which the laboratory has evidence that inhibition is rare, the amplification control may be eliminated from the test request. Similarly gonorrhea testing can be included or not depending on the clinician request.

The assay also utilizes an enzyme in the amplification mix that degrades previously amplified sequences based on use of dUTP rather that dTTP. This provides the user with a safety net to protect against minor splashes and aerosolization that routinely occur when handling a large number of samples and enhances reproducibility of results.

The BDProbeTec® ET chlamydia and gonorrhea assay was the first commercially available real-time assay. This test uses isothermal strand displacement amplification to simultaneously amplify and detect target sequences at 52.5°C. Amplification of a sequence of the chlamydial cryptic plasmid occurs in a sealed plate with a fluorescent energy transfer read-out. This scheme was designed to minimize the potential for environmental carry-over contamination since amplified samples are never opened.

Approved samples include urine, endocervical and urethral swabs. Again evidence suggests that vaginal swabs are a useful sample type and studies are underway investigating the performance of the assay with additional sample types. Swab samples are collected using the kit provided by the manufacturer and are stable at room temperature (RT) for up to 6 days prior to testing. First-catch urine is stable for up to 24 hours at 4°C. If a preservative pouch is added to the sample, stability of urine is extended to 2 days at RT or 4-6 days at 4°C. The extended RT stability of swabs makes this assay attractive for public health settings that ship samples to a reference laboratory. Approximately 45% of laboratories in the US that perform nucleic acid based testing use this assay routinely.

This assay can detect both chlamydia and gonorrhea and has an optional amplification control available. The choice of tests requested is strip-specific (i.e. each strip of 8 samples must be tested for the same combination of organisms) for chlamydia and gonorrhea. However, the use of amplification control is plate-specific such that if the option is chosen, it applies to all samples on that plate. The test is in a 96-well format with separate wells for each target sequence. Therefore, if requesting chlamydia, gonorrhea and amplification control, wells in each of three columns are used and a total of 32 samples and controls can be tested on one plate. Alternatively, if only chlamydia is requested a total of 96 samples can be run on one plate. Other combinations of chlamydia, gonorrhea and amplification control result in an intermediate number of samples per plate.

Since the assay was designed to be a closed system, no enzymatic method to degrade carry-over contaminants from previous amplifications was included. Unfortunately, there have been numerous incidents where gross environmental contamination has occurred. These events may take weeks of clean-up and recovery that can result in very costly delays and often require relocation to an area previously unexposed to the assay. Laboratories using this assay must rigorously adhere to an environmental monitoring plan in order to detect contamination events in a timely fashion. A second generation assay that appears to be more resistant to this type of contamination is under evaluation.

A separate, but related issue involves reliability of the assay. Although the specificity of the assay is acceptable, this test is more prone to spurious non-reproducible results than the Amplicor assay. In a comparison of multiple aliquots of urine, each processed in triplicate and each replicate tested in triplicate, the ProbeTec assay had lower reproducibility than either Amplicor or LCx® (Abbott Laboratories, USA, no longer available)[8]. In this study, the ProbeTec had occasional false positive chlamydia results that were not caused by processing or technician error. This data supports the need for reproducibility testing, weighted toward samples that give positive results, on a regular basis.

The third major NAAT is the Aptima® Combo 2 assay (Gen-Probe, USA). This assay is based on the principle of rRNA target capture followed by amplification of a sequence of the 23S rRNA of *C. trachomatis*. Amplification is detected using the kinetics of light emission from labeled DNA-probes complimentary to the target region. Approved samples include urine, endocervical, vaginal and urethral swabs and samples collected in liquid cytology medium. Swabs are collected using the manufacturer's transport medium and are stable for up to 60 days at RT making them ideal for transport to distant laboratories. First-catch urine is stable for up to 24 hours following collection and once placed in the manufacturer's medium is stable at RT for up to 30 days. As with the other assays, additional sample types are under evaluation. Approximately 200 samples can be run during one shift using the available automated system. Although this assay is currently used in less than 20% of US laboratories that perform nucleic acid based testing, its popularity is rapidly increasing as a result of the extended sample stability and the high throughput.

The Aptima target capture system involves isolation of target rRNA sequences using capture oligonucleotides and DNA magnetic beads. Following the target capture process, samples are washed to remove the extracellular matrix and any other sample components. This is intended to reduce or eliminate the potential for amplification inhibition. As a result, the assay does not include a measure of inhibition. Data confirming the lack of inhibition were obtained primarily through use of negative patient samples spiked with laboratory strains[19].

Since samples remain sealed following amplification, the potential for carry-over environmental contamination is expected to be very low. However, as with the ProbeTec, environmental monitoring is strongly recommended in the absence of an enzymatic or other control measure for degradation of amplified product. Stringent adherence to cleaning and decontamination procedures is strongly recommended by the manufacturer. Reproducibility should be monitored and is facilitated by the availability of a chlamydia stand alone assay that can be used for confirmation of positive results. This assay uses a target sequence different than the Combo 2 assay and is therefore ideal for repeat testing[20].

For an excellent review of the principles and properties of many of the assays mentioned here as well as some not covered, and a full discussion of the issues related to discrepant analysis in assay evaluation, see the "Chlamydiae.com" website at the following URL: http://www.chlamydiae.com/diagnostics_index.asp. This website provides a review of much of the evaluation literature available on these tests and presents relative sensitivity and specificity ranges. The data are presented fully and fairly, but the reader needs to pay attention to the details of the method used for estimating performance characteristics and consider the figures in the appropriate context.

CHOOSING THE RIGHT TEST

The primary consideration when choosing a diagnostic method must be the population served and the setting in which testing takes place. For settings where patients have difficulty returning to clinic for treatment, the less sensitive POC assays may provide a benefit in the numbers of patients treated. When cost is the major determining factor, EIA is often the test of choice, but DNA-probe technology may be a reasonable alternative. In settings with sufficient resources, NAATs offer the most flexibility in terms of specimen type, sample stability and sensitivity. For situations where samples will be mailed to a reference laboratory, sample stability at RT must be a consideration. It is also important for clinicians to recognize the difference between screening and diagnostics and communicate with the laboratory regarding this distinction. This is related to the expectation of infection in those for whom diagnosis is being confirmed with a laboratory test versus a broad screening where infection may or may not be prevalent[12].

This leads to the issue of positive predictive value (PPV), the number of true positives over the total number of positives reported. PPV is a function of both specificity and the prevalence of disease. When testing a population of individuals who have never been sexually active, the PPV of a test with specificity of 99.9% is 0% since no true positives are possible. Although this is a population rarely encountered by those testing for chlamydia, the principle remains. At an STD clinic with a prevalence of 10%, the PPV of our hypothetical test would be 99.0%. If we drop the specificity to 97%, the PPV would be 77%. However, if we drop the likelihood of infection for a given individual, even though seen at the same clinic, her PPV may be lower. An example is the practice of STD testing prior to initiation of sex within a new relationship. If the individual being tested has not been sexually active for several years, it is extremely unlikely that she will have a true positive result. Therefore, although the sample comes from an STD clinic, assumptions about the patient population may not apply in this case. Clinicians should always make the testing facility aware of this type of circumstance and request confirmation of positives when appropriate.

The question of confirmation arises when tests are used in particularly low PPV situations. However, the definition of "low" may vary by setting. A word of caution about confirmation: it can be fraught with difficulties. There are the problems associated with sampling variation if a second sample is required[21]. If the original sample contained DNA from a recent coital exposure, or from a self-cleared infection, a subsequent sample may be negative even in the absence of interval treatment. In these situations, neither test result is inaccurate, but the clinician is left with a puzzling set of results. Finally, if confirmation is performed on the original sample and the confirmatory method is less sensitive that the original test, true infections may go untreated[22]. In the final analysis, all test results should be interpreted in the context of the patient's clinical circumstances.

LYMPHOGRANULOMA VENEREUM

A recent outbreak of lymphogranuloma venereum (LGV) in Western Europe warrants a brief discussion of the diagnostic issues specific to this strain of *C. trachomatis*. Although LGV is a member of the species *C. trachomatis*, the three strains (L_1, L_2 and L_3) constitute a separate biovar as a result of the differential tissue tropism and pathogenicity exhibited by these organisms. LGV results in invasive infection that preferentially replicates in the genital lymph nodes and the rectal mucosa. The outbreak in Europe has been isolated to men who have sex with men and manifested as acute proctitis.

Although commercially available diagnostic assays were evaluated using laboratory strains including the three LGV serovars, no clinical trials have evaluated the sensitivity of these tests for detection of LGV. NAAT testing is recommended since this is the most sensitive format. However, no assay has a claim for rectal swabs and there is little information concerning the potentially interfering substances that may be present in this sample type. DNA isolation prior to testing is recommended and subsequent strain typing or sequencing may be necessary to confirm infection with LGV. Therefore, samples collected specifically for LGV diagnostics should be clearly marked as such and multiple procedures may be required for confirmation of the strain.

THE FUTURE OF CHLAMYDIA DIAGNOSTICS

The Taqman® (Roche Diagnostics, USA) assay for chlamydia is now available in many markets. This assay provides real-time PCR results in a format that supports testing of 96 samples per run. Abbott is evaluating a real-time PCR assay that uses molecular beacon technology and looks promising. As mentioned above, the ProbeTec second generation assay is in development and appears to address some of the issues associated with the current assay and will provide extended sample stability. Finally, POC tests are being taken to new levels with a rapid amplification assay being developed by the Wellcome Trust. Hopefully, this and other POC assays will improve the sensitivity to a point that makes them useful tools in resource poor settings.

What is really needed is improved reliability and reproducibility for the laboratory-based assays, improved sample type flexibility and improved sample stability. Streamlined or automated specimen processing could help reduce laboratory contaminations and improve reproducibility. Many sample types (e.g. vaginal swabs, rectal swabs and liquid cytology) must be evaluated and validated by testing laboratories since the manufacturers have not included these in their regulatory submissions. Therefore, although there is strong evidence that these are useful samples, laboratories without the resources to perform in-house validations are unable to take advantage of these specimen types. Additionally, as testing moves from the clinical setting to field-based screening, it is imperative to have longer sample stability to facilitate transport to the laboratory. We now have the sensitivity to detect what may be exposures and remnant nucleic acids that never would have resulted in active infection. While there is little harm associated with treatment in these cases, we certainly do not have a pressing need for tests with improved sensitivity, with the exception of POC tests.

SUMMARY

It is important to recognize that studies vary by definition of populations (i.e. what constitutes symptomatic or high risk?), infection status and measures of agreement making cross-study comparisons a risky proposition. Additionally, some assays may perform better with a given sample type and worse with another, making it difficult to rank the overall performance of assays being compared. Clinical trials tend to be performed under highly regulated, and perhaps artificially ideal, laboratory conditions. Once a method is adopted for routine use on a daily basis, adherence to protocols may be relaxed resulting in variability in actual performance compared to the reported estimates[9]. For all of these reasons, the choice of diagnostic test should not be based solely on cost or on performance estimates, which may not be highly accurate, but should also include consideration of the patient population.

In conclusion, NAATS are superior in terms of sensitivity while other methods may be more cost-effective (IDEIA PCE) or lead to increases in the number of cases treated (POC tests). Assays exhibit sample-to-sample, lab-to-lab and technician-to-technician variation that needs to be addressed by stringent evaluation prior to adoption of a procedure. Assay performance may vary over time thus requiring ongoing re-evaluation and comparison. All of the nucleic acid based tests have excellent specificity when performed properly with rigorous adherence to protocols and routine monitoring of reproducibility. No test is perfect, but the ones available today are excellent when requested appropriately, performed accurately and interpreted in conjunction with clinical observations.

REFERENCES

1. Gift TL, Pate MS, Hook EW, 3rd, Kassler WJ. The rapid test paradox: when fewer cases detected lead to more cases treated: a decision analysis of tests for *Chlamydia trachomatis*. *Sex Transm Dis.* 1999 Apr; **26**(4): 232–40.
2. Newhall WJ, Johnson RE, DeLisle S, *et al.* Head-to-head evaluation of five chlamydia tests relative to a quality-assured culture standard. *J Clin Microbiol.* 1999 Mar; **37**(3): 681–5.
3. Alonzo TA, Pepe MS. Using a combination of reference tests to assess the accuracy of a new diagnostic test. *Stat Med.* 1999 Nov 30; **18**(22): 2987–3003.

4. Moncada J, Schachter J, Hook EW, 3rd, *et al.* The effect of urine testing in evaluations of the sensitivity of the Gen-Probe Aptima Combo 2 assay on endocervical swabs for *Chlamydia trachomatis* and *Neisseria gonorrhoeae:* the infected patient standard reduces sensitivity of single site evaluation. *Sex Transm Dis.* 2004 May; **31**(5): 273–7.

5. Martin DH, Nsuami M, Schachter J, *et al.* Use of multiple nucleic acid amplification tests to define the infected-patient "gold standard" in clinical trials of new diagnostic tests for *Chlamydia trachomatis* infections. *J Clin Microbiol.* 2004 Oct; **42**(10): 4749–58.

6. Hirose T, Iwasawa A, Satoh T, *et al.* Clinical study of the effectiveness of a dual amplified immunoassay (IDEIA PCE Chlamydia) for the diagnosis of male urethritis. *Int J STD AIDS.* 1998 Jul; **9**(7): 414–7.

7. Modarress KJ, Cullen AP, Jaffurs WJ, Sr., *et al.* Detection of *Chlamydia trachomatis* and *Neisseria gonorrhoeae* in swab specimens by the Hybrid Capture II and PACE 2 nucleic acid probe tests. *Sex Transm Dis.* 1999 May; **26**(5): 303–8.

8. Van Der Pol B, Williams JA, Smith NJ, *et al.* Evaluation of the Digene Hybrid Capture II Assay with the Rapid Capture System for detection of *Chlamydia trachomatis* and *Neisseria gonorrhoeae. J Clin Microbiol.* 2002 Oct; **40**(10): 3558–64.

9. Black CM, Marrazzo J, Johnson RE, *et al.* Head-to-head multicenter comparison of DNA probe and nucleic acid amplification tests for *Chlamydia trachomatis* infection in women performed with an improved reference standard. *J Clin Microbiol.* 2002 Oct; **40**(10): 3757–63.

10. Chernesky MA, Martin DH, Hook EW, *et al.* Ability of new APTIMA CT and APTIMA GC assays to detect *Chlamydia trachomatis* and *Neisseria gonorrhoeae* in male urine and urethral swabs. *J Clin Microbiol.* 2005 Jan; **43**(1): 127–31.

11. Gaydos CA, Quinn TC, Willis D, *et al.* Performance of the APTIMA Combo 2 assay for detection of *Chlamydia trachomatis* and *Neisseria gonorrhoeae* in female urine and endocervical swab specimens. *J Clin Microbiol.* 2003 Jan; **41**(1): 304–9.

12. Horner P, Skidmore S, Herring A, *et al.* Enhanced enzyme immunoassay with negative-gray-zone testing compared to a single nucleic Acid amplification technique for community-based chlamydial screening of men. *J Clin Microbiol.* 2005 May; **43**(5): 2065–9.

13. Van Der Pol B, Ferrero DV, Buck-Barrington L, *et al.* Multicenter evaluation of the BDProbeTec ET System for detection of *Chlamydia trachomatis* and *Neisseria gonorrhoeae* in urine specimens, female endocervical swabs, and male urethral swabs. *J Clin Microbiol.* 2001 Mar; **39**(3): 1008–16.

14. Van Der Pol B, Quinn TC, Gaydos CA, *et al.* Multicenter evaluation of the AMPLICOR and automated COBAS AMPLICOR CT/NG tests for detection of *Chlamydia trachomatis. J Clin Microbiol.* 2000 Mar; **38**(3): 1105–12.

15. Mahony J, Chong S, Jang D, *et al.* Urine specimens from pregnant and nonpregnant women inhibitory to amplification of *Chlamydia trachomatis* nucleic acid by PCR, ligase chain reaction, and transcription-mediated amplification: identification of urinary substances associated with inhibition and removal of inhibitory activity. *J Clin Microbiol.* 1998 Nov; **36**(11): 3122–6.

16. Gaydos CA, Crotchfelt KA, Shah N, *et al.* Evaluation of dry and wet transported intravaginal swabs in detection of *Chlamydia trachomatis* and *Neisseria gonorrhoeae* infections in female soldiers by PCR. *J Clin Microbiol.* 2002 Mar; **40**(3): 758–61.

17. Golden MR, Astete SG, Galvan R, *et al.* Pilot study of COBAS PCR and ligase chain reaction for detection of rectal infections due to *Chlamydia trachomatis. J Clin Microbiol.* 2003 May; **41**(5): 2174–5.

18. Schachter J, McCormack WM, Chernesky MA, *et al.* Vaginal swabs are appropriate specimens for diagnosis of genital tract infection with *Chlamydia trachomatis. J Clin Microbiol.* 2003 Aug; **41**(8): 3784–9.

19. Chong S, Jang D, Song X, *et al.* Specimen processing and concentration of *Chlamydia trachomatis* added can influence false-negative rates in the LCx assay but not in the APTIMA Combo 2 assay when testing for inhibitors. *J Clin Microbiol.* 2003 Feb; **41**(2): 778–82.

20. Boyadzhyan B, Yashina T, Yatabe JH, *et al.* Comparison of the APTIMA CT and GC assays with the APTIMA combo 2 assay, the Abbott LCx assay, and direct fluorescent-antibody and culture assays for detection of *Chlamydia trachomatis* and *Neisseria gonorrhoeae. J Clin Microbiol.* 2004 Jul; **42**(7): 3089–93.

21. Nordbo SA, Lund K, Skjeldestad FE. Retesting and follow-up of first-catch urines from men yield variable results with three *Chlamydia trachomatis* nucleic acid amplification tests. *Apmis.* 2000 Nov; **108**(11): 725–8.

22. Schachter J, Hook EW, Martin DH, *et al.* Confirming positive results of nucleic acid amplification tests (NAATs) for *Chlamydia trachomatis*: all NAATs are not created equal. *J Clin Microbiol.* 2005 Mar; **43**(3):1372-3.

CHAPTER 5

Human genital infections with Chlamydia trachomatis – *is there a role for serology?*

Timothy R Moss
Genito Urinary Medicine, Doncaster and Bassetlaw
NHS Foundation Trust, Doncaster, UK

Sohrab Darougar
University of London, UK

INTRODUCTION

The worldwide prevalence and incidence of *Chlamydia trachomatis* genital infection (CtGI) is estimated to be 700 million and 90 million respectively, and is increasing. In the USA and Western Europe, the number of new cases of CtGI is estimated to exceed 4 and 5.5 million per annum respectively. The true prevalence and incidence of CtGI may be 2 to 3 times higher if cases of chronic CtGI with mild symptoms and asymptomatic cases were included.

Based on first and second generation antigen detection systems several authors have acknowledged the problem of the large number of asymptomatic cases of human genital chlamydial infection (50-80%) in which no clinical presentation is made;[1] or where there are symptoms and signs which are generally mild and indistinguishable from those of other sexually transmitted infections (STIs).

Indeed, it may be appropriate to regard chlamydial genital tract infection in both men and women as a potentially chronic disease with an insidious onset.

In men and women with CtGI spontaneous recovery may occur in a small number of cases.

Frequently CtGI may persist for months or years causing serious complications in both sexes,[2] especially females. Chronic/long term infection may be associated with the shedding of very low numbers of infectious elementary bodies, or intermittent shedding. In these patients the sensitivity of conventional antigen detection tests was low. The recent introduction of Nucleic Acid amplification tests (NAATs) may increase positivity rates by up to 30%.

Immunological responses in human chlamydial diseases vary. In the case of *C. trachomatis* serovars A, B, B & C (trachoma) immunological responses appear to be predominantly cellular.

This contrasts with the serovars L1, L2 and L3 of lymphogranuloma venereum (LGV) where cellular responses deal promptly with the initial skin lesion; but the disseminated lymph node involvement, and other complications (such as polyarthritis) prompt rising antibody titres detectable by the LGV complement fixation test (see chapter 14 LGV). Exposure to the genito urinary serovars (D-K) results in a distinct cellular response. Humoral responses have received increasing attention in recent years.

In this chapter it is intended to discuss the possibility that chlamydial serological responses may offer a useful adjunct to the diagnosis and understanding of genito urinary chlamydial infections and their complications.

Serological responses will be considered within the context of serial observations, in combination with antigen detection systems, and within the context of the clinical complexity, extent, and duration of the disease process.

A new sero-diagnostic and sero-epidemiological renaissance may now be anticipated as a result of technological development and increased awareness of the importance of chlamydia serology.

DIAGNOSIS

The diagnosis of genital chlamydial infection relies entirely on laboratory tests. Methods of diagnosis based on isolation of the organism, detecting its infectious elementary bodies using mononuclear antibodies or detecting its components by enzyme immunoassay (EIA) are sensitive during the acute phase of the infection. They are, however, of low sensitivity in cases of chronic or repeated chlamydial infections. There is debate as to whether these tests are cost effective in low risk populations.[3]

Although high rates of infection were identified in asymptomatic teenage women, Clay[4] emphasised that opportunistic screening and treatment will fail to reduce the prevalence of chlamydia without co-ordinated contact tracing and follow-up. The proposed UK Nationwide screening model sees this process as essential.[5] The range and application of antigen detection in diagnosis is covered by Dr Barbara Van Der Pol (chapter 4 – Diagnosis).

With the introduction of NAATs there has been a considerable increase in our understanding of the prevalence of CtGI. Comparison of the number of chlamydia-positive people reported in National surveillance statistics with estimates of prevalent infections from population based surveys indicates that probably over 80% of infection in the community is asymptomatic and remains undetected and therefore untreated.[5]

The further development and application of serological tests must therefore be regarded as a valid and urgent priority. This is of particular importance with regard to recurrent, latent, subacute and chronic disease.

THE PRESENT STATUS OF CHLAMYDIA SEROLOGY

False positive results can occur in chlamydia serology; for example with L2 based tests due to cross reactivity to antibodies produced to *C. pneumoniae* which is widely prevalent in Europe and the USA. This led to a widespread belief that there was little place for chlamydia serology in the diagnosis of human genital infections.

A variety of serological tests including complement-fixation, agglutination, haemagglutination, immunodiffusion, haemolysis in gel and radioimmune precipitation tests have been used in the past. These tests detect group-specific antibodies and have a very low sensitivity and specificity for detecting specific CtDK antibodies. The methods commonly used today are complement fixation, indirect immunofluorescence (IFT), enzyme immunoassay (EIA) and microimmunofluorescence (MIF) tests.

In IFT or EIA, infected cells with one Ct serotype, purified elementary bodies of a Ct serotype or a pool of Ct serotypes D to K are used as a single antigen. These tests detect group-specific chlamydial antibodies and cannot differentiate between antibody responses to CtDK, *C. pneumoniae* and *C. psittaci*.

In contrast the MIF test detects and separates antibodies to Ct from those to non-genital chlamydia species including *C. pneumoniae* and *C. psittaci*. The original MIF test is a complex technology requiring deposition of microdots of all chlamydial serotype antigens individually and a complicated method of reading, recording and analysis of results. Subsequently, simplified versions of MIF were developed to detect type-specific antibodies to chlamydia species.

In our laboratory we used a modified MIF test developed by Treharne *et al.*[6] In summary the test consists of the following: samples of blood are collected by venepuncture. The sera can be tested immediately or stored at +4°C for testing after a few days or stored at –20°C for a longer period.

The antigens consist of panels of microdots containing egg grown purified elementary bodies of chlamydia serovars. Each panel contains four antigen microdots representing:

1) a pool of *C. trachomatis* serovars D to K,
2) single *C. psittaci* agent, IOL 395 isolated in the virus laboratory, Institute of Ophthalmology, London, from the eyes of a human with acute conjunctivitis. This organism cross-reacts with reference sera against other *C. psittaci* strains including 33L, isolated from a case of lymphogranuloma venereum, A22/18, a ewe abortion agent, and a pigeon chlamydial agent,
3) a single *C. pneumoniae agent* IOL 207, isolated from the eye of a child with clinical signs of trachoma in Iran. IOL-207 is serologically similar to TW183, a *C. pneumoniae* strain isolated from the eye of a patient in Taiwan,
4) a negative control using uninfected yolk sacs prepared the same way as infected yolk sacs.

Serum specimens are tested for the presence of IgG at a starting dilution of 1/16 and IgM at a starting dilution of 1/8 using an indirect immuno-fluorescence staining technique. The presence of specific antibodies to CtDK only or cross-reactive against 2 or 3 species, with the highest level against CtDK are considered to identify a CtDK response.

Thomas *et al.*[7] used the MIF technique to assess the significance of positive serology in fallopian tube disease. They reported a marked association between level of titre and the likelihood of tubal damage. (This association will be discussed later.)

Laparoscopy has been regarded as the Gold Standard diagnostic method for pelvic inflammatory disease but this affords limited information regarding endo tubal morphology. In particular, no insight is afforded with regard to cilial function and physiology.

Screening by NAATs provides evidence of current infection, but gives no indication of the proportion of the population ever infected (cumulative incidence). It does not identify those with pelvic disease as a result of current or past infection.

With antigen tests of cervical and tubal material proving negative in some cases; the need for further development in serological testing is emphasised.

Identification of cases who have ever been exposed requires detection of humoral antibodies. If a rapid, high throughput, specific and sensitive *C. trachomatis* antibody assay were available the proportion of the population ever exposed could be monitored, and would provide one measure of the impact of screening programmes on disease prevalence.

Thomas argued that by using *C. trachomatis* antibody testing more widely it may be possible to reduce the number of laparoscopies performed, and that MIF chlamydia serology should become an integral part of infertility investigation.[7]

The potential value of using both McCoy cell culture systems in isolating *C. trachomatis* and serological tests for chlamydia was argued as early as in 1987.[8] It was suggested that the use of Micro Immuno Fluorescent chlamydia serology may be a useful adjunct to tests for antigen from the endocervix and fallopian tubes. One early conclusion was that the addition of species specific chlamydia serology to the routine investigation of women presenting with pelvic inflammatory disease (PID) undoubtedly aids the identification of those infected with *C. trachomatis*. Furthermore, if recurrences of pelvic infection are to be minimised, these women require prolonged tetracycline or erythromycin therapy as well as investigation and treatment of their sexual partner(s).

Examples of such cases will be discussed later in this chapter.

A preceding local study (1986)[9] supported this concept. The untreated, asymptomatic male partner of a woman with PID is an important aetiological factor in the recurrent nature of this disease.

Seventy-one women were reviewed who had a clinical diagnosis of acute PID. 40.8% of women with acute PID had evidence of chlamydial infection using a combination of McCoy cell culture/antigen detection and MIF serology. All of these women were counselled and advised to ask their current sexual partner/partners to attend the Genito Urinary Medicine (GUM) clinic for investigation. This process was patient led, supported by counselling from health advisers and/or ward based nursing staff.

Forty-five male partners were seen and screened for genital tract infection by conventional methods. Of the 45 male partners investigated >2 out of 3 had recoverable chlamydia in their anterior urethra. It was of particular interest to find that chlamydia was isolated from some men whose female partners were culture negative but D-K IgG sero-positive. These men were frequently asymptomatic carriers.

At this time, chlamydial pelvic inflammatory disease in Doncaster appeared to be five times more common than gonococcal PID. Combined infections were frequently identified. Some of these cases may, represent "quiescent chlamydial infection". Latent chlamydial infection with serovars D-K may (like *C. pneumoniae*) be unmasked by another infection. MIF serology supports this interpretation.

It was concluded that unless regular male consorts are fully investigated and additional consorts are also traced, we cannot anticipate containment of chlamydial genital infection in communities.

The role of serology was subjected to further study by the same group and reported in 1993.[10]

Over 7000 cases attending the GUM clinic in Doncaster between May 1983 and May 1990 were assessed serologically using the modified Micro Immuno Fluorescent serology (MIF) test[10] (described above).

This study showed that antibodies to *C. pneumoniae* and *C. psittaci* accounted for up to 50% of all chlamydia IgG positive cases. Infections with *C. pneumoniae* are universally widespread, and have been demonstrated serologically in up to 50% of the adult population in Europe and the United States.

The demonstration that IgG responses to *C. pneumoniae* and *C. psittaci* (i.e. non-genital pathogens) may account for up to half of all chlamydia sero-positive cases attending GUM clinics is important. This explains why less specific chlamydia blood tests have not been found to be helpful, and why there has been little advocacy for the use of chlamydia serology in clinical practice.

It is clearly necessary to recommend that serological tests which can differentiate antibodies to genito urinary *C. trachomatis* serovars D-K (CtDK) from those to *C. pneumoniae* and *C. psittaci* should be the focus of further sero-epidemiological studies.

Although there is a degree of cross reactivity in the MIF test system referred to, it appears possible to accurately identify D-K responses in most cases.

The accuracy of interpretation is believed to be enhanced by considering the IgG sero status within the clinical context; and preferably against the background of past and present antigen detection results and MIF species specific serology in both the presenting patient and in the sexual partner(s).

Clinical practice over some 25 years has allowed a very large, day to day experience of managing diagnostically discordant couples. The detection of one partner who is antigen positive and the other antigen negative but D-K IgG sero positive calls for the exclusion of complications in both. This may influence treatment considerations and long term follow-up.

Subsequently some 200 chlamydia positive female patients were studied[11]. Infection was found in the same proportion of male partners. This work compared and contrasted McCoy cell culture with sero diagnosis; and also reviewed clinical diagnosis.

It was shown that in contacts of patients with genital chlamydial infection neither cell culture diagnosis, nor serotype specific serology testing (or clinical diagnosis) alone achieved the levels of sensitivity and specificity required for identifying current infection. It was proposed that selective application of both diagnostic modalities (preferably using NAATs for antigen detection) may offer substantial improvement.

To repeat this study with a larger, prospective analysis would be of compelling interest. Clinical assessment should be more comprehensive. Clinical categorisation should distinguish symptomatic from latent/ asymptomatic/'carrier' cases. Evidence of disseminated male chlamydial disease should be sought such as epididymitis, prostatitis and sexually acquired reactive arthrosis (SARA) as well as complications in females.

There remains wide acceptance that improved antigen detection alone is not wholly satisfactory. It may in part be 'site dependent'. Kinghorn (personal communication) observed:- "It is well established that endo-cervical cultures for *C. trachomatis* may be negative in patients with active tubal infection:- (i.e. chlamydia antigen positive – proven by laparoscopically obtained tubal specimens.)"

When species specific chlamydia serology was combined with more modern antigen detection systems a marked increase in the sensitivity of diagnosis was achieved. This combined approach facilitates the identification and treatment of more cases of infectious genital chlamydial disease in populations – which minimises the very serious risk of female patients being subjected to multiple re-exposure to the pathogen from both exogenous and endogenous sources. There is subsequently a decreased risk in these women of 'amplified tissue damage' not only via a reduction of multiple episodes of exposure to D-K *C. trachomatis* in their genital tract, but also, by limiting or avoiding additional mucosal damage either via the conceptualised hypersensitivity response to the highly immunogenic heat shock protein (HSP60)[12] (or other inappropriate host mediated inflammatory responses) which are considered important in the pathogenesis of fallopian tube destruction by this organism (it is also possible that avoidance of multiple re-exposure decreases intra-cellular immune/pathological processes which contribute to tubal damage).

The fact that late, disseminated chlamydial genital infection in women is chronic, crippling and largely incurable provides another reason for improved serological diagnosis.

Chronic chlamydial infection almost invariably produces a scarring process. The pathogenesis of this scarring is unknown in detail despite the correlation with antibodies to certain epitopes on chlamydial heat shock proteins. A greater understanding of the patho-physiology of this scarring process may allow application of/development of drugs that would limit this process. For example Morton and Kinghorn advocated the use of proteolytics within this context.[13]

In 1991[14] Taylor Robinson stated: "the role of serology in diagnosis continues to be a contentious issue" He recommended caution because high titres do not always correlate with the detection of chlamydia. It is well recognised that in late chlamydial disease, diagnosed serologically, negative antigen tests are most frequent. The use of a range of modalities of investigation, including the most recent developments in antigen detection, in combination with serology:- (and ideally, in conjunction with antigen detection and serology in the sexual partner/partners) – may identify female cases justifying therapeutic intervention.

The complexities of genito urinary chlamydial disease surely merit a greater effort to clarify the role of serology in diagnosis.

At a time when the National Chlamydia Screening Programme is undergoing significant expansion, the wider application of serology could enhance our awareness of the prevalence of exposure to this group of pathogens in selected populations.

There has been considerable interest in antibody responses as markers for chronic sequelae of *C. trachomatis* infection. The cellular and humoral responses to the chlamydial heat shock proteins HSP60 and HSP10 have been implicated in the immunopathology of pelvic chlamydial disease.[15]

Antibodies to these proteins have been found to be a specific, but not highly sensitive marker of pelvic disease.[15]

The exact significance of these antibodies is unknown, but may reflect persistent infection.[16]

Akande *et al.*[17] explored the relationship between serum chlamydia antibody titres and the detection of tubal damage using the whole cell inclusion immunofluorescence test. The whole cell inclusion immunofluorescence assay (WIF) is the only test in which all chlamydial antigens are presented. This increases test sensitivity, but as some determinants are common to all chlamydiae, specificity is compromised.[18,19]

A linear trend between chlamydia antibody titre and the likelihood of tubal

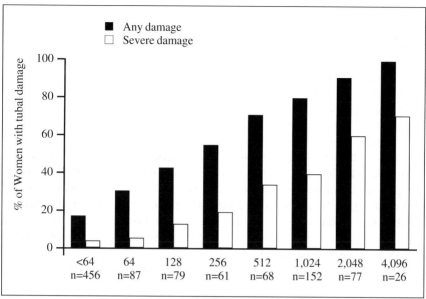

Figure 1. Chlamydia antibody titre.
Reproduced from Akande VA *et al.* Tubal damage in infertile women: prediction using chlamydia serology. *Human Reproduction* 2003; **18**(9): 1841–7 by permission of Oxford University Press.

damage, including severe damage was observed (**Figure 1**).

This Group concluded that chlamydia antibody titres (CATS) are of predictive value in the detection of tubal damage and are quantitatively related to the severity of tubal damage. (These results mirror the clinical findings of the authors of this chapter and this observation is highlighted in the second case history to be described.)

Twenty of these women agreed to undergo laparoscopy and fourteen (70%) had evidence of tubal scarring.[20]

This suggests that WIF antibody titres have the potential to act as a surrogate marker for *C. trachomatis* induced pelvic adhesions. Again, these results mirrored our earlier clinical experience using the MIF test in women with advanced pelvic disease.

If validated – the WIF assay would allow the assessment of changes in age specific prevalence of chlamydial pelvic disease. It would also allow retrospective investigation of the natural history of chlamydial infection at a population level and a range of other factors associated with the development of pelvic disease following CtGI.

Rank[21], suggests that we are now on the threshold of understanding how the basic intracellular molecular interactions of the host cell and the organism may determine the nature of the immune response. It is possible that the interactions that chlamydiae establish within the host cell may actually pre-determine the immune mechanisms (cellular and humoral), which the host may use to limit the infection. Brunham[22] discusses human immunity in the same text and offers a personal view of chlamydial immunity and immuno-pathology. It is suggested that the host facilitates persistent chlamydial infection via a failure to suppress growth at the epithelial cell level. This is due to an induced absence of protective host responses.

Chlamydiae are variably susceptible to inactivation by cellular and humoral defences. High serum antibody to genito urinary chlamydiae suggests persistent infection (see case 2), but the dilemma remains:- How do some organisms survive such defences to initiate and sustain recurrent episodes of infection? Whilst this question remains unanswered, and of fundamental importance, plausible hypotheses are beginning to emerge.[13]

Morton[23] has proposed three (theoretical) types of male carrier status:

1. Urethral carriers.
2. Prostatic carriers.
3. Lymph gland or splenic carriers.
   (Types 2 and 3 may of course present as Type 1)

Positive serology may help identify such carrier states. Treatment of these cases, and their long term serological follow-up alongside treated diseased patients might prove enlightening in terms of understanding residual infection and persistence/latency.

In busy Genito Urinary Medicine Departments the emphasis is on case finding and management of more acute disease. There is a further concern however:- is it possible to detect latent, or asymptomatic active disease by extended clinical surveillance and serological monitoring?

Whilst serodiagnosis of exposure to D-K serovars of *C. trachomatis* may contribute to the identification of 'latent' disease; this concept remains the most challenging in terms of clinical and laboratory diagnosis. Just as the diagnosis of late latent syphilis could only be made after exclusion of neurological or cardiovascular disease activity; so latent chlamydial infection demands at least exclusion of prostatitis in men, SARA in men and women and pelvic disease in women.

With existing serological tests it should be possible to establish a base line in terms of D-K IgG titres and to monitor changing titres against time in the long term surveillance of early disease recurrences and exacerbations of PID and Reiter's syndrome/SARA:- especially in HLA A31 and B27 positive cases.

The presence of type specific antibodies to CtDK suggests that the patient has been exposed to the organism at some time. The natural history of CtGI would support the concept that a number of these patients will have a *current* infection. A judicious application of anti-microbial therapy for these patients *may* have potential benefits.

Whilst acknowledging concerns regarding long term outcomes of chlamydia screening programmes (Dr R Patel – Foreword); work in Scandinavia and the USA has apparently demonstrated that the prevention of pelvic inflammatory disease is achievable by actively screening and treating chlamydial cervical infection. The observation that PID may be present in the absence of detectable antigen in the cervix supports the view that species specific serology may improve the efficacy of this type of screening programme. New serological technologies and studies are anticipated.

CASE REPORTS

Chlamydia and *in vitro* fertilisation embryo replacement (IVF/ER)

Sero-epidemiological studies in patients undergoing IVF/ER further define the avoidable morbidity of female chlamydial infection in the upper genital tract.[24-26]

Chlamydial damage to the epithelial cilia within the fallopian tubes occurs early in both overt and covert pelvic inflammatory disease. Subsequent delay in transfer of the fertilised ovum through the tubal canal predisposes to ectopic gestation.

In women receiving IVF/ER with known tubal disease the serological evidence of exposure to chlamydia D-K was, as expected, much higher than in those with non tubal causes for their infertility. (57% versus 13%).[26]

Of those women with history of both tubal disease and ectopic pregnancy, 69% had serological evidence of previous exposure to D-K serovars of *C. trachomatis*.

Case I

It is believed that the first evidence of a possible relationship between previous exposure to *Chlamydia trachomatis* and failure of IVF/ER was reported by Moss and Steptoe.[27]

This was a case report where chlamydial infection in both husband and wife may have contributed to the loss of an implanted ovum on two occasions following *in vitro* fertilisation.

Extended anti-chlamydial therapy to both partners was followed by a successful ovum implantation and uneventful, successful pregnancy.

(Interestingly, Winston[28] has observed a decline in ovarian function – including a markedly reduced response to oocyte stimulation in women with a history of severe pelvic inflammatory disease).

Case II

In 1990 a middle-aged, monogamous couple, (married for 18 years) were referred to this department. Previous partner changes prior to marriage were openly discussed during joint consultation. The nulliparous female patient, aged 49, was referred (post hysterectomy) for investigation of chronic, recurrent pelvic pain which had run a variable course for most, if not all, of her marriage.

Exacerbations of female pelvic pain were specifically related to the annual surgical dilation of two "mid-penile" strictures in the male anterior urethra. This was invariably followed by a purulent urethral discharge.

All antigen detection attempts (both partners) were negative. The male MIF D-K IgG chlamydia serology was positive at a maximum dilution 1/64.

Female serology identified an astonishing IgM response with D-K positivity to a titre of 1/1024. Extended anti-chlamydial therapy led to an eventual return to sero-negative status in both patients with a concurrent marked clinical improvement maintained throughout two years of follow-up.

Little is known about persistence of antibody titres following acute infection and estimates vary, depending on the sensitivity of the assay. Of 5 tests used in a sero conversion and persistence of Ct antibodies study[29] the MIF IgG seroconversions reverted earliest of negative titres post treatment.

A significant serological response to reinfection was observed only in women with signs of pelvic inflammatory disease. The authors concluded that species specific (serological) tests of high sensitivity and reproducibility are best suited for gynaecological diagnostic purposes.

These two cases illustrate several points of interest.

Concepts of chlamydial reactivation are discussed by Dr Rogstad in chapter 7. The unique development cycle of chlamydia offers a plausible basis for a concept of life-long chlamydial infection in some circumstances.[14]

It is interesting to speculate (Case II):- was this pathological sequence as follows?

1. Surgical intervention in the male leading to reactivation/exacerbation of long term/latent/subacute chlamydial infection (antigen-negative/sero-positive).

   Followed by:
2. Exacerbation of chronic chlamydial-induced pelvic pain in the female partner.
   ±
3. Delayed hypersensitivity response. (60kDa heat shock protein) ± inappropriate host immune response.

(These findings may offer some support for the hypothesis describing reactivation of latent chlamydial genital infection described by the late Dr R S Morton in chapter 16.)

The application of chlamydia serology in couples who are both experiencing features of long term/chronic chlamydial genital tract disease may be more relevant than isolated application of chlamydia serology in individual patients, whatever the stage of disease dissemination.

Case II is particularly unusual. IgM antibody production at very high titres, with a 6-fold reduction in dilution following three months of anti-chlamydial therapy has not previously been seen.

IgM is rarely identified. In the serology study (discussed previously),[11] of 7,002 cases attending Genito Urinary Medicine IgM was detected in only 2.6% of the cases, of which 98% related to *C. trachomatis* D-K.

The low prevalence of IgM in this study compared with other series was thought to be due to the inclusion of a large number of cases with chronic genital infections.

The only other serological study we have undertaken which identified significant numbers of D-K IgM positive subjects referred to a series of women patients who were treated for infertility.

They were all recipients of donated semen prior to the screening of donors for genital tract chlamydia D-K.[30]

IS SEROLOGY A DIAGNOSTIC TEST?

This question merits further discussion.

Until very recently the majority of GUM specialists and microbiologists considered serology tests of little value for the diagnosis of current CtGI, because of its low specificity. This claim is based on the following findings or assumptions:

Presence of chlamydia IgG in a large number of patients with no clinical, epidemiological or microbiological evidence of being infected with chlamydial antigen

In these studies, the serology tests used were either EIA or indirect immuno-fluorescence (IFT) using a single antigen such as LGV prototype strains. Other studies have shown that these tests mostly detect cross-reactive and group-specific chlamydia IgG and that IgG to CtDK accounts for only half of the IgG detected. The remaining IgG detected is related to nongenital *C. pneumoniae* or *C. psittaci*. The results of these studies clearly indicate that commonly used single antigen serology tests such as EIA and IFT lack the ability to differentiate IgG to CtDK from IgG to non-genital chlamydia species and as such produce a large number of false positive results.

Poor correlation between the presence of IgG in the blood and presence of chlamydial antigen in the genital tract

In chlamydial genital infection, the specificity of serology tests is being compared with the presence/absence of chlamydial antigen in the genital tract. We believe that these two tests should not be compared with each other, because of fundamental differences in their sensitivity for detecting IgG or chlamydial antigen during the natural history of CtGI. Antigen detection tests are most sensitive in patients with acute and early infection and least sensitive in those with chronic, recurrent or asymptomatic disease. In contrast, type-specific serology tests are less sensitive during the acute stage of CtGI and most sensitive in patients with chronic disease.

The assumption that IgG generally represents past infection

Our studies of contacts refute such an assumption, because

a)   in nearly half of the contacts with IgG at a level or 1/16 or higher, chlamydial antigen was also detected in their genital tract, indicating that at least in about half of the IgG positive contacts, the presence of IgG is a true indicator of a current CtGI.

b) In approximately two thirds of contacts with IgG levels of 1/64 to 1/256, chlamydial antigen was also present in their genital tract. This finding confirms results of previous studies that the presence of IgG at a level of 1/64 or higher is a reliable indicator of current CtGI.

Studies have shown that CtGI is naturally a chronic disease with a low rate of spontaneous recovery. Without treatment infection may persist for several years
These findings may suggest that in patients with symptoms of non specific genital infections (NSGI) who have not been treated, the presence of IgG may indicate a current CtGI.

Based on our studies and experience it is suggested that a cost effective and efficient strategy for maximising diagnosis, efficacy of treatment and population control of CtGI could be achieved by a combination of both antigen detection tests and type specific serology.

Test selection criteria would include duration of exposure/infection, presence or absence of symptoms, and previous treatment/absence of treatment. The contact tracing of D-K IgG positive, antigen negative individuals may well be justified.

NATURAL HISTORY, PATHOGENESIS AND CHLAMYDIA SEROLOGY

The protected intra-cellular environment in which chlamydia are metabolically active, together with the presence of a metabolically inactive component of the developmental cycle may afford protection against host defence mechanisms, as well as against anti-chlamydial therapy. This means that absolute and complete eradication of chlamydial disease with anti-microbial therapy may be more difficult to achieve than is widely conceptualised. It may also provide an explanation for subsequent development of both asymptomatic and recurrent chronic infection.

There is potential for the continued presence of inert organisms to provide an opportunity for future recrudescence. This occurs in all chlamydial diseases. In the case of serovars D-K it is not always easy to differentiate whether a recurrence has been endogenously or exogenously acquired.

We cannot escape the widespread belief that chlamydia serology has been regarded by many eminent authorities on the subject to be of limited diagnostic significance. The application of test systems based on individual serovars could be a way forward.

Whilst recognising that human papillomavirus (HPV) infection has been established as the cause of cervical cancer, epidemiological studies suggest that *C. trachomatis* infection also confers increased risk for cervical squamous cell carcinoma (SCC). Whether this risk is serotype specific is unknown.

An example of individual serovar investigation has been published by Anttila *et al*[31]. This is believed to be the first study providing longitudinal seroepidemiological evidence of an association between specific serotypes of *C. trachomatis* and cervical SCC. It was demonstrated that the presence of serum IgG antibodies to *C. trachomatis* serotype G was associated with the highest risk of developing SCC. It is suggested that exposure to *C. trachomatis* takes place several years or even decades before the diagnosis of cervical SCC.

It was stated that future studies should address the question of whether there are any specific determinants related to serotype G that may be directly or indirectly carcinogenic

A possible relationship between Ct D-K infection in women and subsequent ovarian cancer has been described by other authors. (Angela Robinson: The case for screening. Karen Rogstad: Complications in the female and their management).

The link between bacterial infections and carcinogenesis is not clear.

Release of nitric oxide and the specific inhibition of host cell apoptosis by *C. trachomatis* may be possible mechanisms occurring in chronic chlamydial infections that could initiate or promote carcinogenesis.

Differences in pathogenicity between serovars have been reported, but no general pattern has emerged.[19]

Genotyping is a powerful epidemiological tool but is not yet ready for clinical use.

Future serological studies and developments may well complement modern diagnostic endeavours. Improved speed and efficiency of contact tracing the infected female or male partner may decrease recurrence rates (especially of male urethral infection) and reduce the burden of disseminated disease. The potential for improvement in diagnosis before treatment is attractive to clinicians as well as to patients.

It is valid to argue for the wider application of chlamydia serology (which identifies immune responses to the D-K serovars of this pathogen) in both individuals and couples. There should be particular emphasis on serial monitoring over time in those patients with early recurrences, suspected latency or with clinical evidence of disseminated, subacute or chronic disease.

CONCLUSION

It would appear that chlamydia serology has been neglected in the United Kingdom and in the USA with regard to genital tract infection.

Current expert opinion considers that no single sensitive and specific *Chlamydia trachomatis* antibody test has been consistently used to investigate the value of chlamydia serology.[18-19]

This contrasts with a rapidly expanding literature relating to the use of serological tests to study the epidemiology and possible disease relationships of *C. pneumonia* (see chapter 13).

Nevertheless, the authors remain of the belief that there is a valid and wide application of serological investigation in genital tract disease, particularly with regard to patients suffering from mild or asymptomatic Ct D-K genital tract infection.

We have no doubt that over many years of screening with Micro Immuno Fluorescence serology many of our patients would have remained undiagnosed should antigen detection systems have been used in isolation.

The interpretation of our MIF investigations was always made in the clinical context, including the clinical and diagnostic information available for sexual partner/s (where available) as well as the individual presenting patient.

Extensive experience with the MIF serological investigation leads us to conclude that large numbers of cases which benefit from treatment are identified. This facilitates the avoidance of complications, and often validates and facilitates partner treatment.

Current literature still refers to the micro immuno fluorescence serological test for chlamydia as the "gold standard".

New technological developments in chlamydia serology include the detection of antibodies to heat shock proteins HSP60 and HSP10. EIA technology has been applied.

Screening by nucleic acid amplification (NAATs) provides evidence of current infection but gives no indication of the proportion of the population ever infected, or those with pelvic disease as a result of current or past infection.

The whole inclusion immuno fluorescence (WIF test) expresses all chlamydial antigens and shows association with disease, as does serology identifying HSP 60.

There may be other chlamydial antigens associated with genital tract infection.

If a rapid, high throughput, specific and sensitive *C. trachomatis* antibody assay were available, the proportion of the population ever exposed could be monitored, and this could provide one measure of the impact of screening programmes on disease prevalence.

The published literature covers a range of different methodologies. It is believed that the content of this chapter strongly supports an advocacy that a new look at Ct serology is urgently required.

We concluded this chapter in the first edition with an appeal for further clinical research, improved technological development and wider application of chlamydia serology.

It is clear that this advocacy was justified and we would urge that current opportunities are afforded high priority.

Acknowledgements

Mrs Joan Pleasance for preparation of all areas of text.

The authors record their appreciation to the following expert advocates of technological developments/application of chlamydia serology: Dr Patrick Horner, Professor Anne Johnson, Professor Myra McClure, Dr David Cahill, Dr Alan Herring.

REFERENCES

1. Oriel JD. The Carrier State. *Chlamydia trachomatis. J Antimicrobiol Chemother* 1986; **18** (Supplement A): 67–71.
2. Schachter J. Infection and Disease Epidemiology in Chlamydia – Intracellular Biology, Pathogenesis and Immunity. Ed Stephens RS. ASM Press. 1999; Chapter 6, 154–157.
3. Howell MR, Quinn TC, Braithwaite W. *et al.* Screening women for *Chlamydia trachomatis* in family planning clinics – the cost-effectiveness of DNA amplification assays. *Sex Trans Dis* 1998; 108–117.
4. Clay JC, Bowman CA. Controlling chlamydial Infection. *Genito Urinary Medicine* 1996; **72:** 145.
5. Pimenta J, Catchpole M, Gray M *et al.* Evidence Based Health Policy Report: Screening for Genital Chlamydial Infection. *Br Med J* 2000; **321:** 629–631.
6. Treharne JD, Darougar S, Jones BR. Modification of the micro-immunofluorescence test to provide a routine serodiagnostic test for chlamydial infection. *J Clin Pathol* 1977; **30:** 510–517.
7. Thomas K, Coughlin L, Mannion PT, Haddad NG. The value of *Chlamydia trachomatis* antibody testing as part of routine fertility investigation. *Human Reproduction* 2000; **15**(5): 1079–1082.
8. Moss TR, Hawkswell J. Clinical and Microbiological Investigation of Women with Acute Salpingitis and their Consorts. *Br J Obstet Gynaecol* 1987; **94:** 187–188.
9. Moss TR, Hawkswell J. Evidence of Infection with *Chlamydia trachomatis* in Patients with Pelvic Inflammatory Disease: Value of Partner Investigation. *Fertility and Sterility.* 1986; March

429–430.

10. Moss TR, Darougar S, Woodland R *et al.* Antibodies to Chlamydia Species in Patients Attending a Genitourinary Clinic and the Impact of Antibodies to *C. pneumoniae* and *C. psittaci* on the Sensitivity and the Specificity of *C. trachomatis* serology tests. *Sex Trans Dis* 1993; **20**(2): 61–65.

11. Moss TR, Darougar S. Sensitivity, specificity and predictive values of symptoms, culture and serological tests for indicating a current chlamydial genital infection in contacts. Unpublished data.

12. Ward ME. Mechanisms of Chlamydia-induced disease. The Role of chlamydial Heat Shock Proteins in the Pathogenesis of Disease in Chlamydia – Intracellular Biology, Pathogenesis and Immunity. Ed Stephens RS. ASM Press. 1999; Chapter 7. 186–187.

13. Morton RS, Kinghorn GK. Genitourinary chlamydial infection: a reappraisal and hypothesis. *Int J of STD & AIDS* 1999; **10:** 765–775.

14. Taylor-Robinson D. Genital Chlamydial Infections: Clinical aspects, diagnosis, treatment and prevention in: Recent Advances in Sexually Transmitted diseases and AIDS 4. Editors: Harris JRW, Forster SM, Churchill Livingstone 1991.

15. Toye B, Lafarriere C, Claman P, Peeling R, Association between antibody to the Chlamydial heat-shock protein and tubal infertility. *Journal of Infectious Diseases* 1993; **168**(5): 1236–40.

16. LaVerda D, Albanese LN, Ruther PE, *et al.* Seroreactivity to Chlamydia trachomatis Hsp10 correlates with severity of human genital tract disease. *Infect Immun.* 2000; **68**(1): 303–9.

17. Akande VA, Hunt LP, Cahill DJ, *et al.* Tubal damage in infertile women: Prediction using chlamydia serology. *Hum Reprod.* 2003: **18**(9): 1841–7.

18. Tuuminen T, Palomaki P, Paavonen J. The use of serologic tests for the diagnosis of Chlamydia infections. *Journal of Microbiological Methods* 2000; **42**(3): 265–79.

19. Persson K. The Role of Serology, antibiotic susceptibility testing and serovar determination in genital Chlamydial infections. *Best Practice & Research in Clinical Obstetrics & Gynaecology* 2002; **16**(6): 801–14.

20. Cahill *et al.* unpublished data.

21. Rank RG. Models of Immunity in Chlamydia – Intracellular Biology, Pathogenesis and Immunity. Ed. Stephens RS. ASM Press 1999; Chapter 9. 239–295.

22. Brunham RC. Human Immunity to Chlamydiae in Chlamydia – Intracellular Biology, Pathogenesis and Immunity. Ed Stephen RS. ASM Press. 1999; Chapter 8. 211–238.

23. Morton RS. Personal communication

24. Rowland GF, Forsey T, Moss TR. *et al.* Failure of *in vitro* Fertilization and Embryo Replacement following infection with *Chlamydia trachomatis. J in vitro Fert and Embryo Transfer.* 1985; **2**(3): 151–155.

25. Rowland GF, Moss TR. *In Vitro* Fertilization. Previous Ectopic Pregnancy and *Chlamydia trachomatis* infection. Letter to the Editor. *Lancet.* 1985; **11:** 8459

26. Moss TR, Rowland GF. Fothergill D *et al.* Is the incidence of ectopic pregnancy rising? Letter to Editor *Br Med J* 1985; 26.10.85.

27. Moss TR, Steptoe PC. *Chlamydia trachomatis*: Importance of *in-vitro* fertilization? *J Royal Soc Med.* 1984; **77:** 70–72.

28. Winston Lord R. Personal communication

29. Clad A, Freidank HM, Kunz EM, *et al.* Detection of sero conversion and persistence of Chlamydia trachomatis antibodies to 5 different serological tests. *European Journal of Clinical Microbiology and Infectious Diseases* 2000; **19**(12): 932–7.

30. Moss TR, Nicholls A, Viercant P. *et al. Chlamydia trachomatis* and Infertility. Letter to the Editor *Lancet* 1986; **II:** 8501 p218.

31. Anttila T, Saikku P *et al.* Serotypes of *Chlamydia trachomatis* and Risk for Development of Cervical Squamous Cell Carcinoma. *JAMA* 2001; **285:** 47–51.

CHAPTER 6

Therapeutic management

Janette Clarke

Leeds General Infirmary, Leeds, UK

INTRODUCTION

In this chapter, studies of therapy for uncomplicated and complicated genital infections with *Chlamydia trachomatis* serovars D-K will be appraised with reference to our knowledge of the lifecycle of the organism and theoretical knowledge of antibiotic sites of action. Factors in assessing microbiological and clinical cure will be discussed. Consideration will be given to treatment options in pregnancy and the potential induction of latent disease by certain antibiotics. Current recommended regimes will be compared, and prospects for improving therapeutic management will be discussed.

THE AIM OF THERAPY IN GENITAL CHLAMYDIAL INFECTIONS

The twin goals of microbiological clearance and clinical cure are obvious aims in any symptomatic patient. However, many people infected with chlamydia have no symptoms, and their partners may or may not be infected. It is this practice of treating asymptomatic cases or contacts of infection that reinforces the need for safe and effective therapy with minimal side effects.

THE LIFE CYCLE OF CHLAMYDIA AND ANTIBIOTICS

An understanding of the unique reproductive cycle of chlamydiae gives the theoretical basis for therapy. The elementary bodies (EBs) transform to reticulate bodies (RBs); RBs divide and finally differentiate back to EBs, which are released by host cell lysis. The metabolic activity within cells means that antibiotics must achieve sufficient intracellular tissue levels to be effective. The whole cycle takes about 40 hours in culture systems; this slow life cycle implies that a long course (over 5 days) of therapy is required or high tissue levels from a single dose therapy must be maintained over such a period. Tetracyclines, azithromycin, ofloxacin and erythromycin work to interfere with chlamydial protein synthesis.

PENICILLINS AND CHLAMYDIA

Penicillin and other beta-lactam antibiotics inhibit the growth of peptidoglycan-containing bacteria by specific inhibition of penicillin binding proteins. Mycoplasmas lack peptidoglycan and are refractory to penicillin. chlamydiae share some structural features with mycoplasmas; however, chlamydiae are interrupted in their life cycle by penicillin. Recent genomic analysis[1] indicates that chlamydiae have the capacity to synthesise peptidoglycan. There is considerable controversy in microbiological circles about whether the walls of chlamydial elementary bodies contain peptidoglycans. The ultrastructural changes associated with penicillin use include the development of abnormal enlarged reticulate bodies. These abnormal forms have a low expression of outer membrane proteins, which may diminish immune recognition and clearance, but maintain intracellular survival - a recipe for latent infection[2].

IN VITRO STUDIES

In laboratory tests that evaluate the growth of chlamydiae in cell cultures[3,4,5] the tetracyclines, erythromycin, rifampicin, certain fluoroquinolones (especially ofloxacin) and azithromycin are all highly active against these organisms. Sulphonamides and clindamycin are also active against *C. trachomatis*, but to a lesser degree. Penicillin and ampicillin suppress chlamydial multiplication but do not eradicate the organism *in vitro*. The cephalosporins appear to be relatively ineffective and streptomycin, gentamicin, neomycin, kanamycin, vancomycin, ristocetin, spectinomycin, and nystatin are not effective at concentrations inhibitory for most bacteria and fungi.

ANTIMICROBIAL RESISTANCE IN CHLAMYDIA

The potential for the development of antimicrobial resistance in *C. trachomatis* has not been widely studied. Wang *et al*[6] reviewed the knowledge and available approaches to evaluating antimicrobial resistance and potential treatment failures in human genital chlamydial infections.

There have been no descriptions either of isolation of strains that display stable resistance to recommended antibiotics or of mechanisms of possible resistance in isolates from patients failing treatment. *In vitro* genetically mediated fluoroquinolone- and rifampicin-resistant variants have been described and 4 clinical isolates demonstrated *in vitro* resistance to macrolides.

RESISTANCE TESTING AND CLINICAL OUTCOMES

There is a lack of a standardised *in vitro* assay, and such studies that have been performed demonstrate very variable levels of inhibitory concentrations of antimicrobials depending on the conditions used for testing, cell lines and timing of inoculation. Moreover, the correlation between the results of existing *in vitro* antimicrobial susceptibility tests and clinical outcome after treatment for *C. trachomatis* infection is unknown. The detection of heterotypic resistance, whereby a single resistant organism propagated in an antimicrobial containing medium yields a mixed population of susceptible and resistant organisms, has been described in clinical isolates but with no consistent link to clinical outcome. One small study indicated that treatment failures were more common in women infected with heterotypic resistant strains[7], but another group found no correlation in 88 isolates between clinical outcome and heterotopic resistance[8]. Homotypic resistance where there is replication of a clonal colony of resistant progeny from a single resistant organism has not yet been described in *Chlamydia trachomatis*, although it has been described in *Chlamydia suis* from pigs.

It can be seen that the existence of true resistance to antimicrobials in *Chlamydia trachomatis* infections is yet to be fully established in human clinical practice. Antimicrobial susceptibility testing is not well validated for chlamydia and is not recommended in the current routine management of patients with chlamydial infection.

ESTABLISHED DRUGS IN PRACTICE

Characteristics of ideal anti-chlamydial therapies are listed in **Box 1.**
Current options for therapy will be discussed by antibiotic class.

Tetracyclines

These are bacteriostatic agents, which interfere with bacterial protein synthesis.

There is equivalent therapeutic action of tetracycline, doxycycline and minocycline, but doxycycline is preferred because of less frequent dosing, fair side effect profile and fewer dietary restrictions. Tetracycline, minocycline and doxycycline have all been shown to eradicate *C. trachomatis* from male urethra (as judged by culture) with failure rates of between 0-3% with 7, 14 or 21 days therapy[3]; in women cervical infections had declared failure rates of 0-8% in similar studies. Single doses are not effective. However, Reedy[9] demonstrated that a 3-day course of doxycycline at standard dosage (100mg twice daily) was equivalent in outcome to a 7-day course in women with uncomplicated chlamydial cervicitis, as judged by three-week post therapy PCR screening.

Side effects of doxycycline are commonly gastrointestinal, with up to 20% compliant patients complaining of nausea and vomiting. Calcium, iron and magnesium containing medications should not be taken with tetracyclines because they interfere with absorption. Food interferes with the absorption of

---

Box 1. Ideal Characteristics of treatments for genital chlamydia

- Microbiological cure - at least 95% efficacy
- Effective in both clinically apparent and asymptomatic infection
- Safe in clinical practice
- Ease of dosing - single dose preferable
- Minimal disturbance of patient lifestyle
- Minimal side effects
- Safe in pregnancy
- Cost effective, low cost
- Occasional missed dosages in a multi-dose regimen not significant
- Agent(s) treat concomitant infections e.g. gonorrhoea

all tetracyclines except minocycline and doxycycline.

Twice daily doxycycline has been shown to have better compliance than tetracycline taken four times daily. Minocycline is less favoured since it is associated with vestibular toxicity, and is more expensive than doxycycline. Triple tetracycline (Deteclo) is probably as good as doxycycline; photosensitisation is more common with Deteclo, and there is little data on efficacy if compliance is poor.

Oxytetracycline at a dose of 250mg four times daily for 7 days has been shown to be effective in limited evidence, but the effects of missing doses is not documented.

Tetracyclines are contraindicated in established or suspected pregnancy and in children under 8 years old because of discolouration of permanent teeth and disturbance of growth in developing bone.

Doxycycline 100mg twice daily for 7 days is a standard therapy with which all new antibiotic regimens have been compared[4,5].

Macrolides

Erythromycin, clarithromycin and azithromycin from this group will be considered[10]. They are bacteriostatic agents that inhibit bacterial protein synthesis.

Erythromycin has similar *in vitro* activity to tetracycline, but is poorly tolerated in doses shown to be clinically effective. Reported failure rates at 7 days of 0-37% in males with NGU and in non-pregnant women with cervicitis of 0-34% are poorer than with azithromycin or doxycycline. Discontinuation due to gastrointestinal upset is common. A 2g daily dose may produce adverse effects in 70% of patients. A seven-day 1g daily dose still had a 34% adverse event profile and a four-fold failure rate compared with successful 2g dosing. Longer dosing schedules such as 500mg twice daily for 14 days have reported efficacy rates between 73% and 95%. Two weeks seems more effective than 7 days at 500mg twice daily, but compliance with longer regimes is likely to be poor. Erythromycin and clarithromycin have important interactions with some drugs. They may potentiate terfenadine, for example, with the risk of ventricular arrythmias.

Clarithromycin has a longer half-life than erythromycin and has been found to be clinically safe and effective in NGU and cervicitis[11] at a dose of 250mg twice daily.

Roxithromycin 300mg daily for 7 days has equivalent effect to erythromycin.

Azithromycin has rapid and extensive penetration into intracellular tissues, with sustained levels with an estimated tissue half-life of a 500mg dose of about 60 hours. This may exceed the minimum inhibitory concentration for *C. trachomatis* by 3- to 10-fold for up to 5 days; clinical trials have been based on double this dose. Side effects are rare, with gastrointestinal upset in less than 10% subjects in reported series. Interactions are also less marked than with other macrolides.

Azithromycin is well established as single dose therapy for uncomplicated male and female infections, for NGU[12] and for treating contacts of infection. There is limited safety data on use in pregnancy. Azithromycin may be more effective for patients with erratic health seeking behaviour, and both cost and use-effectiveness studies[13,14] have demonstrated that single dose azithromycin is superior to 7 day dosing with doxycycline. Carlin and Barton[14] found that men with NGU preferred single-dose azithromycin to a seven day course of doxycycline; this approach was also found to be cost-effective since fewer treatment failures and clinic visits were recorded in those receiving azithromycin. Hillis *et al*[15] found comparable high rates of use and effectiveness between single dose azithromycin and seven days of doxycycline in a randomised controlled study of 196 women and their partners with a PCR follow-up test at four weeks. Failures in both groups were all in women with risk behaviours consistent with re-infection.

Quinolones

The fluoroquinolones, synthetic derivatives of nalidixic acid are bactericidal, inhibiting bacterial DNA gyrase. They vary in anti-chlamydial activity. Norfloxacin and ciprofloxacin are not sufficiently effective for use in suspected chlamydial infections.[16] Ofloxacin, levofloxacin, grepafloxacin, trovafloxacin and sparfloxacin have been assessed in clinical trials. Ofloxacin has been used in varying protocols. Seven-day regimens of 200mg twice daily or 400mg once daily are highly effective, but a 5-day course had a cure rate of only 20%. Levofloxacin, the L- form of the racemic mixture ofloxacin, at a dose of 300mg tds for 7 days was found to have a an eradication rate of 87% in a study of chlamydial cervicitis[17] though the established recommendation for dosage is 500mg daily for 7 days[18]. There are no data on whether a missed dose on the single daily routine has any effect on cure rate. However, ofloxacin is active against mycoplasma and gonoccocal infections, making a relatively expensive group of drugs more cost effective in treating patients with simultaneous infections.

Adverse reactions are rare. Neurological disturbances, usually limited to dizziness and mood alteration, have been reported in less than 5% patients using ofloxacin. There is a concern that tendinitis may be provoked by fluoroquinolones, and this may limit their use in growing adolescents. Interactions with non-steroidal anti-inflammatory drugs may potentiate neurological side effects.

Penicillins

The debate about how and why penicillins have an effect on chlamydiae *in vitro* has been discussed. Clinical response to penicillins is unpredictable, and penicillins have no action against ureaplasmas. Ampicillin, amoxicillin, co-amoxiclav and pivampicillin have been shown to be active clinically. Since suppression rather than elimination of infection is possible, follow-up testing is desirable but rarely documented in trials.

Amoxicillin

Amoxicillin is preferred over ampicillin for oral administration because of better absorption and fewer side effects. Meta-analysis of the use of amoxicillin in chlamydial infections in pregnancy[19] compared with erythromycin indicated a similar cure rate for the two regimens, but a much better side effect profile for amoxicillin.

OTHER ACTIVE DRUGS NOT USED IN CLINICAL PRACTICE

Rifampicin is effective against chlamydiae, as are rifalazil and rifabutin. Resistance to rifampicin and rifalazil develops rapidly *in vitro*; and may appear during therapy.[4,20] This has led to a disinclination to use these drugs in clinical practice. Spiramycin has some effect *in vitro* but is not a drug of choice.

INEFFECTIVE DRUGS (Box 2)

Several classes of antibiotics in common use for urogenital infections are not effective in treating chlamydial infections. These failures may be due to the inability to reach therapeutic intracellular levels. In particular, cephalosporin based combinations for treating suspected pelvic infections should be avoided.

Box 2. Drugs known to be ineffective against genital chlamydial infections

- Aminoglycosides
- Sulphonamides
- Trimethoprim
- Clindamycin
- Cephalosporins

In a detailed study of women treated with ß-lactam antibiotics for acute salpingitis, Sweet *et al*[21] found persistence of endometrial and cervical infection despite completion of antibiotic regimes and clinical improvement.

ANTIBIOTICS ARE ONLY HALF THE STORY...

Microbiological and pharmaceutical studies may not reflect clinical practice in treating real patients. In sexual infections, the social and sexual behaviour of infected persons to be treated can have significant influence on the success of a drug regimen. Patients and partners should understand the infection and proposed therapy, the need for contact tracing, sexual abstinence and the benefits of completing treatment. The treatment should be effective, easy to take, with minimal side effects and cheap for patient and doctor.

Antibiotics chosen should have activity against other likely contemporaneous infection with gonococci, mycoplasma and ureaplasma.

Women may have particular needs from antibiotics in terms of efficacy and safety. Regimens for apparently uncomplicated infection should still show efficacy for pelvic disease. Pregnancy leads to concerns to treat effectively to abolish any risk of fetal infection at delivery.

Serious infections requiring inpatient care may mimic acute abdominal catastrophe and provoke gastrointestinal upset. Parenteral therapies should be available to those unable to tolerate oral therapy.

Patient preference and cost-effectiveness studies are becoming more important in influencing therapeutic choices in treating uncomplicated chlamydial infections.

Critical appraisal of the design of published clinical studies in treating sexually transmitted infections (**Box 3**) reveals that very few fulfil such

---

Box 3. Ideal characteristics of studies in chlamydia therapy

- Randomised, double-blind studies of either active drug vs. placebo or between two treatments.

- Study groups reflect demographic distribution of infection in general population.

- Clear description of inclusion criteria and infection severity (symptomatic/asymptomatic/complicated).

- Method of confirming infection declared.

- Drug dosage, duration and compliance assessments described. Sexual partners of subjects traced and treated.

- Sexual abstinence/condom use/simultaneous therapy of partners documented.

- Follow-up testing of cure clearly described in method and interval.

- Adverse reactions, discontinuations listed.

- Detailed review of persistent positive subjects to determine sexual behaviour risks for re-infection.

---

criteria. Treatment recommendations in national and international guidelines[18,22,23] are heavily based on historical and anecdotal experience, *in vitro* susceptibility testing and small trials. Most data are found on treating men with NGU. There are few studies in women with uncomplicated disease, and very small studies in pregnant women. Follow-up to confirm clearance of infection has either been poorly described or limited to less than two weeks.

ASSESSING SUCCESS OF TREATMENT

The problem of assessing cure in uncomplicated chlamydia, which is usually asymptomatic especially in women, has been compounded by the poor sensitivity of tests such as antigen detection or culture which have been used as markers of infection and tests of cure in most therapeutic trials. There are persistent therapy failure rates, whatever the drug, of 0-37%; even azithromycin has failure rates as high as 15% in some series. There may be poor absorption or bioavailability of the drugs or there may be relative or absolute resistance to treatment. Apparent failure of therapy may be due to re-infection by sexual contact with an untreated partner rather than persistence of original infection. Many methods of ascertaining cure will be positive in the presence of non-viable organisms, and may become negative with interval re-testing.

Complicated presentation, as with pelvic infection, may be polymicrobial and clinical end points may measure efficacy against several organisms.

PROVING EFFICACY OF TREATMENT

Optimal assessment techniques should detect actively reproducing organisms at high sensitivity and specificity. Non-culture tests such as PCR and SDA conducted at less than 3 weeks after completion of therapy for patients who were treated successfully could yield false-positive results because of continued excretion of dead organisms.

Test of cure is recommended after completing therapy in pregnant women and those using erythromycin. Tests should be performed no earlier than 3 weeks after end of therapy. This imposes a five-week episode of sexual abstinence on the treated person. Re-testing is not needed for those treated with azithromycin or doxycycline unless re-infection is suspected or symptoms persist.

SUPPRESSION, TREATMENT FAILURE AND PERSISTENT INFECTION

Some clinical studies have started to address the question of persistence[24,25]. Tests over five months from three genital sites using two sensitive polymerase chain reaction (PCR) assays for detection after seven days doxycycline in a well motivated study group were positive in only 1 of 20 study subjects; she had been re-infected. Recurrent and/or persistent infection has been reported in 10-15% of women treated for *C. trachomatis* infection[25]. Review of compliance with therapy and partner notification success should be seen as integral to treatment to identify patients needing re-treatment.

TREATING IN PREGNANCY

In a meta-analysis of 11 small studies[18], amoxicillin and erythromycin have been found to be equally effective. End points in pregnancy are, however, different – the obvious measure is the documented prevention of neonatal infection. Unfortunately, very few studies have followed the woman to delivery and examined or treated the neonate. Guidance to perform a test of cure by culture three weeks after completion of therapy may be impractical if infection is late in term.

Neonatal treatment of clinical problems are best documented for neonatal ophthalmia. Oral erythromycin, 50mg/kg is the preferred agent, with tetracycline eye ointments having high relapse rates.

COMPLICATIONS

Pelvic inflammatory disease (PID)

As discussed in chapter 9, the clinical presentation of PID lacks sensitivity and specificity. However, there is some evidence to suggest that delay in therapy is associated with increased risk of subsequent tubal infertility. A low clinical threshold to treat in any woman with undiagnosed acute or chronic pelvic pain is recommended. It is important that all empirical therapy of PID should cover three probable infections – chlamydia, gonorrhoea and anaerobic infections. Gonococcal PID may exist in the absence of endocervical infection. Most studies of treating PID are based on inpatient gynaecological care. There are little data to suggest that milder cases managed in office or outpatient settings warrant any modification of these protocols. Intravenous access may be needed if vomiting is marked. There are recommendations that more serious cases should all receive IV antibiotics to ensure maximal efficacy but there are little supporting data. Parenteral therapy should be continued for a further 24 hours *after* sustained clinical improvement is established, before oral treatment is substituted (**Box 4**). Studies of microbial persistence in PID[21] indicate that clinical resolution may not

---

Box 4. Treating chlamydial PID - some suggestions

Note: Antibiotic choice against gonorrhoea should reflect local strain sensitivities. Regimens should be continued for at least 14 days, with change to oral therapy 24 hours **after** clinical improvement.

- Cefoxitin 2g tds IV plus doxycycline 100mg bd IV; continue with oral metronidazole 400mg bd plus doxycycline 100mg bd to complete 14 days' therapy.

or

- Clindamycin 900mg tds IV plus gentamicin 2mg/kg IV loading dose, then 1.5 mg/kg tds; continue as above with metronidazole/doxycycline orally.

- Ofloxacin 400mg bd IV plus metronidazole 500mg tds IV.

- Cefoxitin 2g tds IV *plus* erythromycin 50mg/kg IV (in pregnancy).

be a reliable marker of micobiological cure. Follow-up tests should be linked to sexual abstinence until the sexual partner is treated.

Peri-hepatitis (Fitz-Hugh-Curtis syndrome) is a complication of chlamydial PID. Apart from anecdotal evidence that adhesions could be divided at diagnostic laparoscopy there is no evidence to modify therapy from PID.

Epididymo-orchitis
Empirical therapy is once again the rule, depending to some extent on the age and sexual behaviour of the man. Antibiotics should cover common urogenital pathogens, gonorrhoea and chlamydia. Ciprofloxacin, despite its common use in this condition by European urologists[26], is not recommended as a single agent for epididymitis due to its unreliable action against chlamydia and emerging ciprofloxacin resistance in *N. gonorrhoea* in many centres.

Typical recommendations include ofloxacin 200mg twice daily for 14 days, or doxycycline 100mg twice daily for 10-14 days with initial dosing of ceftriaxone 250mg IM stat, or ciprofloxacin 500mg oral stat. Test of cure is generally regarded as clinical resolution.

Prostatitis is a controversial area of therapy, since the actual etiological causation by chlamydiae is disputed. Nevertheless, long courses of fluoroquinolones such as ofloxacin and ciprofloxacin have been shown to improve symptoms.

Sexually Acquired Reactive Arthritis (SARA)
There is some evidence that eradicating acute chlamydial genital tract infection tends to reduce the risk of relapse in SARA. There is only one study indicating that long term therapy with anti-chlamydial antibiotics has any effect on clinical outcome[27]. A study in Greenland Inuit tribes found that prompt and effective therapy for chlamydia reduced the risk of SARA in this population with high prevalence of both HLA B27 and chlamydia[28].

TREATING GENITAL CHLAMYDIAL INFECTION – CONCLUSIONS

There are relatively few antibiotics active against chlamydiae (**Table 1**), and some are suspected to induce a latent infection rather than produce microbiological clearance. The complex and prolonged life cycle of these

Table 1. Comparing effective therapies

Assessment of recommended drugs for uncomplicated genital infection with *Chlamydia trachomatis* serovars D-K (after Fitzgerald *et al.*)

Drug	Advantages	Disadvantages
Doxycycline 100mg twice daily x 7 days	Efficacy > 95% Relatively cheap Missed doses do not seem to affect efficacy	Contraindicated in pregnancy Photosensitisation Side effects in 20% (gastrointestinal upset)
Deteclo 300mg twice daily x 7 days	Cheap Efficacy >95%	Cannot take with milk Contraindicated in pregnancy Photosensitivity
Azithromycin 1g stat	Efficacy >95% Once only dosing Patient preferred	Expense Limited long term follow-up data Limited data on use in pregnancy
Erythromycin 500mg four times daily x 7 days or 500mg twice daily x 14 days	Cheap Safe in pregnancy	Four times daily or lengthy dosing schedule limits compliance Efficacy<95% Significant side-effects in 25% to discontinuation
Ofloxacin 400mg daily x 7 days	Efficacy >95% Good side-effect profile	Expensive Lack of data about efficacy in missing doses Contraindicated in pregnancy Avoid in young people (risk of joint damage)
Amoxicillin 500mg three times daily x 7 days	Good side-effect profile Safe in pregnancy	Poor efficacy Risk of latency Three times daily dosing

intracellular organisms requires sustained therapeutic levels of antibiotics in the target tissues. Clinical success also depends on patient adherence with effective antibiotic regimes, sexual abstinence during therapy and treating sexual partners.

Future trials of therapy should be compared with current "gold standards" of doxycycline and azithromycin. All such trials should have use- and cost-effectiveness analyses, and assess patient preferences for treatment. Tests of cure using detection of only actively replicating chlamydiae would settle the question of persistence after therapy. New agents for use in pregnancy are required to dispel disquiet around current therapies.

REFERENCES

1. Chopra I, Storey C, Falla TJ, Pearce JH. Antibiotics, peptidoglycan synthesis and genomics: the chlamydial anomaly revisited. (review article 40 refs) *Microbiology* 1998; **133:** 2673–2678.
2. Morton RS, Kinghorn GR. Genitourinary chlamydial infection: a reappraisal and hypothesis. *Int J STD & AIDS* 1999; **10:** 765–775.
3. Toomey KE, Barnes RC. Treatment of *Chlamydia trachomatis* Genital Infection. *Rev Infect Dis* 1990; **12**(suppl 6): S645–655 (review article 114 refs.)
4. Weber JT, Johnson RE. New treatments for *Chlamydia trachomatis* genital infection. *Clin Infect Dis* 1995; **20**(suppl 1): S66–71.
5. Jones RB. New treatments for *Chlamydia trachomatis. Am J Obstet Gynaecol* 1991; **164**(6): 1789–93.
6. Wang SA, Papp JR, Stamm WE *et al.* Evaluation of antimicrobial resistance and treatment failures for *Chlamydia trachomatis:* a meeting report. [Review article 40 refs] *Journal of Infectious Diseases* 2005; **191**(6): 917–23.
7. Schmid G, Van Der Pol B, Jones RB, Johnson R. Further investigating the clinical importance of heterotypic antimicrobial resistance in *Chlamydia trachomatis. Int J STD & AIDS* 2001; **12**(supp 2): 41-3.
8. Suchland RJ, Geisler WM, Stamm WE. Methodologies and cell lines used for antimicrobial susceptibility testing of *Chlamydia* spp. *Antimicrobial Agents & Chemotherapy* 2003; **47**(2): 636–42.
9. Reedy MB, Sulak PJ, Miller SL, *et al.* Evaluation of a 3-day course of doxycycline for the treatment of uncomplicated *Chlamydia trachomatis* cervicitis. *Infect Dis Obstet Gynecol* 1997; **5**(1): 18–22.
10. Alvarez-Elcoro S, Enzler MJ. The macrolides: erythromycin, clarithromycin, and azithromycin. [Review 346 refs]. *Mayo Clinic Proceedings* 1999; **74**(6): 613–34.
11. Stein GE, Mummaw NL, Havlichek DH. A preliminary study of clarithromycin versus doxycycline in the treatment of non-gonococcal urethritis and mucopurulent cervicitis. *Pharmacotherapy* 1995; **15**(6): 727–31
12. Stamm WE, Hicks CB, Martin DH *et al.* Azithromycin for empirical treatment of the non-gonococcal syndrome in men. A randomised double-blind study. *JAMA* 1995; **274:** 545–9.
13. Magdid D, Douglas JMJ, Schwartz JS. Doxycycline compared with azithromycin for treating women with genital *Chlamydia trachomatis* infection: an incremental cost-effectiveness analysis. *Ann Intern Med* 1996; **124:** 389–99.
14. Carlin EM, Barton SE. Azithromycin as the first-line treatment of non gonococcal urethritis (NGU); a study of follow-up rates, contact attendance and patients' treatment preference. *Int J STD & AIDS* 1996; **7**(3): 185.
15. Hillis SD, Coles FB, Litchfield B, *et al.* Doxycycline and azithromycin for the prevention of chlamydial persistence or recurrence one month after treatment in women. A use-effectiveness study in public health settings. *Sex Trans Dis* 1998; **25:** 5–11.

16. Ziegler C, Stary A, Mailer H, *et al*. Quinolones as an alternative treatment of chlamydial, mycoplasmas and gonococcal urogenital infections. *Dermatology* 1992; **185**(2): 128–31.

17. Mikamo H, Sato Y, Hayasaki Y, *et al*. Adequate levofloxacin treatment schedules for uterine cervicitis caused by *Chlamydia trachomatis*. *Chemotherapy* 2000; **46**(2): 150–2.

18. Centers for Disease Control and Prevention. 2002 Guidelines for treatment of sexually transmitted diseases. *MMWR*; 2002; **51**(RR06);1-80. also available at www.cdc.gov/STD/treatment/4-2002TG.htm#Chlamydia

19. Brocklehurst P, Rooney G. Interventions for treating genital *Chlamydia trachomatis* infection in pregnancy (Cochrane Review). In: *The Cochrane Library Issue 2*. 2000; Oxford: Update Software.

20. Kutlin A, Kohlhoff S, Roblin P, *et al*. Emergence of resistance to rifampicin and rifalazil in *Chlamydophila pneumoniae* and *Chlamydia trachomatis*. *Antimicrobial Agents & Chemotherapy* 2005; **49**(3): 903–7.

21. Sweet RL, Schachter J, Robbie MO. Failure of ß-lactam antibiotics to eradicate *Chlamydia trachomatis* in the endometrium despite apparent clinical cure of acute salpingitis. *JAMA* 1983; **250**: 2641–5.

22. UK Clinical Effectiveness Guidelines. Clinical Effectiveness Group. *Sex Trans Infects.* 1999; **75**(suppl 1); also available at www.agum.org.uk

23. FitzGerald MR, Welch J, Robinson AJ, Ahmed-Jusuf IH. Clinical guidelines and standards for the management of uncomplicated genital chlamydial infection. *Int J STD & AIDS* 1998; **9**: 253–262.

24. Whittington W, Kent C, Kissinger P, *et al*. Determinants of persistent and recurrent *Chlamydia trachomatis* infection in young women. *Sexually Transmitted Diseases* 2001; **28**: 117–23.

25. Workowski KA, Lampe MF, Wong KG, *et al*. Long-term eradication of *Chlamydia trachomatis* genital infection after antimicrobial therapy; evidence against persistent infection. *JAMA* 1993; **270**: 2071–5.

26. Drury NE, Dyer JP, Breitenfeldt N, *et al*. Management of acute epididymitis: are European guidelines being followed? *European Urology* 2004; **46**(4): 522–4; discussion 524–5.

27. Lauhio A, Leirijalo-Repo M, Lahdevirta J, *et al*. Double-blind placebo controlled study of three-month treatment with lymecycline in reactive arthritis, with special reference to Chlamydia arthritis. *Arthritis Rheum* 1991; **34**: 6–14.

28. Bardin T, Enrel C, Cornelis F, *et al*. Antibiotic resistance of venereal disease and Reiter's syndrome in a Greenland population. *Arthritis Rheum* 1992; **35**: 190–4.

CHAPTER 7

Partner notification

Karen E Rogstad
Department of Genito Urinary Medicine,
Royal Hallamshire Hospital, Sheffield, UK

INTRODUCTION

Partner notification or contact tracing has been an integral part of the management of bacterial sexually transmitted infections (STIs) for more than 60 years both in the United Kingdom and the USA. It aims to identify often-asymptomatic cases to reduce morbidity in the individual, and reduce onward transmission. Originally used in the 19th century in the form of incarceration of prostitutes suspected of having syphilis, it was not until 1942 in the UK and 1936 in the USA that contact tracing was developed as a means of offering treatment to infected partners in order to control the spread of syphilis and gonorrhoea.

The prevalence of an STI in the community is dependent on biological features of the organism and behavioural factors of the individual[1]. The former includes efficiency of transmission and duration of infectiousness, and varies greatly between the different organisms causing sexually transmitted diseases. Behavioural factors include the rate of partner change, sexual mixing and barrier contraceptive use. As partner notification identifies asymptomatic cases, thus reducing duration of infectiousness and ongoing transmission, then it would be expected that it will help in the control of STIs. Contact tracing should therefore be of benefit to the individual, their partners and to society via improving the public health.

WHAT IS PARTNER NOTIFICATION?

As defined by the World Health Organization[2], partner notification is

That public health activity in which sexual partners of individuals with HIV infection and those sharing injecting equipment are notified, counselled about their exposure and offered services.

This definition is equally applicable for other STIs.

The pressure upon an infected individual to participate in contact tracing varies from country to country, depending on the legal framework and attitudes towards the rights of individuals versus the rights of infected contacts and the public health. Even in countries with similar cultural backgrounds there can be diametrically opposing views, such as in Scandinavia. Norway and Denmark[3] provide absolute confidentiality for those infected with STIs and official contact tracing is opposed, whereas in Sweden index patients are legally obliged to name partners and contacts have a legal requirement to be tested[4]. In the United Kingdom patients are encouraged to co-operate with contact tracing but their participation is voluntary.

HOW IS IT PERFORMED?

Strategies for partner notification (PN) vary. In the UK, where the majority of STIs are managed in free, open access confidential clinics, PN is undertaken by dedicated healthcare professionals known as Health Advisors. These are usually trained nurses, social workers or occasionally individuals from other backgrounds who have received additional training.

When a man or woman is diagnosed as being infected with *Chlamydia trachomatis* (CT) details of sexual contacts should be requested, both current and previous. The length of look-back time varies according to the STI, but for chlamydia would usually be all partners in the previous 3-6 months, or 4-6 weeks for symptomatic men. If there have been no partners in this time then the last partner in 6 months should be determined, although some studies suggest that this should be up to one year or longer.

Partner notification consists of three types:

Patient referral The index case is given one or more contact slips to pass on to sexual partners. This has on it the date, diagnosis, clinic, and index case's clinic number. In order to maintain confidentiality the diagnosis is indicated by a national code (which is part of a coding system, that is standardised throughout the United Kingdom and Ireland).

Provider referral The healthcare worker contacts the sexual partner. This may be done by telephone, letter or home visit, and this system is utilised when the index case will not see the contact again, wishes anonymity or is worried about the threat of violence.

Conditional (or contract) referral Initial PN is undertaken by the patient with the agreement that if the contact has not attended within a specific time then provider notification will be undertaken.

Partner notification has consisted of advising the patient of the need to attend medical services, by provision of a contact slip with the diagnosis coded. Newer methods include provision of a website address, texting, emailing or providing a home testing kit for their partner. Home testing kits improved the number of patients having at least one partner tested in Denmark[5]. It is important to assess patient preference which can vary widely between different methods[6]. New initiatives have been assessed which indicate the diagnosis on the contact slip, if the patient agrees.

Partner notification is discussed as soon as the individual is given a positive diagnosis of chlamydia. It may be undertaken by doctor, nurse or more usually by a health advisor.

It is important that it is undertaken in a non-judgmental fashion and that confidentiality is guaranteed. The patient or index case should be reassured that neither his or her identity nor diagnosis would be disclosed during provider referral. They should be encouraged to disclose both regular and non-regular partners. As much information that is available on the contact should be elicited including name, address, telephone number, and if full details are unavailable, then a description may be useful.

Contacts can be divided into one of three groups:

Treated Partners who have been documented as already having attended for diagnosis, received treatment and not had unprotected sexual intercourse with the untreated index case since their treatment.

Contacts to be sought Some of these will prove to be untraceable if details are incomplete or incorrect.

Untraceable Partners who cannot be notified because their name and/or whereabouts are unknown, or because they are abroad and un-contactable.

An agreement should be made as to which type of PN is to be undertaken and this may vary for each contact. It needs to be accepted that in some rare cases the risk of violence to patient or health advisor may be such that partner notification is not performed. In practice there is usually a way around this, by delaying PN in order to obscure the identity of the index, and the use of letters or phone calls without home visits. Patients ought to be followed-up in order to determine that contacts have been notified and received screening and treatment. Traditionally this has been done by face to face interview but recent studies have suggested that telephone follow-up may be as or more effective, particularly for black ethnic minority groups[7]. The index case may also have managed to find out or be prepared to disclose additional information on contacts during the follow-up interview.

When a patient attends with a contact slip, details of their treatment and date of attendance should be noted and the slip returned to the issuing clinic.

Partner notification needs to be tailored to cultural needs[8] and access to healthcare systems, and the UK system may not be applicable to the developing world.

DOES PARTNER NOTIFICATION WORK?

There have been few properly conducted studies to assess the efficacy of contact tracing either for *C. trachomatis* or any other sexually transmitted disease. There is certainly a benefit at the individual level as a means of preventing re-infection or diagnosing individuals with previously unrecognised infection. However at a population level, as a public health intervention, the efficaciousness of partner notification is less clear, both as a means of reducing prevalence of infection in the community and reducing incidence of complications. There are even less data on cost-effectiveness and cost-benefit. Comparing studies on partner notification is fraught with difficulties, as healthcare systems vary according to country and different criteria for success are used. There is also the added difficulty that the incidence and prevalence of the infection in the community is usually not accurately known.

Studies in the USA have shown that during periods of intensified PN, disease incidence or complications from disease declined relative to the period preceeding the intensified PN[9]. The proportion of contacts notified or attending for treatment is very variable, but can be high. In Indianapolis, for example, 82% of contacts of patients with gonorrhoea, chlamydia or related conditions were contacted[10]. However many medical practitioners do not undertake PN nor refer patients to a service that do. Some General Practice studies have shown only 13% of patients would be referred to a genito urinary clinic for contact tracing[11] whereas in other studies GPs refer more than 50%[12]. In practices where there is no referral to an STI service for PN, contact tracing is undertaken in only a minority[13].

There are little data on the most effective method of partner notification. A systematic review of the efficacy of differing PN strategies in the management of STIs included 11 randomised controlled trials, including 8014 participants[14]. Their conclusions were that:

i. Provider referral alone, or the choice between patient and provider referral, when compared with patient referral among patients with HIV or any STI, increases the rate of partners presenting for medical evaluation;

ii. contract referral, when compared with patient referral among patients with gonorrhoea, results in more partners presenting for medical evaluation;

iii. verbal, nurse given health education together with patient-centred counselling by lay workers, when compared with standard care among patients with any STI, results in small increases in the rate of partners treated.

However conditional and provider notification is between 4 and 8 times more expensive than patient referral[10].

In one study on cost effectiveness, a hypothetical model suggested that in the prevention of chlamydial pelvic inflammatory disease (PID) contact tracing would be cost effective only if 43% of the named male partners of female cases, or 11% of the named female partners of male index cases received treatment[15]. This study did not take into account the prevention of onward transmission therefore the true cost-effectiveness is likely to have been underestimated.

WHAT ARE THE DISADVANTAGES?

There has been little work done to evaluate the psychological and social effects of partner notification. There may violence, breakdown of relationships and anxiety or depression. A Zambian study has shown higher rates of domestic quarrels when men had the choice of provider or patient notification, compared with patient referral alone[16]. Adverse effects may be preventable by careful discussion and counselling.

WHAT INFORMATION SHOULD BE GIVEN?

Patients must be made aware of the sexually transmitted nature of their infection. There should be a clear discussion of the long latent period in some people and that sexual partners can be infected but asymptomatic. The possibility of complications needs to be raised, highlighting that these can occur in those who have no symptoms. Patients must also be made aware of the risk of re-infection from untreated partners, and that it can be acquired *de novo* from new partners.

Women, particularly those with chlamydial PID, should be informed of the risk of ectopic pregnancy and further episodes of PID (which may be CT negative) and advised on accessing healthcare quickly if complications develop. The patient should be made aware of the future risk of infertility, particularly if re-infection with chlamydia occurs.

It is essential that the patient is given time to ask questions and reassured about any anxieties they may have. In some cases referral to a clinical psychologist may be necessary.

All patients should be advised on sexual abstinence until they and their partner have been treated and a test of cure performed if appropriate. There should be education about safer sex and a demonstration of condom use where necessary.

Partner notification remains an integral part of the control of *C. trachomatis* in developed countries. In the developing world PN may not be as feasible because of cost, cultural barriers and stigmatisation of those with infection. Additionally the value of contact tracing where syndromic management of STIs occurs is unclear. The relevance of contract tracing in the 21st century with the possibility of population screening by highly sensitive DNA amplification methods needs to be ascertained. Newer methods of evaluating PN eg use of genotyping, have been used in a research context, although currently this technology does not have proven value in improving contact tracing[17]. Those undertaking PN should audit their performance, but agreeing national standards is difficult[18]. Until there is evidence to the contrary, it should retain its key role in the management of anyone diagnosed with *C. trachomatis*. PN should follow clearly developed protocols with regular auditing of its effectiveness and be tailored to take into account the cultural differences of patients. New approaches such as home testing and the use of new communication technologies should be considered depending on client characteristics, preferences and resources.

Acknowledgement
I would like to thank Gill Bell for her helpful advice.

REFERENCES

1. Heathcote HW, Yoke JA. Gonorrhoea: transmission dynamics and control *Biomathematics* 1984; **56:** 1–105.
2. WHO Consultation document SHO/BPA/ESR/89/2.
3. Blaxter M. AIDS: World-wide policies and problems: London Office of Health Economics 1991.
4. Thelin I, Wennstrom AM, Mardh PA. Contact tracing in patients with genital chlamydial infection *Br J Vener Dis* 1980; **56:** 259–62.
5. Ostergaard L, *et al.* Managing partners of people diagnosed with *Chlamydia trachomatis*: a comparison of two partner testing methods. *Sex Transm Infect* 2003; **79:** 358–362.
6. Tomnay JE, Pitts MK, Fairley CK. Partner notification: preferences of Melbourne clients and the estimated proportion of sexual partners they can contact. *Int J STD & AIDS* 2004; **15:** 415–418.
7. Apoola A, Boothby M, Radcliffe K. Managing genital chlamydial infection: the effects of ethnic origin and method of follow-up. *Int J STD & AIDS* 2004; **15:** 725–727.
8. Mulvey G. Contact tracing and sexually transmitted disease among Aboriginal men on the Anangu Pitjantjatjara Lands. *Aust J Public Health* 1995; **19:** 596–601.
9. Brewer D. Case finding effectiveness of partner notification and cluster investigation for sexually transmitted disease/HIV. *Sex Transm DIS* 2005; **32:** 78–83.
10. Katz BP, Danes CS, Quinn TS, *et al.* Efficiency and cost effectiveness of field follow-up for patients with *Chlamydia trachomatis* infection in a Sexually Transmitted Disease Clinic. *Sex Trans Dis* 1998; **15:** 11–16.
11. Ross JDC, Sutherland S, Copi J. Genital *Chlamydia trachomatis* infections in primary care. *Br Med J* 1996; **313:** 1992–3.
12. Rogstad KE, Kinghorn GR, Horton M. Community control of *Chlamydia trachomatis Int J STD & AIDS* 2000; **11:** 248–249.
13. Rogstad KE , Davies A, Krishna Murthy S, *et al.* The management of *Chlamydia trachomatis*: combined community and hospital study. *Sex Trans Inf* 2000; **76:** 332–334.
14. Mathews C, Coetzee N, Zwaenstein M, *et al.* A systematic review of strategies for partner notification for sexually transmitted dieases, including HIV/AIDS. *Int J STD & AIDS* 2002; **13:** 285–300.
15. Howell MR, Kassler WJ, Haddix A. Partner notification to prevent pelvic inflammatory diseases in women *Sex Trans Dis* 1997; **24:** 287–92.
16. Faxelid E, Tembo G, Ndulo J, Krantz I. Individual counselling of patients with sexually transmitted diseases: a way to improve partner notification in a Zambian setting? *Sex Transm Dis* 1996; **23:** 289–92.
17. Osterlund A, *et al.* Improved contact tracing of *Chlamydia Trachomatis* in a Swedish county – is genotyping worthwhile? *Int J STD & AIDS* 2005; **16:** 9–13.
18. Low N, Welch J, Radcliffe K. Developing national outcome standards for the management of gonorrhoea and genital Chlamydia in genitourinary medicine clinics. *Sex Transm Infect* 2004; **80:** 223–229.

CHAPTER 8

Complications of Chlamydia trachomatis infection in men

David Hicks

Central Sheffield University Hospitals, Sheffield, UK

Chlamydia trachomatis derives its name from the Latin, meaning "to cloak". This term not only describes its life-style as an obligate intracellular energy parasite but also the way in which it is "hidden" from health professionals and patients.

Around 70% of women and 50% of men are asymptomatic when infected genitally but such estimates depend on the diagnostic methodology used. Screening for the organism is not generally employed (but is being introduced to the UK) and therefore estimations of prevalence are always an underestimate. Incidence is highest for men between the ages of 20 and 24 years at about 965 per 100,000 in the UK[1] and USA[2] but in 1997 the UK Health Education Authority carried out a poll which showed that only 27% of adults knew what chlamydia was.

The spread of infection therefore, is aided by ignorance, mis-diagnosis and inadequacies in diagnostic methods and may truly be termed a "hidden epidemic".

This chapter describes asymptomatic, symptomatic and complicated chlamydial disease in men (management and therapy is dealt with in chapters 4 and 6) but first it should be recognised that spontaneous clearance in untreated patients is possible. Just as no organism is 100% infectious then similarly a host can resist infection through a variety of mechanisms and thereby cope with early and established infection.

SPONTANEOUS CLEARANCE

A study[3] from a population attending a sexually transmitted infection (STI) clinic in Birmingham, Alabama is illustrative. The study group consisted of patients who had had positive cultures for *C. trachomatis* who then had repeat specimens performed within 45 days of initial observation, but who did not receive recommended therapy for this infection in the interval between the 2 tests. Of 74 evaluable patients, 24 (32%) had negative follow-up cultures. These cultures were tested with Direct Immuno-Fluorescence (DIF) and Polymerase Chain Reaction (PCR) assays for chlamydia and only 3 of the 24 (13%) proved positive. Rates of positivity declined significantly with increasing age and also duration of follow-up. Whilst Benzathene Penicillin resulted in apparent resolution of infection in 9 of 10 remaining patients, treatment with a cephalosporin, Metronidazole or anti-fungal agent in others was not associated with clearance of infection. Overall, in this retrospective study, resolution of *C. trachomatis* infection occurred in 28% of 74 patients who did not receive currently recommended therapy.

These findings are supported by a more recent study[4] of asymptomatic, chlamydia-positive pregnant women. In this study the prevalence of asymptomatic *C. trachomatis* was 9% (140 of 1,547 women tested) with spontaneous resolution of the infection occurring in almost half of those infected. Older age and screening time interval to spontaneous resolution were notable associated factors.

These data should be borne in mind when considering public health measures to control the infection as well as for proper interpretation of prevalence rates.

ASYMPTOMATIC INFECTIONS

Generally a milder urethritis is caused by *C. trachomatis* when compared to that caused by *Neisseria gonorrhoea*. This, and asymptomatic carriage of chlamydia can be explained by host immune defences to the organism.

The incidence of asymptomatic infections would appear to be rising. This may be due to variables such as the sensitivity and specificity of tests used over time, comparability of populations studied and the depth of questioning taken in a sexual history.

In the 1970s when culture was used for diagnosis 0–5% of men without obvious urethritis had chlamydia isolated from the urethra.

In studies in the 1980s using Enzyme Immuno-Assay (EIA) testing, male asymptomatic carriage was typically found to be around 50%.

With techniques now available such as Polymerase Chain Reaction (PCR) which are highly sensitive and highly specific, one can expect that asymptomatic infection in men will be found to be no less and probably more common than this. In a study[5] of 2,308 teenage boys tested by urine Ligase Chain Reaction test 143 (6.2%) were shown to be infected with over 90% of these being worryingly asymptomatic. Using urine PCR testing a more recent study showed a prevalence of 4.6% in Danish male military recruits who were all asymptomatic[6].

Males who are asymptomatic or who have mild urethritis tend to ignore even minor symptoms longer than do men with obvious problems, remaining sexually active (and infective) for a longer duration without diagnosis and treatment. The fact that these men are more likely to have a long-term persistence of this organism means they may be more at risk of developing one or more of its complications.

PHARYNGITIS

Pharyngeal infection has been little studied but may be 3-6% of the STI clinic chlamydia-positive population. An absence of symptoms is the usual (non) presentation in this area. One study in the UK[7] showed a prevalence of 2.4% in STI patients (only 3 cases) which were all culture negative, asymptomatic and diagnosed by PCR. A study using cell culture and PCR, of 70 men reporting recent oral sex and attending STI Departments, failed to find any confirmed infection[8].

RECTAL INFECTION

C. trachomatis has been isolated from the rectum of asymptomatic homosexuals attending an STI clinic in 6% of men who practised passive rectal intercourse[9].

URETHRITIS

Both *C. trachomatis* and *N. gonorrhoea* produce clinical signs and symptoms due to their preference to infect columnar or transitional epithelium. For both, urethritis is the commonest presentation, although the epididymis, rectum and conjunctivae can also be sites of infection in men. Urethritis can be noted only as a historical event in men who have subsequently developed complications.

The inflammation produced by *C. trachomatis* is usually revealed as a discharge appearing at the urethral meatus with or without meatal inflammation. Symptoms experienced by the patient include discharge, burning on micturition or an itching sensation meatally (or in the urethra). Any discharge tends to be less acute, profuse and purulent than in men with gonococcal urethritis and have a longer incubation period (usually 7–21 days) but differences are qualitative rather than quantitative and, as such, are not helpful in diagnosis.

Frequency, urgency, nocturia, haematuria, perineal pain, scrotal swelling, inguinal lymphadenopathy, pain on opening the bowels and fever can occur but are all unusual.

Microscopic evidence of urethritis depends upon the demonstration (in two or more of five microscopy fields) of urethral leucocytosis (equal to, or greater than 5 polymorphonuclear leucocytes per x 1,000 field) on a Gram-stained slide of urethral secretions. This is accepted by most authorities as the benchmark of urethral inflammation, but some use 10 such cells.

A polymorphonuclear leucocytosis may also be detected in the sediment of a first voided urine. The patient should not have passed urine for 4 hours prior to the test, or preferably overnight. The first 10-20ml of urine voided is collected and centrifuged at 400g for 5 minutes. Sediment can then be removed by a sterile plastic or platinum loop for culture and Gram staining.

Leucocytosis will not pathognomically reveal the presence of *C. trachomatis*, but can demonstrate its effect as inflammation. Microscopy may also differentiate gonococcal from non-gonococcal urethritis with high degrees of specificity and sensitivity in the hands of microscopists experienced in sexually transmitted infection populations.

EPIDIDYMITIS

Many organisms are implicated as causes of acute or chronic epididymitis. Pathogens such as coliforms and pseudomonads are important causes in older men, where there is often a history of urological disease or instrumentation. In keeping with its mode of transmission, *C. trachomatis* is a major cause of acute epididymitis in populations at risk of acquiring sexually transmitted infections. The original studies suggesting this association with chlamydia used an age cut-off of 35 years of age (ie men older than this being more likely to have a bacterial cause). A good (sexual) history is a more sensitive determinant than age.

Classically then, the patient is a younger man who may have had a urethritis (perhaps being asymptomatic) who presents with a unilateral scrotal pain, swelling and tenderness accompanied by fever. The clinical and historical features are again of little help when differentiating between gonococcal, chlamydial and other bacterial aetiologies.

If the patient is not recognised as a contact of chlamydia, or presents as the "acute scrotum", Colour Doppler Imaging (CDI) is the examination of choice in evaluating the condition. Its superior resolution will help to differentiate causes such as torsion of the spermatic cord, epididymal and testicular inflammation and scrotal trauma. It demands a degree of operator experience, sensitive Doppler ultrasound equipment and knowledge of the limitations of its use.

Additional clinical information can be identified by observations of pyuria, positive culture, leukocytosis, accelerated erythrocyte sedimentation rate and a positive C-reactive protein test but these are all non-specific. Microbiological identification by culture or other technique is of most value but should not delay treatment.

A review of histological, immunohistochemical and clinicopathological findings in chlamydial and bacterial epididymitis has been performed[10]. Chlamydial epididymitis is characterised by its minimally destructive nature and periductal and intraepithelial inflammation with active epithelial proliferation. *E. coli,* in contrast, is remarkable for its highly destructive nature, forming large abscesses and xanthogranulomas.

Whilst women with pelvic inflammatory disease are counselled with reference to their subsequent fertility, our lack of knowledge and the (usually) unilateral nature of infection leads to difficulties in extending the same courtesy to men with epididymitis. It is known however that such infections can have a negative impact on fertility[11].

It is estimated that perhaps 5% of men with untreated *Chlamydia trachomatis* will develop epididymitis. In one STI clinic population aged under 35 with epididymitis the prevalence of chlamydia was around 45%[12].

PROSTATITIS

Acute prostatitis is characterised by pyrexia, feverish chills, general malaise, frequency of micturition, perineal ache or pain and occasionally acute retention of urine. A non-acute syndrome exists with less fulminant symptoms. Disturbances of bladder function are common including dribbling of urine post micturition. A urethral discharge may co-exist.

Suprapubic dull aching sometimes radiating to the perineal area, inguinal region, testes and penis is not uncommon with post-ejaculatory pain and haematospermia said to be more frequent in bacterial prostatitis.

The methods for detecting urethral and prostatic inflammation in patients with chronic prostatitis have been reviewed[13] to show that first void or mid-stream urine examination has low sensitivity for detecting urethral inflammation. Examining both expressed prostatic secretions and post prostatic massage urine proves best for detecting inflammation in prostatic fluid. Combining a urethral smear with lower urinary tract localisation in the form of a Meares-Stamey four glass urine test, represents a pragmatic approach to detecting urethral and prostatic inflammation.

Chronic prostatitis is associated with increased blood flow to the prostatic capsule and diffuse flow through the prostatic parenchyma. Colour Doppler Ultrasonography can provide objective documentation of such abnormalities.

There remains, however, no absolute evidence that *C. trachomatis* is a cause of prostatitis. Early studies showed only 10% of patients with non-bacterial prostatitis to have antibodies to *C. trachomatis* in serum or expressed prostatic secretions with none having the organism recovered by culture. Some men with prostatitis respond to drugs which are active against *C. trachomatis* and where other pathogens are not found. *C. trachomatis*, however, is not thought to infect glandular tissue such as the prostate.

One mechanism used to explain the association is that the syndrome is, in part, caused by a hyper-sensitivity reaction to the organism. Some men with chronic non-bacterial prostatitis are more likely than controls to show positive delayed hypersensitivity skin test reaction to the organism[14]. A reduction in the skin test response following Azithromycin treatment goes some way to support this hypothesis.

Whilst chlamydia has been recovered from expressed prostatic secretions in men with acute non-gonococcal urethritis and the prostatic fluid of men with non-bacterial prostatitis the definition of prostatitis used in these studies has been disputed. *C. trachomatis* has been cultured from expressed prostatic secretions of 6 men with negative urethral cultures[15].

In a study using trans-rectal biopsy of the prostate in 30 men with known positive urethral cultures for chlamydia and a diagnosis of prostatitis (prostatic tenderness and swelling on digital examination per rectum) chlamydia was cultured from a third of these[16]. Urethral contamination is a possibility however.

In an attempt to overcome this, a study[17] was performed using ultrasound-directed percutaneous biopsies but this was unable to isolate the organism from any specimen although it did find a chronic inflammatory reaction in the majority of cases.

Chlamydial DNA has been found using PCR in 4 of 135 prostatic biopsies in a study excluding men with microscopically diagnosed urethritis but no other evidence of infection with gonorrhoea, chlamydia or ureaplasma[18].

PROCTITIS

Intestinal involvement is well described in the related lymphogranuloma venereum (LGV) infection and this can cause a severe proctitis (see chapter 14).

The oculogenital serovars of chlamydia can also produce proctitis but this tends to be of a milder nature or even be asymptomatic.

The symptomatic condition is characterised by ano-rectal pain, a bloody mucopurulent discharge, tenesmus and diarrhoea.

With naked eye inspection, the proctitis can take on a granular appearance, but this may be absent. Many infected individuals are diagnosed only during routine diagnostic testing for STIs.

Sigmoidoscopy may be normal or can reveal mild inflammatory changes with small erosions and/or follicles in the lower 10cm of the rectum.

Histologically, rectal biopsy shows polymorphonuclear leucocyte infiltrate within the lamina propria with giant cells, crypt abscesses and granulomas often present.

It may be difficult, on the evidence of histopathological findings, to differentiate this from Crohn's Disease or unexplained proctitis. Where inflammatory bowel disease in a homosexual patient is suspected, chlamydial infection should be considered.

A small number of faecal leucocytes may be present on microscopy of a per rectal swab but the test is not sensitive enough to indicate proctitis.

The diagnosis of chlamydial proctitis is made by isolation or detection of the organism from the rectum and a response to symptoms with appropriate therapy. Serotyping by micro-immunofluorescence can differentiate LGV from non-LGV strains. To date, there have been no studies using Nucleic Acid Amplification Techniques (NAAT) and the best method of detection may be by culture, since the former may be insensitive because of inhibitors.

REITER'S SYNDROME

Reiter's syndrome is defined by the American College of Rheumatology as "an episode of peripheral arthritis of more than one month duration occurring in association with urethritis and/or cervicitis"[19]. A classic presentation of reactive arthritis accompanied by urogenital, mucocutaneous and ocular inflammation is unusual, and *"formes fruste"* are common. The syndrome is often mis-diagnosed as one of the other sero-negative spondylo-arthropathies such as psoriatic arthritis, ankylosing sponylitis or the arthritis of inflammatory bowel disease. This makes accurate epidemiological data difficult to compile.

The syndrome exists both as a Sexually Acquired Reactive Arthrosis (SARA) and a less common epidemic dysenteric form, the latter having been associated with *Shigella flexnerii, Salmonella* spp, *Yersinia enterocolitica* and *Campylobacter jejuni* but *Shigella soneii* is apparently not associated with this complication.

Peak onset of Reiter's syndrome is in the third decade but it may appear in children and the elderly. Incidence is probably around 33 per 100,000 in males[20].

SARA affects men more often than it does women. The male to female ratio was thought to be 20:1 but this was the result of under reporting in women (where cervicitis and less severe disease went unrecognised) and observations in cohorts from predominately male populations. Male to female ratios probably range from 9:1 to 5:1.

The disease is a symptom complex which may be straightforward to diagnose but fewer than one third of patients present with all definitive systems involved. A good sexual history therefore is an important aid to diagnosis.

Urethritis is an early symptom, occurring 2-4 weeks after sexual exposure or diarrhoeal illness. Men may have prostatitis and women cervicitis or vaginitis. These symptoms can also occur in patients with the post-dysenteric form. Ocular findings are seen in 50% of the sexually acquired form and 75% of the dysenteric. Conjunctivitis is common with keratitis, iritis and uveitis less so. All of these may be recurrent.

Arthritis is usually the last clinical feature to appear, being polyarticular and asymetric with effusions. Any joint can be involved but favoured sites are the ankles, knees and toes with later involvement including fingers and wrists. 50% of patients have sacroiliitis and axial spine involvement. Inflammation of the bony insertion of tendons and ligaments is found in some patients, particularly affecting the Achilles tendon and plantar fascia. Dactylitis can produce sausage shaped fingers or toes.

Dermatological involvement is seen in approximately half of Reiters cases with painless, shallow ulcerations on the lips, palate and tongue with circinate balanitis a common feature. Keratodermia blennorrhagica is seen on the soles of the feet or palms of the hands as erythematous macules which form hyper-keratotic papules.

Unusual complications include cardiac conduction abnormalities, myocarditis, aortitis and neurological findings such as hemiplegia and peripheral neuropathy.

Laboratory findings are generally non-specific and unhelpful with raised C-reactive protein levels and erythrocyte sedimentation rate. Mild anaemia and leucocytocis (with a "shift to the left") can be found. About 80% of people with Reiters syndrome are HLA – B27 (a major immuno-histocompability gene) positive. Only 6% of people who have the syndrome do not have the gene.

Joint fluid may reveal a polymorphonuclear lymphocytocis and elevated protein. A Gram stain should be negative for organisms.

C. trachomatis is obviously not the only trigger infection to produce the syndrome but researchers have shown some association. Elementary bodies in joint fluid and synovial biopsies of patients with Reiter's syndrome have been demonstrated[21]. Both PCR and LCR have been used more recently to demonstrate the presence of the organism in stored synovial samples[22] and synovial fluid[23]. It is possible that new developments in chlamydia serology may enhance our understanding of this condition (see chapter 5).

SOME FURTHER CONSIDERATIONS

As can be seen from the above, chlamydia presents a real and increasing danger to the sexual health of men both physically and psychologically. This is not only because of its incidence and clinical manifestations, but also because it is often sub-clinical, with patient/partner(s) and health provider insufficiently aware of the likelihood of its presence.

The situation may be improved by two developments. Firstly, advances in the technology of detection should make testing less invasive, and therefore more acceptable to patients. This should also facilitate the second development, which is screening. Screening should reveal more of the hidden endemic infection present in both the male and female population and thereby reduce not only the numbers of complications arising from infection but also background prevalence overall.

A note of caution, however, should be raised here. Women have traditionally been seen as the ideal (i.e. easiest) population to screen since they access healthcare in appropriate locations where detection can be employed. GU Medicine, Family Planning, Antenatal and Well Women Clinics are locations where sexually active women attend and where screening can be applied. With men the situation is quite different, especially for the young. There exists no focus of healthcare where men can be found *en-masse* and therefore, innovative approaches must be sought. These might include screening at social functions (e.g. music events and youth centres) or even schools or institutions of higher education. In this way men may be brought into screening.

Until they are, the temptation is to screen the easy target i.e. women, but this only addresses half of the problem. It could allow men to permit the responsibility for good sexual health to rest with their female partners. Men may thus be disenfranchised and come to regard chlamydia in the same way some of them presently consider other issues of sexual health such as contraception and termination of pregnancy – as the sole responsibility of women.

Non-invasive screening techniques for chlamydia combined with appropriate educational interventions which raise awareness could make men sexually healthier in the more holistic sense.

REFERENCES

1. Health Protection Agency (*Chlamydia trachomatis*). http://www.hpa.org.uk/infections/topics_ax/hiv_and_sti/sti-*chlamydia*/chlamydia.htm.
2. Centers for Disease Control and Prevention. Sexually Transmitted Disease Surveillance, 2001. Atlanta, GA; US Department of Health and Human Services, September 2002.
3. Parkes KS, Dickson PB, Richie CM. Spontaneous Clearance of *Chlamydia trachomatis* Infection in Untreated Patients *Sex Trans Dis* 1997; **24**(4):229–35.
4. Sheffield JS, Andrews WW, Klebanoff MA, *et al.* Spontaneous Resolution of Asymptomatic *Chlamydia trachomatis* in Pregnancy *Obstet Gynecol* 2005; **105**(3): 557–62.
5. Cohen DA, Nsuami M, Martin DH, *et al.* Repeated School Based Screening for Sexually Transmitted Diseases: A Feasible Strategy for Reaching Adolescents. *Paediatrics* 1999; **104**(6): 1281–1285.
6. Van de Brule AJC, Munk C, Winthers FJ *et al.* Prevalence and persistence of *Chlamydia trachomatis* infection in urine specimens from Danish Male Military recruits. *Int J STD AIDS* 2002; **13**(Supplement 2): 19–22.
7. Jebakumar SPR, Storey C, Lusher M *et al.* Value of screening for oro-pharyngeal *Chlamydia trachomatis* infection. *J Clin Path* 1995; **48:** 658–61.
8. Winter AJ, Gilleran G, Easttick K *et al.* Comparison of a Ligase Chain Reaction Based Assay and Cell Culture for Detection of pharyngeal Carriage of *Chlamydia trachomatis. J Clin Microb* 2000; **38**(9): 3502–4.

9. Quinn TC, Goodell SE, McKritchian E, *et al. Chlamydia trachomatis* Proctitis. *N Eng J Med* 1981; **305**: 195–200.

10. Hori S, Tsutsumi Y. Histological Differentiation between Chlamydial and Bacterial Epididymitis: non-destructive and proliferative *vs.* destructive and abscess-forming – immunohistochemical and clinicopathological findings *Human Pathology* 1995; **26**(4): 402–7.

11. Idhal A, Boman J, Kumlin U *et al.* Demonstration of *Chlamydia trachomatis* antibodies in male partner of the infertile couple is correlated with reduced likelihood of achieving pregnancy. *Hum Reprod* 2004; **19**(5): 1121–6.

12. Mulcahy FM, Bignell CJ, Rajakumar R *et al.* Prevalence of Chlamydia infection in acute epididymo-orchitis. *Genitourin Med* 1987; **63**(1): 16–18.

13. Krieger JN, Jacobs R, Ross SO. Detecting Urethral and Prostatic Inflammation in Patients with Chronic Prostatitis. *Urology* 2000; **55**(2): 186–192.

14. Ballard RC, Koornhof HJ, Mausenbaum E, *et al.* The Role of *Chlamydia trachomatis* in the Aetiology of Chronic Prostatitis and Treatment of the Condition with Azithromycin. 12th International Congress of Chemotherapy. Florence 1981 Abstract 233.

15. Bruce A W, Reid G. Prostatitis Associated with *Chlamydia trachomatis* in 6 Patients. *J Urol* 1989; **142**: 1006–7.

16. Poletti F, Medici MC, Alinovi A *et al.* Isolation of *Chlamydia trachomatis* from the prostate cells in patients affected by acute abacterial prostatitis. *J Urol* 1985; **134**: 691–3.

17. Doble A, Thomas BJ, Walker MM, *et al.* The Role of *Chlamydia trachomatis* in Chronic Abacterial Prostatitis: A Study Using Ultrasound Guided Biopsy. *J Urol* 1989; **141**: 332–3.

18. Krüger JN, Riley DE, Roberts MC *et al.* Prokaryotic DNA sequences in patients with chronic idiopathic prostatitis. *J Clin Microbiol* 1996; **34**: 3120–8.

19. Willkens RF, Arnett FC, Bitter T, *et al.* Reiter's Syndrome: Evaluation of Preliminary Criteria for Definite Disease. *Arthritis and Rheum* 1981; **24**(6): 844–9.

20. Cush JJ, Lipsky PE. Reiter's Syndrome and Reactive Arthritis in Arthritis and Allied Conditions: McCarty D J, Koopman W J, eds. 12th Edition Philadelphia: Lea and Febiger: 1993; **106**, 1–78.

21. Keat A, Thomas D, Dixey J. *Chlamydia trachomatis* and reactive arthritis: the missing link *Lancet* 1987; **1**: 72–74.

22. Nikkari S, Puolakkainen M, Yli-Kerttula U *et al.* Ligase chain reaction in detection of chlamydial DNA in synovial fluid cells *Br J Rheumat* 1997; **36**: 763–5.

23. Taylor-Robinson D, Gilroy CB, Thomas BJ. Detection of *Chlamydia trachomatis* DNA in joints of reactive arthritis patients by Polymerase Chain Reaction. *Lancet* 1992; **340**: 81–82.

SUGGESTED FURTHER READING

Centers for Disease Control and Prevention Recommendation for the prevention and management of *Chlamydia trachomatis* infections *Morbid. Mortal. Weekly Report* 1993; **42** (RR-12): 1–39.

Stamm WE, Holmes KK. *Chlamydia trachomatis* infections of the adult.Sexually Transmitted Diseases: Eds: Holmes KK, Mårdh P-A, Sparling PF, Wiesner PG New York: Mc Graw Hill; New York: 1990; 181–194.

Herbner TD. Ultrasound in the Assessment of the Acute Scrotum. *J Clin Ultrasound* 1996; **24**(8): 405–21.

Purvis K, Christiansen E. The Impact of Infection on Sperm Quality *Human Reproduction* 1996;. **11**: 2 Suppl; 31–41.

Hughes RA, Keat AC. Reiter's Syndrome and Reactive Arthritis: A Current Review. *Seminars in Arthritis & Rheumatism* 1994; **24**(3): 190–210.

Complications in the female and their management

Karen E Rogstad
Department of Genito Urinary Medicine,
Royal Hallamshire Hospital, Sheffield, UK

INTRODUCTION

Chlamydia trachomatis (CT) infection of the female genital tract can vary from an asymptomatic self-limiting infection to a severe debilitating illness with serious long-term complications both of the reproductive tract itself and also as a more disseminated disease. Whilst in the asymptomatic phase, ongoing damage to the fallopian tubes may be occurring and the diagnosis may only be made many years later, when complications are detected.

Initial entry to the body usually occurs through penetrative sexual intercourse, with organisms being deposited in the urethra, vagina and endocervix. Ascending infection then occurs, via the uterus, to the fallopian tubes to cause silent or overt pelvic inflammatory disease (PID), with resultant complications. Dissemination may then progress to the liver. Autoimmune responses to the bacteria complicate the picture resulting in worsening of PID or a reactive arthritis. Potential complications are shown in **Table 1** and illustrated in **Figure 1**.

Direct or auto-inoculation results in conjunctivitis, and anal sexual intercourse can result in a proctitis although this appears to be rare in women. Similarly, pharyngitis in women is unusual. If present in a pregnant woman, chlamydia can result in neonatal infection and post-partum complications in the mother.

Symptoms may appear soon after infection, or many months later and untreated latent infection may be reactivated at a later date.

Table 1. Complications of *Chlamydia trachomatis* in women

Site		symptoms, signs and complications
Urethra	urethritis	frequency/dysuria
Cervix	cervicitis	mucopurulent vaginal discharge
Uterus	endometritis	vaginal discharge irregular bleeding post coital bleeding
Fallopian tubes	salpingitis	pelvic inflammatory disease ectopic pregnancy tubal infertility chronic pelvic pain
Liver	perihepatitis	right upper quadrant pain
Bartholins gland	bartholinitis	swelling and pain of vulva
Conjunctiva	conjunctivitis	discharge from eye
Systemic	Reiter's syndrome	arthritis (large joints) iritis keratodermia blenorrhagica
Pregnancy/Neonate	pneumonitis conjunctivitis post-partum endometritis	

PATHOPHYSIOLOGY

C. trachomatis enters into columnar or transitional epithelial cells of the genital tract, rectum and peritoneum. The reticulate body of the chlamydia replicates and, when new elementary bodies are assembled, they leave the cell, with resultant cell death. In the fallopian tube, there is subepithelial inflammation, epithelial ulceration and scarring. The cellular and humoral immune responses to the chlamydial heat shock proteins HSP60 and HSP10 have been implicated in the immunopathology of pelvic chlamydial disease[1,2]. Antibodies to these proteins have been found to be a specific but not highly

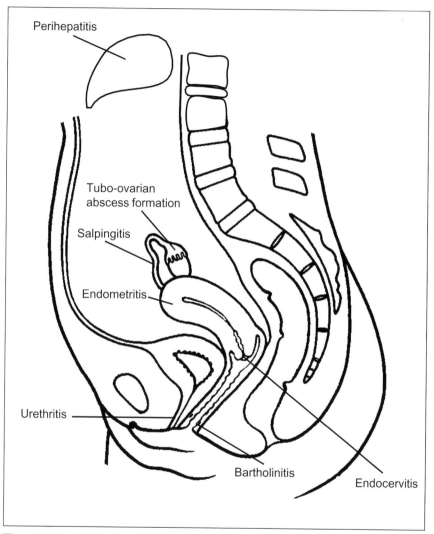

Figure 1. Sites of infection with *Chlamydia trachomatis*.

sensitive marker of pelvic disease[2-6]. The exact significance of these antibodies is unknown. The continued production of HSP60 by latent chlamydial infection or a breakdown in self tolerance to HSP60 have been proposed as possible mechanisms by which the immune response to HSP60 causes disease[7-9].

Recent work has suggested that the cellular responses of non-immune infected host cells may have an important role[7].

ACUTE URETHRAL SYNDROME

This develops as a result of urethral infection, although the majority of women with chlamydial infection of this site are asymptomatic

The diagnosis should be considered in women presenting with symptoms of cystitis, particularly where the dysuria has been present for more than one week. Examination may reveal meatal discharge, erythema or swelling but is usually normal. A clue to a urethral rather than bladder cause for the symptoms is suggested by lack of suprapubic tenderness, absence of haematuria and a urethral smear showing more than 10 polymorphs per high power field. A mid-stream urine specimen will reveal a culture negative pyuria.

CERVICITIS

Women with cervicitis can be asymptomatic or complain of vaginal discharge, which may be yellow or green. If there is coexistent bacterial vaginosis (BV) (which is often the case) then they may also complain of odour. Post-coital bleeding occurs in some.

The cervix may appear completely normal despite being infected with chlamydia. However, at least a third may show evidence of infection with either a hypertrophic ectopy of the endocervix, as manifested by cervical oedema, congestion and bleeding (19%), or have a mucopurulent discharge (37%)[10].

A cotton tipped swab inserted into the endocervix detects mucopus in the presence of a mucopurulent chlamydial cervicitis. Contact bleeding, on taking swabs or when performing cervical cytology, is also suggestive of chlamydial infection.

Cervicitis can also be diagnosed by microscopy of an endocervical swab, with a finding of more than 30 polymorphonuclear leucocytes (PMNs) per x 1000 field suggesting a diagnosis of chlamydia or gonorrhoea. However, the diagnosis of chlamydia itself requires specific testing and is discussed elsewhere. The inflammatory response associated with chlamydial cervicitis can obscure the endocervical cells on PAP smears, resulting in inadequate cervical cytology. Any woman who has a smear reported as "inflammatory changes" requires testing for the detection of *C. trachomatis*.

Although there is an increased prevalence of *C. trachomatis* in those with cervical ectopy the reason for this is unclear. It may be either because the organism itself causes ectopy, because those with ectopy are predisposed to acquiring chlamydia, or ectopy of the cervix in women increases shedding of the organism.

ENDOMETRITIS

Nearly half of patients with chlamydial cervicitis will also have an endometritis. This can be asymptomatic or the patient may complain of menorrhagia, metrorrhagia or post-coital bleeding. Endometrial biopsy shows plasma cells in the stroma and polymorphonuclear leucocytes in the superficial epithelium, but is rarely undertaken. Tests for CT from the endocervix may be negative.

PELVIC INFLAMMATORY DISEASE

Pelvic inflammatory disease (PID) occurs when there is upper genital tract infection and can be used to refer to salpingitis alone or include endometritis. It can be acute, sub-acute, chronic or silent. Up to 80% of cases of acute PID in the developed world are due to a sexually transmitted infection, and European studies suggest CT is the cause of at least 60% of cases. Accurate diagnosis is difficult without the use of invasive techniques such as laparoscopy therefore data on frequency are difficult to interpret. However it appears that between 10 and 40% of women infected with *C. trachomatis* develop PID[11]. There is often co-infection with BV associated organisms and *Neisseria gonorrhoeae* may also be present.

The incidence is greatest in 15-19 year olds, and the relative risk of acquiring PID in women is also highest in this group. The combined oral contraceptive pill confers some protection against ascending infection, and if PID does occur it is usually less severe. The risk of CT causing PID is increased by the presence of an intrauterine contraceptive device (IUCD), particularly at initial insertion or when it is changed. Certain types of IUCD e.g. those with progesterone appear to pose less risk than other types. The risk of CT causing salpingitis is also increased by manipulation of the cervix during termination of pregnancy or other gynaecological procedures.

Recurrences of PID are frequent and can be due to chlamydia persistence because of incomplete treatment, re-infection as a result of failure to perform partner notification or a new infected partner. Recurrences also occur as an ascending infection of other bacteria from the lower genital tract into the already damaged fallopian tubes.

PID presents as acute lower abdominal or pelvic pain. There may be deep dyspareunia, vaginal bleeding and discharge as well as pyrexia of more than 38°C. Clinical examination can reveal lower abdominal tenderness, adnexal tenderness and cervical excitation (pain on cervical movement). Bilateral masses may be felt, particularly if there is tubo-ovarian abcess formation. In some, investigations show a raised white cell count, ESR and C reactive protein. However, in silent chlamydial PID no symptoms or signs may be present although ongoing tubal damage is occurring. Previous tubal ligation does not exclude the diagnosis as was previously thought[12].

Definitive diagnosis can be difficult, with clinical signs and symptoms having a positive predictive value of only 65-90% compared with laparoscopy[13]. Laparoscopy is not justified routinely and may fail to detect milder cases. Similarly, endometrial biopsy or ultrasound may be helpful but their routine use is not advocated at the current time. The absence of endocervical or vaginal pus cells has a good negative predictive value of 95%, but their presence has a positive predictive value of only 17%.

The management of PID is described in chapter 6 and consists of oral or intravenous antibiotics active against *C. trachomatis*, combined with metronidazole to cover anaerobes which are also usually present. Bed rest and analgesia may be required and advice on abstinence from sexual intercourse, partner notification and a patient information leaflet should be given (available from www.rcog.org.uk). The presence of tubo-ovarian abcesses may require surgical intervention.

Physicians should have a low threshold for diagnosis and initiation of therapy particularly in adolescents, as even a 3-day delay in treatment can cause a threefold increase in risk of infertility[13]. It is therefore recommended that empiric treatment of PID should be initiated in sexually active young women and other women at risk for STDs if uterine/adnexal tenderness or cervical motion tenderness are present and no other cause(s) for the illness can be identified[14]. If an intrauterine contraceptive device is present its removal should be considered as it may be associated with better short-term clinical outcomes, but must be balanced against the risk of pregnancy[15].

Whenever a diagnosis of PID is made, testing for other sexually transmitted infections and pregnancy testing should be performed, as recent data have shown that ectopic pregnancy may be an acute as well as a long-term complication of chlamydial infection.

COMPLICATIONS OF CHLAMYDIAL PELVIC INFLAMMATORY DISEASE

As PID worsens, tubo-ovarian abcesses can form and peritonitis develop, as well as Fitz-Hugh-Curtis syndrome. Long-term complications of PID include ectopic pregnancy, tubal infertility and chronic pelvic pain. The risk of sequaele increases disproportionately with subsequent infections. For ectopic pregnancy or tubal infertility the odds ratio increases from 6 after one episode of PID to 17 after two episodes[16].

An ectopic pregnancy is life threatening, resulting in 10% of deaths in England that occur as a complication of pregnancy, childbirth or the puerperium. In women who have had PID the risk of ectopic pregnancy is increased by 7–10 times, and 43% of cases of ectopic pregnancy may be due to chlamydia, either recognised or unrecognised[17]. Evidence from Sweden suggests that ectopic pregnancy may be an acute, as well as, long-term complication of infection with *C. trachomatis*. Researchers found a strong correlation between ectopic pregnancy rates and rate of chlamydial infection in the same year for women 20–24 years of age[18].

As well as causing ectopic pregnancy, the tubal damage which occurs as a result of tubal inflammation, scarring and subsequent occlusion can result in primary or secondary infertility. It is estimated that 50% of cases of infertility are due to tubal factors of which 50% of these are caused by *C. trachomatis*, and many give no history of previous PID[19].

Chronic pelvic pain occurs in more than 15% of women with previous episodes of PID, increasing from an incidence of 11% after one episode to 66% after 3 or more episodes. It appears to be correlated with the presence of peritoneal adhesions.

BARTHOLINITIS

The Bartholins ducts open into the posterior third of the labia minora, and although infection with subsequent abscess formation is more usually associated with gonococcal infections, Bartholinitis can also be caused by chlamydia. It typically presents with local pain and swelling and examination reveals a tender abscess of the lower labia, which may be fluctuant.

Management is by antibiotic therapy but surgical treatment with marsupialization may be necessary.

FITZ-HUGH-CURTIS SYNDROME

The term Fitz-Hugh-Curtis Syndrome (FHC) is used for the perihepatitis associated with genital chlamydial or gonococcal infection. Although first described in the latter it is more frequently associated with chlamydia. There is an acute inflammatory reaction on the liver capsule and adjacent peritoneum, but there is no involvement of the liver parenchyma. *C. trachomatis* organisms can sometimes be isolated from the hepatic surface. This condition occurs in 5–15% of women with laparoscopically diagnosed salpingitis and symptoms suggestive of it are found in 20%. It may result from direct spread of chlamydia from the fallopian tubes via the peritoneum. However it is likely that spread through the lymphatic system and haematogenous spread may also occur, as it has been found in women who have had tubal ligation and also rarely in men with gonococcal urethritis. Evidence suggests an association with previous chlamydial infection, as titres of antibody to CT are significantly higher in those with the syndrome compared to those women with CT PID and no perihepatitis. Patients with FHC also have high titres of antibodies to chlamydial 60kDa heat shock protein.

Patients present with right, upper quadrant pain which may occur alone or with symptoms of vaginal discharge or PID. Fever, nausea and vomiting may be present. The pain can be pleuritic and there may be referred pain to the shoulder and back. Symptoms can be exacerbated by breathing, coughing and movement. The upper abdominal pain can precede the pelvic pain by several days and may be so severe that the PID symptoms are ignored. On examination, there is tenderness under the right costal margin and a rub may be present in severe cases. Signs of general peritonitis can occur. White cell count and ESR are raised in approximately 30% and mild bilirubin and liver enzyme increases are found in less than 50%. Chest X-ray may show pleural fluid. Diagnosis is usually based on clinical suspicion, in the presence of a normal ultrasound of the gallbladder and common bile ducts.

A definitive diagnosis is made by laparoscopy when purulent fibrinous peritonitis of the liver capsule is found. Adhesions between the liver and abdominal wall can occur and typical thin, avascular "violin-string" adhesions may be found in more advanced cases.

PREGNANCY AND THE NEONATE

There is little and conflicting evidence to implicate CT in chorioamnionitis and adverse pregnancy outcome. DNA amplification has found it to be present in the amniotic fluid of 6.7% of women with pre-labour amniorrhexis but the significance of this is not known[20]. However late post partum endometritis is well recognised and occurs in 30% of women with antenatal CT infection. On examination there may be mild uterine tenderness, or the patient may be asymptomatic, and if unrecognised and untreated secondary infertility may result.

Infants of mothers with chlamydial infection will develop conjunctivitis in 18-50% of cases and pneumonia in 11–20%. Although these are thought to result from contact with infected vaginal secretions, there have been cases reported where neonatal chlamydial infection was found in infants delivered by caesarean section in the presence of intact membranes[21]. Chlamydial conjunctivitis presents 5-10 days after delivery whereas pneumonitis usually presents at 2-3 weeks. Rarely there may be severe respiratory failure, and there is some evidence to suggest long-term respiratory disease may result[22,23]. Whether serous otitis media, small for dates babies and failure to thrive in infancy occur secondary to vertically acquired chlamydia is controversial.

REACTIVE ARTHRITIS

This term replaces the former term of Reiter's syndrome which, by definition, requires the presence of conjunctivitis, arthritis and urethritis, thus contributing to the high male:female ratio. Viable chlamydiae have now been found in synovium and synovial fluid using nucleic acid amplification techniques. It is thought the chlamydiae are transported from the genital tract in macrophages or dendritic cells and that chlamydial persistence may play a role[24]. The presence of HLA-B27 appears to increase susceptibility, severity and persistence. There is an association with the other spondyloarthropathies.

The arthritis typically affects large weight-bearing joints and occurs several weeks after infection. There may also be iritis, conjunctivitis and keratodermia blenorrhagica (circinate balanitis is an associated feature in male cases).

Management is of the underlying chlamydial infection, non-steroidal anti-inflammatory drugs and physiotherapy. Bed rest may be appropriate in the early stages. One trial has shown possible benefit of long-term tetracycline[25] and results of a further trial using azithromycin are awaited.

OTHER COMPLICATIONS

Although there have been occasional case reports of pneumonitis in immunocompetent adults, there is no real evidence. There have been some suggestions that genital *C. trachomatis* may be implicated in culture-negative endocervicitis, meningo-encephalitis, peritonitis and post-menopausal vaginitis. A recent case-control study has suggested a link between past or chronic infection with chlamydia and ovarian cancer but further studies are awaited[26].

The early diagnosis and management of chlamydial infection of the female genital tract is essential to protect the reproductive health of women. Every doctor and nurse must consider chlamydial infection a possibility in any sexually active girl or woman, and in neonates with respiratory or conjunctival problems. Only by doing so will women and babies be protected from the debilitating acute and long-term sequelae of this disease.

Acknowledgement

I would like to thank Dr Paddy Horner for information and advice on the pathophysiology of chlamydia.

REFERENCES

1. Paavonen J, Eggert-Kruse W. *Chlamydia trachomatis:* impact on human reproduction. *Hum Reprod Update* 1999; **5:** 433–47.
2. LaVerda D, Albanese LN, Ruther PE, *et al.* Seroreactivity to *Chlamydia trachomatis* Hsp10 correlates with severity of human genital tract disease. *Infect.Immun.* 2000; **68:** 303–9.
3. Toye B, Laferriere C, Claman P, *et al.* Association between antibody to the chlamydial heat-shock protein and tubal infertility. *Journal of Infectious Diseases* 1993; **168:** 1236–40.
4. Dieterle S, Wollenhaupt J. Humoral immune response to the chlamydial heat shock proteins hsp60 and hsp70 in chlamydia-associated chronic salpingitis with tubal occlusion. *Hum. Reprod.* 1996; **11:** 1352–6.
5. Sziller I, Witkin SS, Ziegert M, *et al.* Serological responses of patients with ectopic pregnancy to epitopes of the *Chlamydia trachomatis* 60 kDa heat shock protein. *Hum. Reprod.* 1998; **13:** 1088–93.

6. Land JA, Evers JL. Chlamydia infection and subfertility. [Review] [59 refs]. *Best Practice & Research in Clinical Obstetrics & Gynaecology* 2002; **16:** 901–12.

7. Stephens RS. The cellular paradigm of chlamydial pathogenesis. [Review] [103 refs]. *Trends in Microbiology* 2003; **11:** 44–51.

8. Morrison RP, Belland RJ, Lyng K, Caldwell HD. Chlamydial disease pathogenesis. The 57-kD chlamydial hypersensitivity antigen is a stress response protein. *Journal of Experimental Medicine* 1989; **170:** 1271–83.

9. Bavoil P, Stephens RS, Falkow S. A soluble 60 kiloDalton antigen of *Chlamydia* spp. is a homologue of *Escherichia coli* GroEL. *Mol Microbiol* 1990; **4:** 461–9.

10. Harrison HR, *et al*. Cervical *Chlamydia trachomatis* infection in university women: Relationship to history, contraception, ectopy and cervicitis. *Am J Obstet Gynaecol* 1985; **153:** 241–4.

11. Stamm W, Guinan M, Johnson C, *et al*. Effects of treatment regimens for *N. gonorrhoea* on simultaneous infection with *Chlamydia trachomatis*. *N Engl J Med* 1984; **310:** 545–9.

12. Leugur M, Duvivier R. Pelvic inflammatory disease after tubal sterilization: a review. *Obstetrical & Gynaecological Survey* 2000; **55:** 41–50.

13. Hillis S, Jeosoef R, Marchbanks P *et al*. Delayed care of pelvic inflammatory disease as a risk factor for impaired fertility *Am J Obstet Gynaecol* 1993; **168:** 1503–9.

14. Workowski KA, Levine WC. Sexually Transmitted Diseases Guidelines 2002 MMWR 2002 51(RR-06); 1-80. www.cdc.gov/mmwr/PDF/RR/RR5106.pdf

15. Ross J. United Kingdom Guideline for the Management of Pelvic Inflammatory Disease, February 2005 www.BASHH.org

16. Westrom C. Sexually transmitted diseases and infertility *Sex Trans Dis* 1994; **21:** 532–37.

17. Sexually transmitted diseases quarterly report: genital chlamydial infection, ectopic pregnancy and syphilis in England and Wales. *Commun Dis Rep CDR wkly* 2000; **10:** 116–117.

18. Egger M, Low N, Smith GD, *et al*. Screening for chlamydial infection and the risk of ectopic pregnancy in a county in Sweden: ecological analysis. *Br Med J* 1998; **316:** 1776–80

19. World Health Organization Task Force on the prevention and management of infertility Tubal Infertility: Serologic Relationship to Post Chlamydial and Gonococcal Infection *Sex Trans Dis* 1995; **22:** 71–77.

20. Ville Y, Carroll SG, Watts P, *et al*. *Chlamydia trachomatis* infection in pre-labour amniorrhexis *Br J Obstet Gynaecol* 1997; **104:** 1091–1093.

21. Ratelle S, Keno D, Hardwood M, Etkind PH. Neonatal chlamydial infections in Massachusetts 1992–1993, *Am J Prev Med* 1997; **13:** 221–224.

22. Harrison HR, Phil D, Taussig LM *et al*. *Chlamydia trachomatis* and chronic respiratory diseases in childhood *Pediatr Inf Dis* 1982; **1:** 29–33.

23. Weiss SG, Newcomb RW, Beem MJ. Pulmonary assessment of children after chlamydial pneumonia of infancy *J Paediatr* 1986; **108:** 659–64.

24. Gaston JSH. Immunological basis of chlamydia induced reactive arthritis *Sex Trans Infects* 2000; **76**(15): 6–161.

25. Lauhio A, Leirisalo Repo M, Lahdevirta J *et al*. Double-blind, placebo – controlled study of three-month treatment with lymecycline in reactive arthritis with special reference to chlamydia arthritis. *Arthritis Rheum* 1991; **34:** 6–14.

26. Ness RB, Goodman MT, Shen C, Brunham RC. Serologic evidence of past infection with *Chlamydia trachomatis*, in relation to ovarian cancer. *J Infect Dis* 2003; **187:** 1147–52.

BIBLIOGRAPHY

Holmes KK, Sparling PF, Mårdh P-A *et al*. (1999). Sexually Transmitted Diseases 3rd edition, McGraw – Hill. ISBN 0-07-029688-X

Chlamydia trachomatis *infection in fallopian tube disease – the Swedish experience*

Per-Anders Mårdh
Department of Obstetrics and Gynaecology,
University Hospital, Lund, Sweden

INTRODUCTION

The Swedish effort to reduce the pool of carriers of *Chlamydia trachomatis* is a textbook example of a highly successful public health intervention programme to reduce a disease and thereby also its sequelae. Thus the intensive screening programme of the agent performed on a national basis resulted in a massive reduction of pelvic inflammatory disease (PID) and also of chlamydial infections in the newborn, e.g. of eye and lung infections. The efforts are also likely to have reduced late sequelae, e.g. of asthma, obstructive lung disease, as well as of infertility, ectopic pregnancy and chronic abdominal pain. The present study reviews the initial Swedish chlamydia research and the national public health efforts regarding screening and counselling activities in the field.

HOW DID IT ALL START?

After a visit to Seattle and contact with Dr Say-Ping Wang, the author, and later also the author's PhD students, started research into how to simplify the diagnosis of chlamydial infections. When this research became fruitful we started to study the local epidemiology of genital *C. trachomatis* infections. In 1975, at a meeting in Lake Placid, US, we were able to present a method that meant a breakthrough in the diagnosis of infections by *C. trachomatis*, i.e. the use of cycloheximide-treated McCoy cell cultures[1]. At the same meeting, we presented evidence for *C. trachomatis* being an etiological agent of PID[2]. In 1977, we published a study confirming such an etiological relationship[3].

By the end of 1976, we offered the possibility for routine diagnosis of *C. trachomatis* for our laboratory's catchment area. We carried out routine testing of women attending the outpatient department of Obstetrics and Gynaecology at Lund University Hospital, as well as women hospitalised at the clinic. These studies confirmed that genital chlamydial infections were common in these cohorts. Thus, 25% of all women with vaginal discharge at that time had a genital chlamydial infection[4]. Of those with gonorrhoea, one in four also had an infection by *C. trachomatis*. The opposite was also true. Partner notification detected a chlamydial infection in more than half of the sexual contacts to an index case[5].

EVIDENCE OF CORRELATION BETWEEN PID AND GENITAL CHLAMYDIAL INFECTION

In any study of salpingitis, it is essential that the diagnosis is correctly confirmed. So far, laparoscopy/laparatomy have ranked highest in accuracy among diagnostic methods[6]. In laparoscopically confirmed cases of salpingitis, samples that we collected from the fallopian tubes revealed the presence of *C. trachomatis* by the use of tissue cell cultures[3,7]. In such cases, we also found a significant antibody response to the agent[7,8]. Also histological findings supported a causal relationship[9]. In animal models, e.g. in grivet monkeys, *C. trachomatis* provoked salpingitis[10,11].

We presented data supporting a canalicular spread of chlamydia organisms to the tubes by showing evidence of endometritis in PID cases being caused by *C. trachomatis*[12], where histological sections showed a characteristic plasma cell infiltration.

In women with chronic abdominal pain[13] and in those with involuntary childlessness[14], there is evidence of a past infection with *C. trachomatis*. We also found evidence of complications of PID being due to an agent, as in periappendicitis[15], perihepatitis[16-18], peritonitis, perisplenitis and perisigmoiditis as a consequence of chlamydial infection spreading from the tubes to the abdominal cavity.

Use of oral contraceptives may modulate the course of PID and therefore also the rate of sequelae of chlamydial salpingitis[19,20]. We found that perihepatitis was a rather uncommon complication in chlamydia PID cases in women on the pill, but rather common in such cases *not* taking the pill.

POSITIVE IMPACT ON PUBLIC HEALTH BY SCREENING FOR *C. TRACHOMATIS*

Knowledge of a high prevalence of genital chlamydial infections in the general Swedish population at the beginning of the 1980s led to the start of an impressive national screening programme for *C. trachomatis*. For some years during the mid-1980s the number of chlamydia samples collected exceeded half a million (the Swedish population at that time was approx. 8.5 million). The outcome of the programme was a marked drop over the next few years in the number of diagnosed PID cases[21] and some years later of ectopic pregnancy cases[22].

There was a simultaneous drop in the number of chlamydial infections and of gonorrhoea cases after diagnostic possibilities of the former were established. The reduction of both these infections started some years before similar trends were seen in other countries. It should be noted that tests for *C. trachomatis* and *Neisseria gonorrhoea* were generally done simultaneously in the Swedish screening programmes. A tetracycline (often doxycycline or lymecycline) was the drug generally chosen to treat chlamydial infections in Sweden; a therapy which at that time was also curative for the vast majority of gonorrhoea infections. Thus screening for genital chlamydial infections also meant a concomitant decrease in the carrier rate of gonococci in the general population. This contributed to a decrease in the rate of gonococcal salpingitis and its complications and sequelae.

The rate of ectopic pregnancy in Sweden decreased in parallel with that of PID, but with some years delay. In a group of Swedish women, a mean time lag of 7.5 years was found between a diagnosed episode of PID and that of ectopic pregnancy. The time delay may partly reflect the trend among Swedish women to wish to conceive at a much later age than when they generally contract their first chlamydial infection.

There is evidence that a genital chlamydial infection may induce hypersensitivity reactions, (*via* similarities between human and chlamydial heat shock proteins [HSP-60]), that can interfere with the ability to conceive and also contribute to failure of *in vitro* fertilisation (IVF) attempts[23].

As a consequence of the wide spread of genital chlamydial infection in young Swedes, "youth clinics" were opened in many Swedish cities. Teenagers can attend these clinics, without pre-booking consultation time. At the clinics the teenagers meet midwives, who are supported by gynaecologists if necessary. The midwives often gain the teenager's confidence, so that counselling in risk reduction is very successful. Contraceptive advice also plays a central role in the youth clinic programme; the clinics were also intended to try to reduce teenage pregnancies.

MOTIVATIONS FOR SCREENING PREGNANT WOMEN

We found evidence of intrauterine infections by *C. trachomatis*, i.e. in cases of Premature Rupture of Membranes (PROM)[24] and we demonstrated serological evidence of a past *C. trachomatis* infection in many cases of ectopic pregnancy[25].

There is new evidence that *C. trachomatis* may also play an important role in premature birth in women who have an intrauterine infection by the agent.[26] Thus up to 10% of children born prematurely may be already infected *in utero*, as evidenced by tests of cord blood for antichlamydia IgM antibodies.

We and other Swedish researchers also reported on evidence of pelvic chlamydial infection after elective abortion performed within 14th week of gestation[27,28]. In the later study, positive *C. trachomatis* cervical cultures supported a causal relationship.

INFECTIONS IN NEWBORNS

Transfer of *C. trachomatis* at delivery from an infected mother to the offspring may cause pneumonia in infants. The pneumonia often presents several weeks after delivery when the child has developed the capability to react with delayed hypersensitivity reactions to the agent[29]. It is notable that newborns are often transiently colonised in the eyes by *C. trachomatis*[30], but will never develop any signs of infection.

CHOICE OF THERAPEUTIC AGENT IN PREGNANT WOMEN

Therapy of genital chlamydial infections in pregnant women is restricted to the choice of a tetracycline (often doxycycline), erythromycin or azithromycin. In a study comparing Tetralysal® and Azithromax®, we found no difference in their efficiency to cure genital chlamydial infections in females, as evidenced from negative post-therapy cultures of *C. trachomatis*[31].

We also stressed the importance of early partner notification in any therapy of an index case infected by *C. trachomatis*[5].

As the infection in the pregnant woman may have been contracted before she conceived, the infection has had the chance to ascend to the uterine mucosa. Thus pregnant women should be treated as if they have a PID (even if the chlamydia diagnosis is only based on a positive test from the lower genital tract or by analysis of voided urine samples).

COST ESTIMATES OF GENITAL CHLAMYDIAL INFECTION

Cost estimates of screening programmes for genital chlamydial infections have shown that they (on a local or national level) are cost-effective if the carrier rate in the population is 6%[32,33], if one does not include an assumed percentage of clinical silent PID. When including a percentage of such cases, other workers found screening programmes to be cost-effective at a carrier rate of only 3%. However, all cost estimates presented so far have never considered the enormous costs of life-long sequelae, e.g. of obstructive lung disease, in persons infected at delivery by a chlamydia-infected mother. Other costs seldom considered are those related to giving birth to premature born twins after IVF (motivated by a previous chlamydial infection that had resulted in tubal occlusion). Thus to be realistic, any cost estimates should also include life-long sequelae in persons prematurely born, as a consequence of a chlamydial infection in his/her mother.

REFERENCES

1. Ripa T, Mårdh P-A. A new simplified culture technique for *Chlamydia trachomatis*. In: Holmes KK, Hobson D, eds. Non-gonococcal Urethritis and Related Infections. Washington DC: *Am Soc Microbiol* 1977; 32–37.
2. Mårdh P-A, Ripa KT, Wang S-P, Weström L. *Chlamydia trachomatis* as an aetiological agent in acute salpingitis. In: Holmes KK, Hobson D, eds. Non-gonococcal Urethritis and Related Infections. Washington DC: *Am Soc Microbiol* 1977; 77–83.
3. Mårdh P-A, Ripa KT, Svensson L, Weström L. *Chlamydia trachomatis* infection in patients with acute salpingitis. *N Engl J Med* 1977; **23:** 1377–9.
4. Svensson L, Weström L, Mårdh P-A. *Chlamydia trachomatis* in women attending a gynaecological outpatient clinic with lower genital tract infection. *Br J Vener Dis* 1981; **57:** 259–62.
5. Thelin I, Wennström A-M, Mårdh P-A. Contact tracing in patients with genital chlamydial infection. *Br J Vener Dis* 1980; **56:** 259–62.
6. Weström L, Mårdh P-A. Salpingitis. In: Holmes KK, Mårdh P-A, Sparling F, Wiesner P, eds. Sexually Transmitted Diseases. New York: McGraw-Hill, 1984: 615–63.
7. Svensson L, Weström L, Mårdh P-A. Acute salpingitis with *Chlamydia trachomatis* isolated from the fallopian tubes: clinical, cultural and serological findings. *Sex Trans Dis* 1981; **8:** 51–5.
8. Treharne JD, Ripa KT, Mårdh P-A, Svensson L, Weström L, Darougar S. Antibodies to *Chlamydia trachomatis* in acute salpingitis. *Br J Vener Dis* 1979; **55:** 26–9.
9. Möller BR, Weström L, Ahrons S, *et al. Chlamydia trachomatis* infection of the Fallopian tubes. Histological finding in two patients. *Br J Vener Dis* 1979; **55:** 422–8.
10. Möller BR, Freundt EA, Mårdh P-A. Experimental pelvic inflammatory disease provoked by *Chlamydia trachomatis* and *Mycoplasma hominis* in grivet monkeys. *Am J Obstet Gynecol* 1980; **138** Suppl: 1017–21.
11. Möller BR, Mårdh P-A. Experimental salpingitis in grivet monkeys by *Chlamydia trachomatis*. Modes of spread of infection to the Fallopian tubes. *Acta Path Microbiol Scand* 1980; **88B:** 107–14.

12. Mårdh P-A, Möller BR, Ingerslev HJ, *et al.* Endometritis caused by *Chlamydia trachomatis. Br J Vener Dis* 1981; **57:** 191–5.

13. Wölner-Hanssen P, Mårdh P-A, Weström L, Svensson L. Laparoscopy in women with chlamydial infection and pelvic pain. A comparison of patients with and without salpingitis. *Obst Gynecol* 1983; **61:** 299–303.

14. Svensson L, Mårdh P-A, Weström L. Infertility after acute salpingitis with special reference to *Chlamydia trachomatis. Steril Fertil* 1983; **40:** 322–9.

15. Mårdh P-A, Wølner-Hanssen P. Periappendicitis and chlamydial salpingitis. *Surg Gynecol Obstet* 1985; **160:** 304–6.

16. Wølner-Hanssen P, Weström L, Mårdh P-A. Perihepatitis and chlamydial salpingitis. *Lancet* 1980; **i:** 901–4.

17. Wølner-Hanssen P, Weström L, Mårdh P-A. Perihepatitis and chlamydial salpingitis. *Obst Gyn Survey* 1981; **36:** 44–5.

18. Wølner-Hanssen P, Svensson L, Weström L, Mårdh P-A. Isolation of *Chlamydia trachomatis* from the liver capsule in Fitz-Hugh-Curtis syndrome. *New Engl J Med* 1982; **306:** 113.

19. Svensson L, Mårdh P-A, Sandström E. Susceptibility of *Neisseria gonorrhoeae* to rifampicin and thiamphenicol: correlation with protein I antigenic determinants. *Sex Trans Dis Suppl* 1984; **11:** 366–70.

20. Wølner-Hanssen P, Svensson L, Mårdh P-A, Weström L. Laparoscopic findings and contraceptive use in women with signs and symptoms suggestive of acute salpingitis. *Obstet Gynecol* 1985; **66:** 233–8.

21. Weström I. Decrease in incidence of women treated in hospital for acute salpingitis in Sweden. *Genitourin Med* 1998; **64:** 59–63.

22. Thorburn J. Ectopic pregnancy. The "epidemic" seems to be over. *Läkartidning* 1995; **92:** 4701–6. (in Swedish with English summary).

23. Neuer A, Spandorfer SD, Giraldo P, *et al.* The role of heat shock proteins in reproduction. *Hum Reprod Update.* 2000; **6:** 149–59.

24. Mårdh P-A, Johansson H, Svenningsen N. Intrauterine lung infection by *Chlamydia trachomatis* in a premature infant. 1984; *Acta Paed Scand* **73:** 569–572.

25. Svensson L-O, Mårdh P-A, Ahlgren M, Nordenskjöld F. Ectopic pregnancy and antibodies to *Chlamydia trachomatis. Fertil Steril* 1985; **414:** 313–7.

26. Mårdh P-A, Novikova D. Impact of chlamydial infections on pregnancy outcome, perinatal health and long-term sequelae of offsprings – a review of novel studies and reappraisal of earlier data. *Italian J Gynae & Obs* 2000; **12:**

27. Möller BR, Ahrons S, Laurin J, Mårdh P-A. Pelvic infection after elective abortion associated with *Chlamydia trachomatis. Obstet Gynecol* 1982; **59:** 210–13.

28. Osser S, Persson K. Postabortal pelvic infection associated with *Chlamydia trachomatis* and the influence of humoral immunity. *Am J Obstet Gynecol* 1984; **100:** 699–703.

29. Hallberg A, Mårdh P-A, Persson K, Ripa T. Pneumonia associated with *Chlamydia trachomatis* infection in an infant. *Acta Paed Scand* 1979; **68:** 765–7.

30. Mårdh P-A, Helin I, Bobeck S, *et al.* Colonisation of pregnant and puerperal women and neonates with *Chlamydia trachomatis. Br J Vener Dis* 1980; **56:** 96–100.

31. Brihmer C, Mårdh P-A, Osser S, *et al.* Efficiency and safety of azithromycin versus lymecycline in genital chlamydial infection in non-pregnant women. *Scand J Infect Dis* 1996; **28:** 451–4.

32. Genc M, Mårdh P-A. A cost-effectiveness analysis of screening and treatment for *Chlamydia trachomatis* infection in asymptomatic women. *Ann Int Med* 1996; 124: 1–7.

33. Genc M, Ruusavaara L, Mårdh P-A. An economic evaluation of screening for *Chlamydia trachomatis* in adolescent males. *JAMA* 1993; **17:** 2057–64.

CHAPTER 11

Economic implications of Chlamydia trachomatis

Farzana Malik

Health Economist, drfarzanamalik@yahoo.co.uk

INTRODUCTION

When referring to the economic implications of chlamydia, we usually have two different types of economic issues in mind. The first is associated with the estimation of the overall impact on society of chlamydia in terms of direct and indirect cost of disease. This is usually referred to as cost of illness or burden of illness and crucially depends on factors such as prevalence of the disease; the costs associated with the complications and how it affects the capacity of people to participate in productive work (see **Figure 1**).

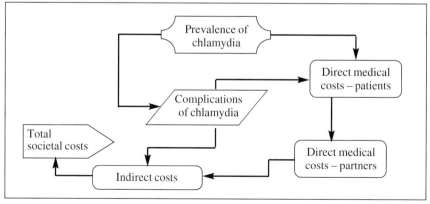

Figure 1. A cost of illness model for *Chlamydia trachomatis*.

Table 1: Economic Evaluation of Alternative Strategies of Managing Chlamydia

- Cost-effectiveness of:
    - screening strategies in women
    - screening in pregnant women
    - screening strategies in adolescent males
    - partner notification
    - empirical vs laboratory confirmed treatment
    - treatment regimens
- Cost-benefit evaluation of routine tests after treatment

The second category of economic issues arise from the economic evaluation of alternative strategies for the management of chlamydia. The latter category covers a variety of issues some of which are presented in **Table 1.**

PREVALENCE AND INCIDENCE OF CHLAMYDIA TRACHOMATIS

Chlamydia trachomatis infection is the most common sexually transmitted bacterial disease in England and Wales[1]. Estimates of the overall prevalence show infection figures of 2.8% in men and 3.6% in women[2] (see chapter 2). The main features of this infection are threefold: infection is often asymptomatic, sequelae may be severe and if left untreated, infection can persist for more than a year[3]. Data from various surveys of individuals attending health services suggest infection may be asymptomatic in up to 70% of infected women[4,5] and in 4-11% of men[6,7]. More recently, very much higher figures of asymptomatic male infection have been suggested[8] (see chapter 2). The most serious sequelae of infection occurs in women where infection with *Chlamydia trachomatis* may lead to pelvic inflammatory disease (PID), ectopic pregnancy and infertility. These sequelae may have important lifetime consequences and are extremely costly to treat. According to the World Bank, chlamydial infection represents the most economically important sexually transmitted disease (STD) after HIV[7].

In the European region, approximately 10 million new cases of chlamydial infection occur each year[9]. Further, an estimated 600,000 cases per annum of salpingitis may be caused by *Chlamydia trachomatis* and approximately

120,000 cases will become infertile. Prevalence rates collated for the European Region range between 1% and 33% in women who are screened and 10-20% for men who undergo screening. Prevalence rates in persons with signs or symptoms of infection are much higher and may be as high as 80% in men with epidymitis and 70% in women with PID.

ECONOMIC BURDEN OF CHLAMYDIA

There is limited research on the economic burden of chlamydia with only two US based studies that address this important issue. At the time of writing, there are no published cost of illness studies for chlamydia in Europe however some research suggests the economic burden of chlamydia in the UK may be as high as £100 million.[10]

In an incidence based evaluation, Chesson *et al.* estimated the direct medical costs of chlamydia and seven other major STDs among American youth.[11] The authors reviewed the existing literature on the costs of chlamydia and then multiplied these costs per case estimates by the approximate number of new cases of chlamydia acquired by youth aged 15-24. All costs were adjusted for inflation to year 2000 dollars. The average cost per case of chlamydia was based on costs of diagnosis and treatment of acute infections, screening tests that yielded positive results and sequelae resulting from untreated acute infections or from delayed or improper treatment. The diagnostic and treatments cost of acute infection included costs for office visits, treatment visits, diagnostic testing and treatment. Costs of sequelae included potential costs associated with PID (chronic pelvic pain, ectopic pregnancy and treated infertility) in women and for epididymitis in men. The model assumed that acute infections were asymptomatic in 78% of men and 32% of women. The results showed chlamydia results in a total economic burden of $248 million for the 1.5 million new cases occurring in 2000. The average cost per case of chlamydia infection for women ($244) and for men ($20). The largest cost component, 82% in women was due to costs associated with sequelae, whereas in men, 78% was attributable to costs associated with an acute infection. Chlamydia represented the fourth most costly STD in the USA.

Since the study is based on literature rather than research, the results are highly sensitive to the limitations of the individual investigations that provide the source for costs and probability estimates. Furthermore, this study excludes indirect costs and therefore significantly underestimates the real economic burden of chlamydia.

A landmark study of the economic burden of chlamydia in the US population was conducted by Washington *et al.*[12] Washington *et al.* used the methodology of a prevalence-based approach to evaluate the cost of illness for chlamydia. This type of methodology estimates the direct and indirect costs of chlamydia accrued in a given year with the exception of future lost earnings of those patients who die as a result of chlamydia (eg death from ectopic pregnancy). This study estimates healthcare costs for chlamydia in men and for chlamydia and its sequelae in women.

The economic burden was calculated as $1.4 billion dollars annually. When these costs are updated to 1998 values, they represent a total cost of $2.64 billion. The vast proportion of costs is attributed to the management of infections in women, and in particular the costs of managing the sequelae, mainly PID. Treatment of infections in women account for almost 80% of the total costs of treating chlamydia.

Although this study demonstrates that chlamydia represents a significant economic burden, the actual figures are likely to be an underestimate of the full costs of managing chlamydia and its sequelae. The authors used the lower range of estimates for the direct healthcare costs of managing each of the chlamydia and associated conditions. Secondly, the cost of managing complications in men (e.g. Reiter's syndrome) was excluded. Thirdly, infant costs exclude estimates for adverse pregnancy outcomes or mortality. Fourthly, costs of sequelae associated with asymptomatic infections were excluded even though these make up the majority of infections in both men and women. Finally, the psychosocial costs of chlamydia for patients, partners and the community were excluded.

Despite the exclusion of significant direct costs, Washington *et al.* provide the best estimates of the economic burden of chlamydia in the USA. Similar studies have not been conducted in the UK or indeed in other English speaking countries. It is hoped that the following analysis will be found useful to those about to extend screening facilities and who propose to evaluate their cost-effectiveness.

COST-EFFECTIVENESS OF SCREENING STRATEGIES IN WOMEN

Asymptomatic infections represent the majority of *C. trachomatis* infections in both sexes. It is vital therefore to identify and treat these infections before further transmission takes place. Various methods for the detection of asymptomatic infections are currently available. These methods include the use of different types of tests including culture tests and more recently, non-culture methods. Detection of asymptomatic chlamydial infection is a function of type of test, levels of sensitivity and specificity for the diagnostic test used, type of population and the expected prevalence rate in the population to be screened.

Research from the late 1980s to early 1990s in the US and Europe showed screening to be cost effective[13-16].

Phillips *et al.*[13] developed an economic model that showed the use of rapid tests (DFA or EIA) followed by appropriate treatment in women with positive results would reduce overall costs where prevalence of *C. trachomatis* infection was 7% or more. However, if only direct costs are considered the prevalence rate at which screening is considered to be cost effective increases to 25%.

Nettleman and Jones[14] produced an economic model which showed that screening all women at moderate risk (7.9%) of urogenital infections with *C. trachomatis* with a direct antigen test costing less than $12 (1987 values) was more cost-effective than a strategy of no screening and no treatment. However, this was achieved with a high rate of false positive results, with only 53% of women with true positive results.

Marazzo *et al.*[15] developed simple selective screening criteria for chlamydial infection in women to evaluate the contribution of clinical cervicitis to screening criteria and the cost-effectiveness of selective versus universal screening in women attending family practice and STD clinics from 1989-1993. Selective screening was cost-effective in both cohorts of women, family planning clinics and STD clinics. The effect of using azithromycin, a more expensive but more effective therapy, was not evaluated by the authors.

In Europe, the Genc and Mardh model[16] of a Swedish cohort of women showed screening with any of the three diagnostic screening methods (tissue cell culture, confirmed enzyme immunoassay, and DNA amplification assays by either polymerase chain reaction or ligase chain reaction) was cost-effective, compared to no screening. In addition, DNA amplification combined with azithromycin treatment for patients with a positive test was the most cost-effective strategy, compared with doxycyline treatment. This was due to the fact that treatment with doxycycline resulted in significantly lower cure rates than treatment with azithromycin due to patients' poor compliance with a twice-daily regimen for 7 days.

Table 2 illustrates the key findings of recently published literature on the economic implications of screening strategies. Whilst there has been a significant increase in the literature to address cost-effectiveness of screening

Table 2: Selected studies evaluating the economic impact of screening strategies for *Chlamydia trachomatis*.

Author/date	Type of study	Key findings	Case of PID prevented
Adams *et al.* (2004)	Economic model to evaluate cost of screening strategies	Total cost of £49,367 for cohort Average cost per screening (£14-38)	N/A
Norman *et al.* (2004)	Cost effectiveness analysis of various populations	£771 per PID prevented	64 cases of major squelae
Hu *et al.* (2004)	Cost effectiveness analysis of 4 screening strategies	Annual screening in women 15-29 + semi-annual screening in women with a history of infection most cost effective strategy (Cost per QALY <$20,000)	N/A
Howell *et al.* (1999)	Model using real data from records and previous cohort studies (prevalence = 9.2%)	Age based testing or universal treatment in high prevalence groups	233 cases of PID prevented, saving $800/PID
Howell *et al* (1998)	Cost effectiveness of screening strategies (prevalence = 9.2%)	DNA amplification in urine or cervical swab in asymptomatic women < 30yrs	306 cases of PID prevented, saving $3,689/PID
Howell *et al.* (1998)	Cost effectiveness model	Cost effective in low prevalence (3.9%) population using DNA based test assuming 90% return rate	85 cases of PID prevented, saving $3,585/PID per case of chlamydia
Paavonen *et al.* (1998)	Cost effectiveness model	Cost effective in asymptomatic women in FPC with DNA based test at 6% prevalence, positive treated with azithromycin	50% of sequelae prevented cost $45 per case of chlamydia

strategies in different populations, the vast majority of the literature is based on the development of models. Such models have limitations and as noted by Honey *et al.*[17] many of these models suffer from a lack of strong evidence to support assumptions and may therefore be vulnerable to bias in their findings and conclusions.

The exception is perhaps a study published in 2004 by Adams *et al.*[18] in which the authors evaluate the costs of a screening programme offered to a cohort of women in England aged 16-24 by developing a model based on an observational study of patients. This analysis provides estimates of the average cost of screening from the healthcare perspective. The average cost per screening offer was about £15 including partner management, £21 per person tested and £38 per person positive. Although partner management comprised only 5% of the overall costs, the authors state it is an important part of any screening programme as it can help to prevent re-infection and onward transmission of chlamydia. Whilst this is the first study to provide an accurate price estimation of a screening programme, from an economic perspective it falls short as it does not evaluate the cost effectiveness of the screening programme. Thus, the potential benefits of screening in terms of averted costs from preventing infection and sequelae were not evaluated.

However, Norman *et al.* have recently published a cost effectiveness evaluation of screening programme[19]. They conducted an economic evaluation of screening in hospital-based antenatl and gynaecology clinics, and community-based family planning clinics. The estimated cost of screening 250 women in each group was £49 367, while preventing 64 major sequelae, representing a net cost of £771 per major sequelae prevented. The model suggests selective screening of all women under 20 years and all patients attending abortion clinics were shown to be the most cost effective strategies.

COST-EFFECTIVENESS OF SCREENING IN PREGNANT WOMEN

Pregnant women are considered to be at high risk of *C. trachomatis* infection. The prevention of transmission to infants can result in the avoidance of additional costs incurred as a result of treating conjunctivitis and pneumonia in the babies. Additionally, prevention of transmission to the infant may result in lower mortality rates for newborns.

Nettleman and Bell[20] evaluated the cost-effectiveness of screening pregnant women for *C. trachomatis* by a third-party payer. Screening and treatment strategies are more complex in pregnant women as treatment options are more limited. Both mother and infant require therapy while sequelae for infection are more varied. The authors compared the direct medical costs associated with culture in all patients, followed by treatment for positive results, DFA in all patients followed by treatment for positive cases, or culture confirmation for positive DFA results and no screening tests. The treatment regimen was erythromycin for 7 days. Treatment for a single sexual partner was also included in the analysis. If the cost of DFA was less than US$6.30 (1990 values) or prevalence was >6.1% in pregnant women, routine screening with DFA followed by treatment for positive results was the most cost-effective option. Where the cost of DFA was <US$3.90 (1990 values) or the prevalence was higher than 6-7%, confirmation of positive DFA results followed by treatment was the more cost-effective strategy. If the prevalence of infection was >14.8% or the cost of culture was less than US$7.50 (1990 values), culture followed by treatment for positive results was the preferred option. Where the mean cost of uncured infection was >US$284, DFA followed by treatment was the most cost-effective option. Sensitivity analysis showed that the variables affecting the outcome of results were prevalence of infection, cost of direct antigen test, cost of culture and mean cost of a persistent infection.

The authors of this study concluded that screening of pregnant women was not a cost-effective option in low prevalence populations (≤5%). The main disadvantage of this study was the use of charge data as a proxy for costs. However, it could be argued that from the perspective of the third-party payer, it is the charges incurred which represent the real burden of infection with *C. trachomatis*, according to the authors. Additionally, the authors did not allow for non-compliance of therapy with erythromycin in their estimation of efficacy of 92%.

In an interesting evaluation, van Bergen *et al.* conducted an evaluation of pharmacy-based screening programme in the Netherlands.[21] During a two-year period, women aged 15-29 years who collected their contraceptives at the pharmacy were offered chlamydia test material. Home collected urine samples could be mailed to the laboratory and the general practitioner received the results. Nine percent of respondents tested positive. The net cost per PID prevented ranged from cost-saving up to €3872 in a low complication rate/high testing cost scenario.

In Sweden, Novak *et al.*[22] conducted a similar community-based screening programme where participants mailed the urine samples. Their analysis also confirms the cost effectiveness of this screening programme. In this case, screening became more cost effective when prevalence exceeded 5.1% in women and cost-saving in males where prevalence was over 12.3%.

Finally, clinical guidelines have traditionally advised screening for women aged 16-24. However recently proposed screening programmes suggest changing the age groups. Thus, Hu *et al.*[23] assessed the cost-effectiveness of alternative screening strategies in women aged 15-19, 15-24 and 15-29. In this evaluation the results show annual screening in women aged 15-29 followed by semi-annual screening for those with a history of infection was the most effective and cost-effective strategy. This strategy had an incremental cost-effectiveness ratio less than $25,000 per quality-adjusted life-year (QALY). This falls below the generally accepted threshold of $50,000 below which a health intervention is considered to be cost-effective.

COST-EFFECTIVENESS OF SCREENING STRATEGIES IN ADOLESCENT MALES

Adolescent males have the highest rates of infection and associated female complications compared with any other age groups[24-26]. Approximately 50% of nongonococcal urethritis infections and more than 50% of cases of epididymitis are caused by *C. trachomatis*[27]. Epididymitis is a serious condition which can occasionally lead to sterility. Further, this age group represents a major source of transmission to teenage girls.

Randolph and Washington[28] evaluated the costs and benefits of screening tests for chlamydia in adolescent males. The authors developed a model to evaluate three screening methods in a hypothetical cohort of 1,000 sexually active adolescent males. The model considered direct medical costs only: treatment, screening, complications in sexual partners and complications in infected men. The results showed that the leukocyte esterase (LE) test had the lowest average cost-per-cure ($51) compared with direct-smear DFA ($192) and culture ($414). Compared with DFA, the authors estimated that the LE test would save more than $9,727 per cohort of 1,000 sexually active adolescent males, screened. The highest cure rates (56%) were achieved by the screening strategy, although they were more costly. DFA achieved cure rates of 51%, the LE test achieved cure rates of 49% and the no testing strategy achieved the lowest cure rates of 5%. A significant component of overall costs were those related to the treatment of infected female partners ($365 per infected case). Sensitivity analysis revealed robustness of model at clinically feasible values for major assumptions (prevalence, sensitivity, specificity of tests, PID rates, compliance, lost to follow-up rates). The analysis showed that the LE test would result in lower cost-per-cure and lower overall costs per cohort than culture and DFA at any prevalence of *C. trachomatis* infection. Compared to no screening, LE test would result in lower overall costs per cohort at prevalence rates >21%.

In an earlier study, Genc *et al.*[29] evaluated the cost-effectiveness of identifying asymptomatic carriers of *C. trachomatis* in a hypothetical cohort of 1,000 adolescent males and their sexual partners/contacts. This study used a model to evaluate the impact of using enzyme immunoassay on either leukocyte esterase positive urine samples (LE-EIA strategy) or on all urine samples (EIA strategy), compared with no screening strategy. Treatment regimens evaluated were doxycycline, 100mg orally twice a day for seven days and azithromycin, 1g orally single dose. Analysis was carried out with the aid of two decision trees for all possible outcomes for both adolescent males and their sexual contacts. The study evaluated both direct and indirect medical costs. Direct costs were those related to costs of samples, tests, counselling sessions, appointments and treatment of initial *C. trachomatis* infection and its sequelae for both index cases and their partners. Indirect costs were those related to lost productivity as a result of participating in a healthcare programme.

The results showed, compared with no screening, that the LE-EIA and EIA screening strategies reduced the overall costs where the prevalence of chlamydia was more than 2% and 10% respectively. The EIA strategy improved overall cure rates by 12% but reduced the incremental savings by at least $2,144 per cured male, compared with LE-EIA strategy. Confirmation of positive EIA tests reduced overall cost of the LE-EIA screening strategy where prevalence of *C. trachomatis* was less than 8%. In terms of antibiotic treatment, a single dose of azithromycin administered under supervision improved the cure rates of both screening strategies by 12-16% compared with a 7-day course of doxycycline, whilst reducing overall costs by 5-9%. However, the incremental cost-effectiveness ratios for the treatment strategies were not provided by the authors, making an economic comparison difficult.

In summary, DFA screening was cost effective in populations >5% prevalence, and although cell culture has a higher predictive value, it is more costly. DNA amplification is more cost effective in populations with a prevalence of >6% than other models. The authors concluded that use of LE-EIA screening in combination with treatment of positive cases with azithromycin was the most cost-effective strategy, however in low risk populations, positive EIA tests should be confirmed.

COST-EFFECTIVENESS OF TREATMENT REGIMENS

A number of different antibiotic treatment regimens are available for the treatment of *C. trachomatis* as outlined in chapter 6. The availability of newer antibiotics such as the fluoroquinolones and azithromycin and cost containment measures by healthcare systems have led to research efforts to identify cost-effective treatment options. Newer drugs are more expensive than older, generic antibiotics, however they may offer the advantages of fewer side-effects and increased compliance with therapy when compared to traditional treatment options[30-32]. Nuovo *et al.*[33] evaluated the cost-effectiveness of five different antibiotics for the treatment of *C. trachomatis* in non-pregnant women from the perspective of a healthcare system in California (erythromycin, tetracycline, doxycycline, ofloxacin, azithromycin). The authors developed a model and based their estimates of probability values and costs on published literature, State health plan reports and health insurance companies. Extensive sensitivity analysis was undertaken on the parameters: probability of PID and hospitalisation after treatment failure, cost of treatment for inpatient and outpatient PID, and cost and efficacy of azithromycin and doxycycline.

This model showed that the most cost-effective treatment regimes were the doxycycline and tetracycline strategies, followed by azithromycin, ofloxacin and erythromycin. In those patients who were non-compliant, azithromycin may be the best strategy because of the single dose, however, this was not accounted for in the analysis. Marra *et al.*[34] criticised this study for its simplistic model. Further sequelae beyond PID (e.g. chronic pelvic pain, infertility and ectopic pregnancy) were not considered in the analysis. Additionally, the authors did not include the impact of non-compliance with older treatment regimens on the overall cure rates nor the costs incurred in managing adverse drug reactions. This is particularly pertinent as some of the older treatments such as erythromycin and tetracycline have been shown to have higher adverse events than newer agents[30, 35]. Costs of treating secondary transmission to sexual partners were not considered in the analysis.

Haddix *et al.*[36] also developed a model to evaluate the cost-effectiveness of treatment regimens for uncomplicated chlamydial infection. The authors compared treatment with azithromycin 1g with doxycycline 100mg twice daily for 7 days in a cohort of 10,000 non-pregnant women. Additionally, the authors evaluated the treatments based on two diagnostic strategies; laboratory-confirmed *C. trachomatis* infection and presumptive diagnosis, based on clinical signs and symptoms.

This study evaluated the economic impact from the perspectives of the US healthcare system and the publicly funded clinic. In the latter perspective, costs related to sequelae of infection would be managed on an out-patient basis. Probability estimates were obtained from published clinical trials. The effectiveness of doxycycline was adjusted for a compliance rate of 80%, and non-compliant patients were assumed to be treatment failures. For azithromycin, compliance was assumed to be 100% since it is a single dose regimen and was administered in the clinics. The costs included in the model were those relating to treatment, treatment of PID and its sequelae (chronic pelvic pain, ectopic pregnancy and infertility). Costs for sequelae which would occur in future years were discounted at an annual rate of 5%. Costs relating to PID were taken from Washington and Katz (1991)[37]. Additionally, the model assumed 25% of women with tubal-factor infertility would seek treatment. Sensitivity analysis was carried out for prevalence rate of infection in those women treated presumptively, doxycycline compliance rates, cost of PID and its sequelae, probabilities of developing PID in compliant and non-compliant patients, and the risk of developing further sequelae.

The results from the healthcare payer perspective revealed that the use of azithromycin would cost an additional US$290k (1993 values) to treat chlamydial infections in a cohort of 10,000 women under a laboratory confirmed strategy, resulting in savings of US$1.2 million for treating the PID that had been prevented. In the presumptively treated model, use of azithromycin would cost an additional US$290k and would save US$240k to treat a cohort of 10k women. This would result in incremental cost savings of US$800 per additional case of PID prevented for azithromycin versus doxycycline in treated patients. Extensive sensitivity analysis revealed the robustness of model to the extent that azithromycin achieved savings for all plausible values. However, the results of the presumptive model were more sensitive to changes in probability and cost estimates used in the model.

From the perspective of the public health clinic, azithromycin would cost an additional US$220k (1993 values) for a cohort of 10k women in a laboratory-confirmed model, but would result in savings of US$29k from reduced treatment costs of PID. This would result in net savings of US$709 per additional case of PID prevented. In the presumptive treatment model, azithromycin treatment would cost an additional US$220k but would save US$5,670 from reduced treatment costs of PID. This would result in net costs of US$3,969 per additional case of PID prevented. Sensitivity analysis for both strategies revealed that azithromycin becomes more cost-effective in public clinics with non-compliant populations and where prevalence of *C. trachomatis* infection is higher. The authors concluded that the use of azithromycin is more cost-effective under laboratory confirmed conditions from the healthcare-system perspective. In patients who are presumptively treated, azithromycin continues to be cost-effective resulting in incremental cost savings of US$800 (1993 values) per case of PID prevented. Although, azithromycin is cost-effective, from the perspective of a publicly funded clinic, only a small percentage of treatment costs relating to PID and its sequelae is incurred by the clinic; thus this option is also more expensive. The remainder of the costs incurred in treatment of PID and its sequelae will be absorbed by other public or non-public organisations; thus from a societal perspective, such savings are non-existent or artificial.

Marra *et al.*[34] further developed the models constructed by Haddix *et al.*[36] to evaluate the cost-effectiveness of azithromycin and doxycycline from the perspective of the Canadian healthcare system for a cohort of 5,000 non-pregnant women. The costs of managing complications of PID are lower in the Canadian system (the justification used by Marra for developing this model). Probability estimates and costs for resources were obtained from the literature, hospital costing departments and expert opinion. The results showed that azithromycin in a laboratory confirmed model would result in savings of Can$279,150 (1995 values) for a cohort of 5,000 women. In the presumptively treated model, use of azithromycin would result in savings of Can$1,700 for this cohort. In conclusion, the authors state that widespread use of azithromycin in Canada for laboratory confirmed cases of *C. trachomatis* would result in savings of Can$3 million in direct medical expenses per year. However there are a number of limitations to the studies conducted by both Haddix *et al.* and Marra *et al.*; the cost of managing adverse effects of antibiotic therapy were not included; cost of secondary transmission to sexual partners was not evaluated; different screening strategies were not evaluated; and both models evaluated direct medical costs only. Thus the full economic impact from a societal perspective has not been evaluated.

Finally, Magid *et al.*[38] conducted an economic evaluation very similar to that of Haddix *et al.* and Marra *et al.* in evaluating the impact of azithromycin compared to doxycycline in the treatment of women with *C. trachomatis* infection. The advantage of this study over the two previous studies is that it includes the impact of adverse events related to treatment with antibiotics and the costing of sequelae which occur as a result of secondary transmission of infection. Additionally, Magid *et al.* identified cure rates for different levels of non-compliance with doxycycline. The results of this study were similar to Haddix *et al.* and Marra *et al.* When base-case assumptions are used, azithromycin was the more cost-effective treatment option for uncomplicated *C. trachomatis* infection in women. Azithromycin resulted in a reduction in major complications of infection by 2,392 compared to doxycycline at approximately 57% of the cost per patient. Nevertheless, the authors recognised that the higher initial cost of acquiring azithromycin may limit widespread use of this treatment option in the essentially fragmented healthcare system in North America.

SUMMARY AND CONCLUSION

Chlamydial infections continue to represent a significant economic burden. Asymptomatic infections greatly exceed symptomatic infections in both men and women. Detection and appropriate management of asymptomatic infections may lead to a reduction in the total costs of treating chlamydia and its sequelae. Women account for a significant component of the total costs of chlamydia, especially the costs of complications such as PID. Additionally, adolescent males represent a high-risk population and a major source of transmission to young women. A variety of diagnostic tests are available for detection of asymptomatic infections.

The currently available economic literature suggests screening of asymptomatic individuals is a cost-effective strategy, particularly in adolescent males and in young women. Treatment of chlamydial infections with a single dose of azithromycin appears to be the most cost-effective treatment strategy. Further research to explore the benefits of screening programmes is encouraged in order to inform policy makers. The extent of a reduction in societal costs is a function of the types of tests used, costs of treatment and the expected prevalence in the population being screened.

Acknowledgement
I would like to acknowledge the contribution of Professor Mo Malek, who died in 2000. He was co-author of the first edition of this book, which provided the foundation of the present chapter.

REFERENCES

1. Communicable Disease Report. Sexually transmitted diseases quarterly report: genital infection with *Chlamydia trachomatis* in England and Wales. 1998; **6**(22).
2. Macleod J, Salisbury C, Low N, *et al.* Coverage and uptake of systematic postal screening for gential *Chlamydia trachomatis* and prevalence of infection in the United Kingdom general population: cross sectional study. *BMJ* 2005; **330:** 940–942.
3. Brunham RC. A General Model of Sexually Transmitted Disease Epidemiology and its Implications for Control. *Medical Clinics in North America* 1990; **74**(6): 1339–52.
4. Zimmerman H, Potterat J, Dukes R, *et al.* Epidemiological differences between Chlamydia and Gonorrhea. *Am J Public Health* 1990; **80:** 1338–42.
5. Lycke E *et al.* The risk of transmission of genital *Chlamydia trachomatis* infection is less than that of genital *Neisseria gonorrhoeae* infection. *Sex Trans Dis* 1980; **7**(1): 6–10.
6. Karam G, Martin D, Flote T *et al.* Asymptomatic *Chlamydia trachomatis* infections among sexually active men. *J Infect Dis* 1995; **154:** 900–03.
7. World Bank World Development Report 1993. Investing in health. Oxford: Oxford University Press, 1993.
8. McKay L, Clery H, Carrick-Anderson K, *et al.* Genital *Chlamydia trachomatis* infection in a subgroup of young men in the UK. *Lancet* 2003; **361:** 1792.
9. Mardh PA, Westrom LA. Working Group Report on Chlamydial Infections. Sweden (unpublished document) Ref EUR/ICP/CDS 199 (243 8G).
10. Malik F. The economic burden of Chlamydia. Doctoral thesis. 1998. University of St Andrews.
11. Chesson HW, Blandford JM, Gift TL *et al.* The Estimated Direct Medical Cost of Sexually Trasmitted Diseases Among American Youth, 2000. *Perspectives on Sexual and Reproductive Health* 2004; **36**(1): 11–19.
12. Washington A *et al.* *Chlamydia trachomatis* Infections in the United States: what are they costing us? *JAMA* 1987; **257:** 2070–72.
13. Phillips R *et al.* Should tests for *Chlamydia trachomatis* cervical infection be done during routine Gynecologic visits? *Annals of Internal Medicine* 1990; **107:** 188–194.
14. Nettleman M, Jones R. Cost-effectiveness of screening women at moderate risk for genital infections caused by *Chlamydia trachomatis*. *JAMA* 1988; **260**(2): 207–213.
15. Marrazzo J *et al.* Performance and cost-effectiveness of selective screening criteria for *Chlamydia trachomatis* infection in women. *Sex Trans Dis* 1999; **24**(3): 131–141.
16. Genc M, Mardh P. A Cost-effectiveness Analysis of Screening and Treatment for *Chlamydia trachomatis* Infection in Asymptomatic Women. *Ann Intern Med* 1996; **124**(1): 1–7.
17. Honey E, Augood C, Russell I *et al.* Cost effectiveness of screening for *Chlamydia trachomatis*: a review of published studies. *Sex Transm Infect* 2002; **78:** 406–412.
18. Adams EJ, LaMontagne DS, Johnston AR *et al.* Modelling the healthcare costs of an opportunistic Chlamydia screening programme. *Sexually Transm Inf* 2004; **80:** 363–70.
19. Norman JE, Wu O, Twaddle S *et al.* An evaluation of economics and acceptability of screening for *Chlamydia trachomatis* infection, in women attending antenatal abortion, colposcopy and family planning clinics in Scotland, UK. *BJOG* 2004; **111**(11): 1261–8.
20. Nettleman M, Bell T. Cost-effectiveness of prenatal testing for *Chlamydia trachomatis*. *Am J Obstet Gynecol.* 1991; **164**(5): 1289–94.
21. Van Bergen JE, Postma MJ, Peerbooms PG *et al.* Effectiveness and cost-effectiveness of a pharmacy-based screening programme for *Chlamydia trachomatis* in a high risk health centre population in Amsterdam using mailed home-collected urine samples. *Int J STD AIDS.* 2004 Dec; **15**(12): 797–802.
22. Novak DP, Lindholm L, Jonsson M *et al.* A Swedish cost-effectiveness analysis of community-based *Chlamydia trachomatis* PCR testing postal urine specimens obtained at home. *Scand J Public Health* 2004; **32**(5): 324–32.

23. Hu D, Hook EW, Goldie SJ. Screening for *Chlamydia trachomatis* in women 15 to 29 years of age: a cost-effectiveness analysis. *Ann Intern Med* 2004; **141**(7): 501–513.
24. Washington A, Sweet R, Shafer M-A. Pelvic inflammatory disease and its sequelae in adolescents. *J Adolescent Health Care* 1985; **6**: 298–310.
25. Stamm W *et al. Chlamydia trachomatis* urethral infections in men. *Annals of Internal Medicine* 1984; **100**: 47–51.
26. Handsfield H, Jasman L, Roberts P *et al.* Criteria for selective screening for *Chlamydia trachomatis* infection in women attending family planning clinics. *JAMA.* 1986; **255**: 1730–34.
27. Thomson S, Washington A. Epidemiology of sexually transmitted *Chlamydia trachomatis* infections. *Epidemiology Review* 1983; **5**: 96–123.
28. Randolph A, Washington E. Screening for *Chlamydia trachomatis* in adolescent males: a cost-based decision analysis. *AJPH* 1990; **80**(5): 545–550.
29. Genc M, Ruusuvaara L, Mardh P. An economic evaluation of screening for *Chlamydia trachomatis* in adolescent males. *JAMA* 1993; **270**(17): 2057–64.
30. Hopkins S. Clinical toleration and safety of azithromycin. *Am J Med* 1991; **91** Suppl. 3A: 40–5.
31. Bauchmann LH, Stephens J, Richey CM, *et al.* Measured versus self-reported compliance with doxycyline therapy for Chlamydia associated syndromes. (abstract) 36th Interscience Conference on Antimicrobial agents and Chemotherapy. 1996 Sep 15-18; New Orleans: 256.
32. Augenbraun M, *et al.* Compliance with Doxycyline Therapy in an STD clinic. (abstract) 36th Interscience Conference on Antimicrobial agents and Chemotherapy. 1996 Sep 15-18; New Orleans: 37.
33. Nuovo J *et al.* Cost effectiveness analysis of five different antibiotic regimens for the treatment of uncomplicated *Chlamydia trachomatis* cervitis. *J Am Board Fam Pract* 1995; **8**(1): 7–16.
34. Marra F, Marra C, Patrick D. Cost effectiveness of azithromycin and doxycyline for *Chlamydia trachomatis* infection in women: a Canadian perspective. *Can J Infec Dis* 1997; **8**(4): 202–208.
35. Bowie W *et al.* Efficacy of treatment regimens for lower urogenital *Chlamydia trachomatis* infection in women. *Am J Obstet Gynecol* 1982; **142**(2): 125–129.
36. Haddix A, Hillis S, Kassler W. The cost-effectiveness of azithromycin for *Chlamydia trachomatis* infections in women. *Sex Trans Dis* 1995; **22**(5): 274–280.
37. Washington AE, Katz P. Cost of and payment source for pelvic inflammatory disease. Trends and projections, 1983 through 2000. *JAMA* 1991; **266**(18): 2565–9.
38. Magid D, Douglas J, Schwartz S. Doxycyline Compared with Azithromycin for Treating Women with Genital *Chlamydia trachomatis* Infections: an Incremental Cost-effectiveness Analysis. *Ann Intern Med* 1996; **124**: 389–399.

CHAPTER 12

Is the global elimination of trachoma feasible?

Sohrab Darougar
University of London, UK

Timothy R Moss
Genito Urinary Medicine, Doncaster and Bassetlaw
NHS Foundation Trust, Doncaster, UK

Dayshad Darougar
Research Assistant

INTRODUCTION

In 1998, the World Health Organization (WHO) adopted a resolution for the Global Elimination of Trachoma (GET) by the year 2020[1]. Subsequently the WHO Alliance for the global elimination of trachoma (GET Alliance) has taken the initiative for coordinating trachoma control programmes of member countries, to mobilise resources required and to develop technologies, strategies and policies for achieving the aim of GET by the year 2020[1]. The GET Alliance consists of representatives of governments, non-government agencies, charities, academics, research organisations, pharmaceutical companies and other institutions with interest in community healthcare and WHO representatives.

In mid 2005 trachoma still remains one of the world's leading causes of preventable blindness and continues as the target of the WHO campaign to eradicate the disease by the year 2020.

The knowledge, experience and expertise gained by the WHO during the eradication of smallpox, the elimination of poliomyelitis as a major public health problem and in controlling major preventable infections is the subject of international respect. This expertise in combination with modern technologies and more effective anti-trachoma drugs has led to confidence that the goal of eliminating trachoma by the year 2020 is achievable. However, a number of clinicians, scientists and health specialists believe that the objective of GET by the year 2020 may possibly be compromised, because of the absence of adequate financial and human resources and lack of political commitment in some of the developing countries where trachoma is hyperendemic.

In this chapter we examine important features of trachoma complex. We also discuss a range of therapeutic interventions and their potential impact on the success or failure of the GET programme.

Trachoma is one of the oldest and most common eye diseases worldwide. The disease and its blinding complications were known in China in the 27th century BC, in Sumaria in the 21st Century BC, in Greece in the 5th century BC and Rome in the 1st century BC. Trachoma was extremely common in Greece and the Middle-East during the medieval period. In Europe, trachoma was spread by crusaders returning from Palestine and after the Napoleonic wars. However, trachoma in Europe and Northern America disappeared in the early 20th century. It is interesting to note that trachoma was eradicated from Europe and Northern America long before active anti-trachoma drugs became available.

CAUSE

Trachoma is caused by *Chlamydia trachomatis* (Ct) an obligate intra-cellular bacteria. The Ct serotypes causing trachoma are A, B, Ba and C. However occasionally Ct serotypes D and E (common genital pathogens) have been isolated from the eyes with trachoma. The original *Chlamydia pneumoniae* isolates; TW-183 and IOL-207 were isolated from the eyes of children with trachoma in Taiwan and Iran respectively[2]. The role of *C. pneumoniae* in causing trachoma has not been established. Serological studies in Iran showed that the child and some members of his family had type-specific IgG to IOL-207, whereas other children in the adjacent families had no antibodies to IOL-207. The potential pathogenicity of the IOL-207 isolate in causing eye disease was shown in a laboratory accident[3]. A technologist who was propagating IOL-207 isolate in eggs and cell cultures was accidentally infected with the agent and developed a severe keratoconjunctivitis. The eye infection was cured after intensive topical and systemic treatment with tetracyclines exceeding one month. In this patient, cell culture failed to detect the causative organism. Eventually IOL-207 was isolated after inoculation of conjunctival specimens into hens' fertile eggs and passing several times. Concurrently,

IOL-207 was also isolated from the yolk-sac of fertile eggs after inoculating with infected cell culture materials and repeated passing of egg cultures. Serological tests on this patient showed absence of chlamydia antibodies in blood collected before the infection and presence of type-specific IgG to IOL-207 and four-fold rising titre of IgG after the infection.

CLINICAL FEATURES

Trachoma is a chronic infection of the conjunctiva and cornea (keratoconjunctivitis). Pathological changes may also develop in the sub-epithelial connective tissues, tarsal plates, lacrymal gland and ducts, nasal mucosa, pre-auricular lymph nodes and in the upper respiratory tract. The disease generally affects both eyes.

Incubation period

The incubation period of trachoma remains unclear. In experimental inoculation of the eye of human volunteers with trachoma agents, the incubation period was between 1 to 3 weeks. In rural communities, Ct was isolated from the eyes of 6 week old babies[4]. This may suggest that under those conditions the incubation period may be less than six weeks[4].

Symptoms

Common symptoms of trachoma may include watering, mucopurulent discharge, redness, irritation, discomfort, itching and foreign body sensation. In advanced cases of trachoma and particularly in those with severe scarring, patients may complain of heavy and thick lids, dryness, moderate to severe foreign body sensation and blurred vision. In rural communities with high prevalence of trachoma and bacterial conjunctivitis, patients generally do not consider the above symptoms as abnormal, and hence do not complain.

Signs

Clinical signs may occur in the palpebral and bulbar conjunctiva, limbus and cornea.

In the palpebral conjunctiva the major signs are hyperaemia, diffuse infiltration, papillae, follicles and scarring. Papillae may present in various forms. At early stages, they appear as small red spots in the conjunctiva. At later stages, they are much larger, each containing a dense collection of inflammatory cells around congested vessels in a thickened conjunctiva.

Follicles may vary in size and presentation. In the early stages of infection, the follicles are generally small and may appear as yellowish to grey-white nodules against a background of red papillae. However in chronic trachoma, the follicles (particularly in the fornices) may become very large. The follicles contain a collection of inflammatory cells. In well developed follicles, the inflammatory cells are organised around a germinal centre.

Conjunctival scars may develop with variable intensity and shape. In mild cases, scars may appear as fine, focal or linear, while in severe cases they may present as diffuse or synechial or as a broad fibrovascular membrane.

Limbal signs may include vascular congestion, diffuse infiltration, transient follicles and depressions called Herbert's pits.

Corneal signs may include focal or circumcorneal vascularisation, punctate epithelial keratitis, sub-epithelial punctate keratitis, diffuse infiltration and corneal scar. Pannus, the specific corneal sign of trachoma consists of corneal vascularisation with punctate epithelial and punctate sub-epithelial keratitis and diffuse infiltration between vessels. At early stages of trachoma, pannus is small and may be detected only by slit-lamp or high magnification lens. In advanced cases of trachoma, pannus is generally visible to the naked eye.

Complications
Trachoma complications may be categorised as blinding and non-blinding. Blinding complications may include severe conjunctival scarring, severe sub-conjunctival and peri-tarsal fibrosis and tarsal degeneration which may cause lid deformity, trichiasis and entropion. The entropion and trichiasis cause misdirected lashes to abrade the cornea, leading to infected corneal ulcers, scarring and ultimately loss of vision. Non-blinding complications may include dry eye, corneal and conjunctival keratinisation, post-trachomatous cystic degeneration and symblepharon (conjunctival synechiae). The blinding complications generally occur in the older age group and mostly affect the population over the age of sixty.

Clinical variants
In hyperendemic areas, trachoma may present in various clinical forms. The classical form of trachoma consists of the presence of various amounts of papillae and follicles in the palpebral conjunctiva and active pannus. It is common in pre-school children. In young babies under one year, trachoma may present as moderate to severe papillary conjunctivitis resembling bacterial conjunctivitis. Follicles generally appear in older babies and become

prominent in pre-school children. In older school children, scarring may appear in addition to follicles, papillae, diffuse infiltration in the conjunctiva and pannus. In adolescents and adults, scarring may be the main feature of trachoma. However, in adults (mainly female) who are living in large families with several young children with active trachoma, follicles and papillae may be found along with the conjunctival scarring.

In communities with a low prevalence of trachoma, clinical forms are different from those in hyperendemic areas. Mild and moderate papillary trachoma are common in older babies and in pre-school children. Mild follicular trachoma is mainly found in children aged between 4 and 10 years. Mild focal scarring may develop in school children and adults. In these communities the disease is classified as non-blinding trachoma, because of the absence or very low prevalence of severe scarring, entropion and trichiasis.

Natural history

Trachoma is generally considered as a chronic keratoconjunctivitis which may last for several years. It is stated that trachoma may start as a mild or moderate papillary conjunctivitis with a few small follicles progressing towards a florid trachoma with large papillae, mature follicles and pannus. At a later stage, fine, focal or linear scars may develop alongside papillae and follicles in the palpebral conjunctiva. In a late or inactive trachoma, follicles and papillae are no longer present but scars and/or fibrovascular membrane are present in part or whole of the palpebral conjunctiva. However, with better understanding of immunopathological processes, substantial changes in the natural history of trachoma have been identified, particularly in relation to its reduced pressure of transmission. This modified natural history of trachoma has been observed in most communities.

Experimental inoculations of the eye of human volunteers with trachoma agent have shown that infection starts as a moderate papillary conjunctivitis, progressing into a follicular conjunctivitis. The ocular infection generally lasts up to three months and is followed by spontaneous recovery without treatment. It is interesting that none of these volunteers developed pannus or scars.

Experimental studies in laboratory animals inoculated with their own natural chlamydial pathogens or in non-human primates inoculated with Ct have shown that:

- primary infection recovered spontaneously in the course of a few weeks without treatment. None of the inoculated animals developed conjunctival scarring or pannus.

- When the animals were inoculated repeatedly, the eyes developed a chronic conjunctivitis lasting for several months or longer. Conjunctival scarring and corneal vascularisation developed in most of the eyes.

In communities with low prevalence of active trachoma, where pressure of transmission and rate of re-infection are low, the natural history of trachoma is different from those communities with hyperendemic trachoma and high prevalence of severe trachoma. The differences in low prevalence areas include:

- primary trachoma occurs in older babies and in young children;
- in pre-school and school children, trachoma presents as a mild follicular conjunctivitis and its prevalence is low;
- in most of the older school children and adolescents, trachoma recovers spontaneously without causing scarring or pannus or may produce mild scarring;
- the prevalence of newly developed blinding complications of trachoma including trichiasis, entropion and corneal scarring are very low.

In conclusion, trachoma in communities with low prevalence of active trachoma is no longer considered as a blinding disease.

EPIDEMIOLOGY

Trachoma is the most prevalent eye disease worldwide and is second to cataract in causing blindness. Trachoma is considered a major health problem in the rural communities of dry and hot regions of North, East and South Africa, the Middle East, Northern India and South-East Asia. Foci of endemic trachoma also exist in some areas of South America, Australia and some of the tropical and sub-tropical Pacific islands.

Incidence
It is difficult to quantify the incidence of trachoma in the rural communities. This is due to the exacerbation of signs in patients with mild trachoma following re-infection, the masking of clinical signs during seasonal outbreaks of bacterial conjunctivitis or relapse of trachoma in patients who have been treated. However, studies in communities with high prevalence of active trachoma have shown:

- The incidence of trachoma in babies is very high. In babies under the age of one, approximately 50% develop trachoma and by the age of two, over 80% may have trachoma.
- The incidence of trachoma in villages untouched by trachoma control programmes may be as high as 20% per annum.
- The incidence of new cases of trachoma in the rural communities who have been treated with topical or systemic drugs was between 5 to 15% per annum.

In communities with low prevalence of active trachoma, the incidence of trachoma is very low, because of the low level of shedding of trachoma agent from a smaller reservoir of infection. This results in a low rate of transmission in the community.

Prevalence
A few decades ago, the WHO estimated that about 500 million people were suffering from trachoma. More recently the WHO revised the global prevalence of trachoma and estimated that approximately 150 million people have active trachoma, over 10 million are suffering from entropion/trichiasis, six million are blind in both eyes and that over 10 million are blind in one eye or have low vision due to trachoma.

The prevalence of trachoma varies considerably. In most countries of the Middle-East, Indian sub-continent, South-East Asia, Latin America and Australia, the prevalence of active trachoma has decreased substantially due to economic, environmental and public health improvements. In these countries, the overall prevalence of active trachoma is at present estimated to be less than 30%, with the rate of severe trachoma in children less than 10%.

In rural areas of North, East and South Africa where trachoma is still hyperendemic, up to 50% of the population may have active trachoma. Of these, 10 to 20% are suffering from severe trachoma. In pre-school children in these areas, the prevalence of active trachoma may be as high as 70%, with the prevalence of entropion/trichiasis as high as 10%. In adults over the age of 60, entropion/trichiasis may reach 50%[5].

Age
In areas where trachoma is hyperendemic, active trachoma can be detected in 2 to 3 month old babies. In pre-school children, trachoma may be present in up to 70% and over 50% of them may have moderate to severe trachoma. In older

children and those attending schools, the prevalence of trachoma declines gradually and active trachoma may be present only in a minority of children. In adults, active trachoma is commonly associated with conjunctival scarring and may be present in 5 to 40%. Laboratory studies have shown that a large number of pre-school children are shedding detectable trachoma agent and as such they are a major reservoir of infection[5].

Solomon *et al.* used quantative PCR to try and establish the burden of ocular *C. trachomatis* infection in two trachoma endemic communities in Tanzania and in one community in the Gambia.[6] As would be expected, children had the highest ocular loads of *C. trachomatis* and individuals with intense inflammatory trachoma had higher loads of ocular chlamydial infection than did those with other conjunctival signs.

At the site with the highest prevalence of trachoma it was found that individuals with conjunctival scarring, but no sign of active disease, were PCR positive. Clearly quantative PCR would be difficult to apply as a routine test in the field in developing countries.[7]

In communities with a low prevalence of trachoma, babies are commonly free of trachoma. In pre-school children, the disease is mild. In older children, only a minority have a mild trachoma and most adults show no signs of active trachoma or severe conjunctival scarring.

Sex
In pre-school children the prevalence and severity of trachoma is similar in both sexes. In older children and young adults, females have a markedly higher prevalence of active trachoma and more severe disease than males. In older women, the prevalence of trachoma and its blinding complications (ie entropion and trichiasis) are at least 2 to 3 times higher than in older men[8].

Family and village distribution
Both the prevalence and severity of trachoma are generally higher in large families with three or more young children. In these families, almost all children may have active trachoma. Most suffer from moderate to severe disease. Young mothers of these children, commonly have active trachoma with moderate to severe scarring. Older members of these families (and in particular females) may have more entropion, trichiasis, corneal opacity or blindness compared with those in families with two or less young children. Prevalence and severity of trachoma is lower in villages with a small population, in villages with scattered houses and in those with accessible clean water. Trachoma is uncommon among

nomads who have small and widely scattered family units[4].

In villages, trachoma is generally distributed in clusters. The prevalence and severity of trachoma is higher among groups of families living in large houses or in houses built close to each other. Distribution of trachoma in clusters within the village has been shown by serotyping of Ct or by detecting type-specific IgG to Ct agent. In a study in Southern Iran, it was found that a particular Ct serotype was present in a cluster of families in one part of the village and that a majority of members of the families within the cluster showed type-specific IgG to the same serotype. A second cluster of families living in another part of the village were infected with a different Ct serotype and members of these families had type-specific IgG to that serotype (Treharne *et al* unpublished data).

Reservoir of Ct

Babies and pre-school children constitute a large reservoir of infection[4,8]. In areas with high prevalence of trachoma, over 50% of babies and most pre-school children have moderate to severe trachoma. In these cases, Ct has been isolated commonly from their conjunctival specimens, occasionally from ocular and nasal discharges and infrequently from the throat. Older children and young adults with active trachoma and women with severe chronic disease may occasionally shed Ct and as such may remain a reservoir of infection. However, eyes of infants and young children are the major reservoirs of Ct.

Transmission

There is no intermediate host for transmission of trachoma. In rural communities, infectious eye and nose discharges containing Ct may be transmitted by hands, face to face contacts, by cloths used to remove eye and nasal discharges, bedding where children are sleeping in one bed and by house flies.

Studies have shown that eye-seeking house flies, *Musca domestica* and to a greater degree *Musca sorbens* can transmit infectious materials from eye to eye. In a study in Southern Iran, flies have successfully transmitted a colour marker from eyes of children to the face and eyes of other children playing nearby within 30 minutes[4]. In a laboratory study, Ct was isolated from the legs and proboscis of flies fed on Ct infected materials. In the villages, control of houseflies led to a substantial decrease in the prevalence and incidence of trachoma[9].

It is suggested that children who have had severe trachoma and who are exposed to repeated re-infection and adults with severe scarring, trichiasis and entropion who are economically under-privileged are at risk of remaining locked in a vicious circle of repeated transmission of infection from children to children, children to adults and adults to children. This is a particular problem for those living in large families with several young children, where an unhygienic environment also facilitates transmission[4].

CONTROL OF TRACHOMA

In the past few decades, a number of countries in Africa, the Middle-East and South East Asia have established with WHO support, national programmes for control of trachoma. It is reported that in some of these countries, trachoma control programmes have been successful in reducing the prevalence of trachoma and its blinding complications. A number of experts and clinicians have challenged these claims. They argue that most of these programmes relied almost entirely on the efficacy of intermittent application of tetracycline eye ointment for interrupting transmission of trachoma and less on sanitation, health education and establishing a basic primary healthcare network. It is also suggested that mass therapy with topical antibiotic was not entirely successful, because of the erratic and inadequate supply of tetracycline eye ointment at the point of use, inability of individuals to apply eye ointment correctly to their own eyes or in the eyes of their children, and lack of compliance by villagers. They also point out that where reduction of trachoma has been achieved, this was mostly due to improvements in the economy of the country as a whole (for example: oil producing countries), better standards of housing, sanitation, schooling and the development of a primary healthcare system in the rural areas.

> *"For control of trachoma and blindness, we must realise that this is not merely a medical issue. It is a developmental issue with social and economic ramifications. To overcome the problem we will need to recognise the multiple barriers involved. These include: geographic, social, cultural, political, economic and professional".[10]*

To control trachoma **with the aim of its elimination**, there is a need for protecting susceptible persons, stopping shedding of the agent by infected cases, interrupting the transmission of Ct between persons or by involving all of these measures together.

There is no natural immunity to trachoma. Acquired immunity may develop which provides a partial or transient protection. Patients with active trachoma are susceptible to re-infection. In these patients, re-exposure to Ct may produce a more severe follicular response and pannus and enhance development of conjunctival and sub-conjunctival diffuse cellular infiltration, scarring and sub-epithelial fibrosis. In patients with healed trachoma, re-exposure to live Ct or its antigenic components may enhance development of lid deformity, trichiasis and entropion.

At present there is no effective anti-trachoma vaccine available. Early attempts to develop a trachoma vaccine and subsequently to immunise populations in Taiwan, Iran and Egypt showed only a mild and transient protection against trachoma. In addition, it was found that vaccinated groups developed delayed hypersensitivity and when further exposed to Ct, they developed more severe trachoma in comparison to those who had not been vaccinated[11].

Interruption of transmission can be achieved by health education, provision of accessible clean water, improved housing, hygiene, public healthcare and waste disposal. These improvements can substantially and permanently reduce the prevalence and incidence of trachoma, but require substantial financial resources for a prolonged period of time.

Mass therapy of communities with hyperendemic trachoma or treatment of individuals in communities with a low prevalence of active trachoma using effective anti-chlamydial antibiotics may stop shedding of Ct. In order to achieve a substantial and lasting reduction in Ct shedding in the community, it is essential to find a drug and/or a delivery system which requires a single application only with a minimum of supervision. This must be affordable by poor countries. It must also be possible to provide re-treatment annually for several years.

GLOBAL ELIMINATION OF TRACHOMA

Since 1996, the WHO GET Alliance has convened several meetings to develop policies, strategies, procedures and technologies required for the global elimination of trachoma by the year 2020. During these meetings, it was proposed and agreed that a number of member countries with WHO support, should implement the following operational research projects in order to develop highly effective and practical programmes for elimination of trachoma:

Operational Research Projects
Rapid trachoma assessment
The following simple method for rapid assessment and recording of the presence and severity of trachoma, trichiasis and entropion has been recommended for field evaluation:[12]

TF Presence of follicles in the upper tarsal conjunctiva.
TI (intensive or severe trachoma) – This is diagnosed by the presence of papillae and diffuse infiltration masking more than half of the palpebral conjunctival vessels.
TS Trachoma with scarred conjunctiva.
TT Presence of entropion and trichiasis.
CO Corneal opacity.

The practicality and validity of this rapid assessment method was tested under the field conditions by involving ophthalmologists, general practitioners and ophthalmic nurses. The results showed reasonable inter-observer agreement in assessment. The universal application of the rapid trachoma assessment method is recommended in order to achieve the following:-

i)   uniform diagnosis;
ii)   reproducible recording of diagnosis in studies of prevalence and incidence of trachoma;
iii) evaluating the results of mass antibiotic therapy in the treatment of trachoma;
iv)   validating the impact of improved environmental conditions.

Mapping of trachoma
The WHO GET Alliance with the support of other WHO agencies and national trachoma control programmes, initiated a very important and interesting project for worldwide mapping of trachoma distribution[1]. The aim of this project is to map countries, regions and areas with high prevalence of active trachoma, trichiasis and entropion (blinding trachoma) as well as with low prevalence of trachoma (non-blinding trachoma). The mapping of trachoma may play an important role in planning control programmes by giving priorities to countries, regions, areas and villages with blinding trachoma.

Efficacy of azithromycin
Early studies demonstrated that a single oral dose of azithromycin is as effective as topical therapy with tetracycline eye ointment applied twice daily for a duration of six weeks[13]. It is also shown that two or three doses of azithromycin given at weekly intervals achieved a cure rate of >90%[13]. The WHO GET Alliance with the support of a pharmaceutical company, and some non-

government agencies and national trachoma control programmes in some African countries, initiated a large-scale research project to assess the efficacy of various regimens of azithromycin oral therapy. They also studied logistic problems with regard to supply and distribution of drugs, supervision of treatment at village and family levels, compliance of villagers and adverse effects.

Elimination policy

The WHO GET Alliance has devised a novel and multi-disciplinary strategy for elimination of trachoma by the year 2020. The strategy which is called 'SAFE' consists of:

(S) surgery for entropion and trichiasis
(A) antibiotic therapy
(F) face washing and
(E) environmental improvement

Pilot projects were then commenced to assess the efficacy of 'SAFE', logistics for application of 'SAFE' strategy, incorporation into existing primary healthcare systems, and materials and human and financial resources required[1].

Surgery

Over 40 surgical techniques are being used for correcting trichiasis and entropion and re-directing lashes away from the cornea[14]. None of these operations provides a lasting result. In some cases, the failure rates may reach up to 20% in the first year and increase substantially in the following years. In 1999 the WHO GET Alliance recommended a bilamellar tarsal rotation procedure which is simple and has a lower failure rate compared with other commonly used operations[1].

It is possible that some ophthalmologists and experts have failed to recognise the fact that surgical procedures are only providing a cosmetic correction. These operations have no influence on the ongoing trachomatous immunopathological processes in the lids. As described earlier, patients with trachoma when re-exposed to Ct or its antigenic components, may develop strong cell-mediated responses and delayed hypersensitivity.

Peeling and colleagues reported that higher antibody levels to chlamydia heat shock protein 60 are found in subjects with trachomatous scarring compared with controls lacking the disease from endemic communities.[15]

It is this phenomenon which is responsible for conjunctival scarring, sub-conjunctival and peri-tarsal fibrosis and tarsal degeneration, causing shrinkage and deformity of lids. These immunopathological processes are not affected by lid surgery and will continue and may become exacerbated by further exposure to Ct and possibly by operational trauma. In our studies in Iran and Oman, we found that the severity of trachomatous immunopathological processes and the failure rate of lid surgery can be reduced substantially by weekly doxycycline oral therapy for several weeks; and by additional topical therapy with anti-inflammatory drugs.

Unfortunately, in most countries with high prevalence of trichiasis and entropion, patients are not enthusiastic towards having corrective lid surgery. Statistics have shown that in some countries (after several years of offering free lid surgery locally or at the nearby hospitals) less than 30% of patients agreed to have the operation.

This misperception appears to be maintained in mid 2005. "The tragedy is that this (visual) loss could have been prevented at the time by surgical correction of the lid deformity, a procedure which WHO claim can be performed in rural villages, takes about 15 minutes and costs roughly $20."[16]

It might be argued that in order to convince patients with trichiasis and entropion who are already suffering from partial visual defects or who are potentially in danger of losing their sight, to accept surgery, the WHO GET Alliance and national control programmes should base these projects on:

a   an effective health education programme
b   the provision of surgery locally or at nearby hospitals, with
c   free transport for patients and their companions, and free accommodation if they have to stay overnight.

Novel approaches to increase availability of surgical intervention in trachoma include the collaboration with African Traditional Healers for the Prevention of Blindness. "The intent behind involving traditional healers in prevention of blindness activities is not to integrate healers into National Eye Care Programmes but to build on their existing capabilities so that they can provide the best possible primary eye care within the structure of their relationship with patients in the community".[17]

Antibiotic therapy
C. trachomatis is sensitive to sulphonamides, tetracyclines, macrolides

(including erythromycin and more recently developed azithromycin), rifamycin and some quinolones.

Aureomycin eye ointment used twice daily for six weeks is shown to cure trachoma in up to 70% of cases. However, it was found that intensive and continuous topical treatment is not practical for the mass therapy of trachoma in rural communities. As an alternative, the WHO recommended an intermittent regime with aureomycin eye ointment, twice daily, for five consecutive days a month for a period of six months per year. The aim of this method of therapy was to interrupt transmission of Ct during the transmission season, when the fly population is at its greatest and outbreaks of bacterial conjunctivitis are common. Intermittent therapy with topical antibiotics failed to reduce prevalence and incidence of trachoma substantially. This failure was mainly due to inadequate and erratic supply of the antibiotic ointment to the villages and families, inability of adults to apply eye ointment correctly into their own eyes or into the eyes of children and a very low level of compliance (see control of trachoma).

Azithromycin is shown to be highly effective against Ct. The minimum inhibitory concentration (MIC) of azithromycin is shown to be about 0.10–0.25µg per ml[18]. Studies have shown that after a single oral dose of azithromycin (20mg per kg) the drug can be detected in tears and serum in concentrations well above its MIC for 96 hours or longer[18]. The release of azithromycin in body fluids for a long period is due to its high tissue binding and its slow release from tissues into the blood and other body fluids.

Recent studies on the efficacy of azithromycin oral therapy in hyperendemic trachoma have shown that a single oral dose of azithromycin (20mg per kg) is as effective as topical therapy with aureomycin eye ointment applied twice daily for six weeks. It has also been shown that 2 to 3 oral doses of azithromycin given at weekly intervals have cured trachoma in up to 90% of patients[18].

Azithromycin oral therapy may provide a highly effective tool for the elimination of trachoma. However, adoption of azithromycin oral therapy requires substantial financial resources for purchasing the drug, an efficient chain of supply and distribution and close supervision.

We are aware that IO International Ltd, a UK based company, is developing an ocular insert device for sustained and continuous delivery of drugs in the eye. The results so far have shown that the ocular insert device can be retained in the eye for a period of 3 to 6 months without causing an unacceptable level of irritation and adverse effects. The ocular insert device is capable of continuous release of drugs at a predetermined level and duration. This novel development may provide an opportunity to incorporate azithromycin into the delivery system which would then release the antibiotic continuously for the whole trachoma transmission season. We believe that this concept may provide a much cheaper, more effective and practical alternative to oral therapy. For this development to become operational, there is an urgent need for support by WHO or other international agencies and/or pharmaceutical companies.

Face washing
As described earlier, regular face washing of children can remove Ct contaminated eye and nasal discharges, hence interrupting the transmission chain of trachoma. To encourage mothers to wash the faces of their children regularly, firstly, there is a need for a supply of clean water accessible to all inhabitants and secondly, a comprehensive and continuing programme of health education.

Environment
It is known that environmental improvements, including improved standards of housing, sanitation and waste disposal have substantial and continuing effects on the prevalence and incidence of trachoma. Major economic investment in infrastructure is a fundamental requirement to improve the standard of living and health of trachoma-affected communities.

CONCLUSION

While the objective and philosophy of GET by 2020 is of course fully supported, we believe that the above objective may not be achieved without wider specific recognition and subsequently resolution of the following difficulties:

* Magnitude of the problem which involves over 150 million people, spread over 30 countries.
* Inadequate financial, technological, administrative and managerial resources at the national level.
* Lack of political commitment in countries where trachoma is hyper-endemic.
* Insufficient financial provision by international agencies and industrialised countries to support the WHO GET programme.

Frick *et al.* estimated the burden and economic impact (productivity loss of trachoma).[19] It was concluded that from a resource allocation viewpoint, the economic burden of disease was roughly comparable with the expected costs of eradicating blindness due to trachoma.

We are of the opinion that with resources currently available or which may become available, it is feasible to eliminate blinding trachoma by the year 2020. This would, however, require the following:

a) reducing the prevalence, incidence and severity of trachoma using effective mass antibiotic therapy supplemented by improvement in the standards of hygiene, sanitation and public health;

b) eliminating trichiasis and entropion through the development and application of effective surgical procedures supplemented by chemotherapy to prevent the progress of trachomatous immunopathological processes after surgery; and

c) a comprehensive, sustained and continuing health education programme.

Acknowledgement

Mrs Joan Pleasance for preparation of all areas of text.

REFERENCES

1. World Health Organization. (1999). *Report of the third meeting of the WHO Alliance for the Global Elimination of Trachoma.* WHO/PBD/GET/99.3.
2. Dwyer RStC, Treharne D, Jones BR *et al.* Chlamydial infection. Results of micro-immunofluorescence tests for the detection of type-specific antibody in certain Chlamydial infections. *Brit J Vener Dis* 1972; **48:** 452–459.
3. Forsey T and Darougar S. Acute conjunctivitis caused by atypical chlamydial strain: Chlamydia IOL-207. *Brit J Ophthalmology* 1984; **68:** 409–411.
4. Darougar S and Jones Barrie R. Trachoma. *Br Med Bull* 1983; **39:** 117–122.
5. Lietman TM, Dawson CR, Osaki SY *et al.* Clinically active trachoma versus actual chlamydia infection. *MJA* 2000; **172:** 93–94.
6. Solomon AW, Holland MJ, Burton MJ, *et al.* Strategies for control of trachoma: observational study with quantative PCR. *Lancet* 2003; **362:** 198–204.
7. Taylor HR, Daks EM. New precision in measuring trachoma infection. *Lancet* 2003; **362:** 181–182.
8. West SK, Rapoza P, Munoz B *et al.* Epidemiology of ocular chlamydial infection in a trachoma-hyperendemic area. *J Infect Dis* 1991; **163:** 752–756.
9. Emerson P, Lindsay SW, Walraven GEL *et al.* Effect of fly control on trachoma and diarrhoea. *Lancet* 1999; **353:** 1401–1403.
10. Rafei UM, WHO Regional Office South-east Asia Prevention of Blindness 6th Conference of SAARC Ophthalmologist, Kathmandu, November 1999 from selected speeches by Dr Uton Muchtar Rafei; Regional Director WHO South-East Asia Region Vol 2 – 1997-2000 http://w3.whosea.org/en/Section980/Section 1162/Section 1167/Section 1171-4756 htm.
11. Schachter J and Dawson CR.Human chlamydial infections. 1978; PSG Publishing, Littleton, MA.

12. Thylefors B, Dawson CR, Jones BR *et al.* A simplified system for the assessment of trachoma and its complications. *Bull World Health Organization* 1987; **65:** 477–483.
13. Negrel AD, Marriotts SP. WHO Alliance for the global elimination of blinding trachoma and the potential use of azithromycin. *Int J Antimicrobial Agents* 1998; **10:** 259–262.
14. Reacher MH, Taylor RH.The management of trachomatous trichiasis. *Rev Int Trachoma* 1990; **67:** 233–261.
15. Peeling RW, Bailey RL, Conway DJ, *et al.* Antibody response to the 60-kDa chlamydial heat-shock protein is associated with scarring trachoma. *Int J Infect Dis.* 1998 Jan; **177**(1): 256–9.
16. WHO Prevention of blindness programme website www.chlamydiae.com/restricted/docs/infection/trachomagrading.asap.
17. Courtright P, Chirambo M, Lewallen S, *et al.* Collaboration with African Traditional Healers for Prevention of Blindness. 2000 World Scientific Publishing Co. Pte Ltd., Section 18 ISBN 981-02-4374-4.
18. Karcioglu ZA, El-Yazigi A, Jabak MH *et al.* Pharmacokinetics of azithromycin in Trachoma patients, serum and tear levels. *Ophthalmology* 1998; **105:** 658–661.
19. Frick K, Basilion E, Hanson C, Colchero A. Estimating the burden and economic impact of trachomatis visual loss. *Ophthalmic Epidemiology* 2003; **10:** 121–132.

RECOMMENDED FURTHER READING

Markel H. "The Eyes have it" Trachoma, the perception of disease, the United States Public Health Service, and the American Jewish Immigration Experience 1897-1924. *Bull Hist Med* 2000; **74**(3): 525–560.
"This description of the impact of trachoma on global migration in the early twentieth century provides both historical and epidemiological narrative which makes compelling reading". (TRM)

CHAPTER 13

Chlamydia pneumoniae
and heart disease

Pekka Saikku
Department of Medical Microbiology,
University of Oulu, Finland

Chlamydiae are known to cause various heart diseases. Endo-, myo- and pericarditides were associated with chlamydial infections during the first epidemics of psittacosis due to *Chlamydia psittaci*. The commonest Chlamydia of humans, *Chlamydia pneumoniae* has also been incriminated in these disease pictures. Recently, however, greatest attention has been afforded to the association of *C. pneumoniae* with atherosclerosis and coronary heart disease (CHD), and nearly one thousand publications have so far appeared on the subject.

The discovery of disease associations of the chlamydial strain TW-183 in 1985 led to speculation on its ability to cause chronic inflammations typical for other chlamydial species. Since this agent causes about 10% of all pneumonias, its association with chronic obstructive pulmonary disease, asthma and sarcoidosis was in a way natural. Totally unexpected however, was the association of this respiratory agent, now called *C. pneumoniae*, with acute myocardial infarction and chronic coronary heart disease.

The alert came in 1988, when paired serum samples, collected during acute myocardial infarction episodes, showed a seroconversion against an epitope of chlamydial lipopolysaccharide (LPS). This seroconversion was lacking in patients with chronic coronary heart disease, but in both patient groups elevated antibody titres against *C. pneumoniae* were found when compared to healthy matched controls. It was suggested that chronic coronary heart disease patients had a chronic *C. pneumoniae* infection and acute myocardial infarction was associated with an acute exacerbation of this infection[1]. Later on the antibody rises against chlamydial LPS was suggested to be due to release of the antigen from damaged areas leading to a temporal drop in titres when immune complexes are formed with circulating antibodies[2].

The seroepidemiological association has been verified in well over hundred studies in many laboratories with different methods of serology. However, antibodies alone, especially of IgG type, seem to be a marker of atherosclerosis in common and thus have a poor predictive value for cardiac events, which are complications of this extremely prevalent disease condition. Moreover, in prospective studies samples collected years before a cardiac event, do not reliably predict what will be the final course of a possible chronic process. Cross-sectional studies and samples collected one to five years before infarction from relatively young persons give understandably higher risk evaluations[3]. IgA antibodies, with their short half-life time, have generally been better predictors of future cardiac events than IgG antibodies. Presence of IgA antibodies can also be a marker of the shift of immune response from the T helper cells type Th1 to Th2, which is not effective against intracellular parasites. The lack of standardised methods for antibody titrations further confounds the picture and the very high prevalence of antibodies in older persons and smokers leads to underestimations of *C. pneumoniae* as a risk factor. Immune complexes have also been used as markers, but their study is difficult and demands expertise. However, chlamydial proteins in these complexes point to the presence of the agent in the immediate vicinity of the coronary circulation. One should always remember that antibodies alone do not show the site of the infection and how active it is. They should be combined with inflammation or autoimmunity markers. The persistent simultaneous presence of anti- *C. pneumoniae* IgA antibodies, elevated markers of systemic inflammation like elevated hsCRP, and markers of autoimmunity like anti-Hsp-60 antibodies, all together are associated with a highly elevated risk for cardiac event[4].

Seroepidemiology cannot prove or disprove a causal association. The next important finding in these studies was the demonstration of the agent directly in atherosclerotic lesions, even in some patients without antibodies. There are now nearly a hundred studies, in which the presence of *C. pneumoniae* in atherosclerotic plaques has been shown by electron microscopy, immune electron microscopy, immunohistochemistry, polymerase chain reaction, *in situ* hybridisation and culture. Only rarely has it been found in healthy areas of arteries. The results between different laboratories are variable but about half of the atherosclerotic plaques have been reported to contain *C. pneumoniae* elementary bodies, antigens or nucleic acids. The amount of viable pathogen in this chronic process seems to be minimal, which explains negative reports from some laboratories[5]. On the contrary, even claims that all atherosclerotic plaques are in fact positive if studied carefully enough, have been presented[6]. This finding is unique, since among infectious agents only herpes viruses (cytomegalovirus, HSV-1) have sometimes been found in atherosclerotic plaques[7]. *C. pneumoniae* is present in early atherosclerotic lesions and may even be identified in teenagers. Some studies have found the amount of the agent to be greater in advanced plaques or inflamed plaques tending to rupture, but this association has not been uniformly reported.

The problem is: what is this pathogen doing in the plaques? Atherosclerosis is nowadays accepted as an inflammatory condition[8]. Some consider *C. pneumoniae* only as an innocent bystander that has achieved entry into plaques carried within inflammatory cells, which have entered the lesion. Several studies have reported circulating monocytes containing *C. pneumoniae* nucleic acid. However, granulomas filled with inflammatory cells only exceptionally show the presence of this agent. Evidence supporting the active participation of *C. pneumoniae* in the atherosclerotic inflammatory process is steadily accumulating[9]. *C. pneumoniae* can multiply in the endothelial and smooth muscle cells of the vessel wall and this leads to production of adhesins, cytokines, growth – and tissue factors. A considerable proportion of inflammatory cells extracted from atherosclerotic lesions are targeted against the pathogens present. Macrophages turning to foam cells are the key cells of atherosclerotic lesions. *C. pneumoniae* can multiply in monocytes and macrophages with the respective cytokine induction. Moreover, *C. pneumoniae*-infected macrophages start to ingest low-density-lipoprotein and oxidise it, resulting in formation of foam cells. Some of these reactions can be induced with purified chlamydial components, like lipopolysaccharide (LPS) and chlamydial heat-shock protein 60 (Hsp60). In chronic chlamydial infection, chlamydial Hsp60 is produced in large amounts and it is found in plaques alongside human Hsp60. The continuous presence of chlamydial Hsp60 may eventually lead to autoimmunity against human Hsp60, due to cross-reactive epitopes shared by these highly conserved proteins. Altogether there seem to be several mechanisms by which *C. pneumoniae* could contribute to the development of atherosclerosis[9].

Atherosclerosis is a multifactorial disease. There are many risk factors, which may be implicated in the pathogenesis. Several risk factors may be associated with chronic *C. pneumoniae* infection or may be partly a reflection of it (**Table**). Since the majority of individuals are exposed to *C. pneumoniae*

Table 1. Risk factors for coronary heart disease, which have been associated with chronic *C. pneumoniae* infection

A. Affecting the outcome	B. Caused by the infection
– age	– chronic bronchitis
– male gender	– cytokine induction (TNF-alpha, IL-1)
– smoking	– elevation of C-reactive protein
– heredity	– altered lipid profile
– physical activity	– obesity
– diet	– hypertonia
– infections	– fatigue and depression
– stress	– autoimmunity to Hsp60

infection during their lifetime, dose, route of infection and genetic factors of both the host and the pathogen may determine the final outcome. Some HLA-associations and genetic polymorphisms with *C. pneumoniae*-associated CHD have been reported. When *C. pneumoniae* reaches the lungs, it can participate in the development of chronic obstructive pulmonary disease (COPD), a recently recognised risk factor for CHD. The frequent persistence of *C. pneumoniae* in the lungs of even apparently healthy persons provides a continuous source of infectious monocytes leaking into circulation[10,11]. Chronic infection leads to elevated cytokine production, which in turn may lead to fatigue and depression, which are also risk factors. Physical activity improves immune defence mechanisms and protects against cardiac events. Chronic *C. pneumoniae* infection is associated with a lipid profile typical for CHD (elevated triglyceride and cholesterol concentrations and lowered high-density-lipoprotein). Markers of inflammation found in atherosclerosis, like C-reactive protein, can be due to chronic *C. pneumoniae* infection. Immune defence mechanisms of smokers are hampered and in our studies on discordant identical twins, the smoking twin had higher IgA antibody levels and lowered cell-mediated immune response against *C. pneumoniae* than the non-smoking twin. Some reports have associated the presence of chronic *C. pneumoniae* with obesity and elevated blood pressure and *C. pneumoniae* also seems to be a factor in the metabolic syndrome

Animal models are important in the study of atherosclerosis and fortunately several models are available for *C. pneumoniae*. When rabbits are inoculated intranasally by *C. pneumoniae*, those on a normal diet develop atherosclerotic lesions, and in rabbits on a diet enriched with cholesterol, the development of lesions is enhanced. This effect is prevented by macrolides if given early in the disease. Mycoplasma pneumoniae given intranasally to rabbits produces a generalised infection, but it does not lead to focal lesions in arteries[12]. In mouse experiments[13], both normal and gene-knock-out mice have been used. Cholesterol must usually be added in the diet of mice. The development of the atherosclerotic lesions is accelerated by repeated intranasal inoculations of *C. pneumoniae*. Interestingly, *Chlamydia trachomatis* (strain mouse pneumonitis), produces similar systemic infection in mice and can be detected in the aorta after intranasal inoculation. However, it does not persist there and does not cause the development of atherosclerosis. Pigs are also infected and apes are chronically infected with *C. pneumoniae*, but studies on possible atherosclerosis induced in them are lacking.

Final evidence can be found after intervention and vaccination trials. Original small studies were encouraging and several large-scale placebo-controlled intervention studies were started even before anyone knew of an effective treatment for chronic chlamydial infection. The results of these large trials, typically in advanced atheroslerosis in order to prevent secondary myocardial infarctions, have been disappointing[14]. Even prolonged one or two year monotherapy was not effective[15-16]. There can be reasons for this failure. Perhaps when trying to prevent secondary events the disease has proceeded so far that it cannot be treated with antibiotic therapy. Moreover, in animal experiments monotherapy has not eradicated chronic *C. pneumoniae* infection[17]. *C. pneumoniae* infection of human monocytes has been resistant to antibiotics[18] as is a chronic infection cell culture model[19]. In intervention trials, no similar fall in specific antibodies after successful eradication of helicobacter has been reported[14]. Azithromycin treatment alone for *C. pneumoniae* in mice was not successful but in combination with rifampicin, it was effective in eradicating the agent from chronically infected mice[20]. This type of experimentation is essential to ensure that the history of monotherapy in tuberculosis or helicobacter infections does not repeat itself. The problem of the treatment of chronic *C. pneumoniae* infection should be solved in cell cultures and animal experiments before new human intervention trials. Until then, we can continue to use coronary heart disease drugs that have a demonstrated anti-*C. pneumoniae* activity – aspirin[21] and statins[22].

The sequencing of the whole genome of *C. pneumoniae* has offered a shortcut for development of candidate vaccines against the pathogen. We do not yet know whether a therapeutic vaccine is either realistic or achievable, but after successful eradication a vaccine should protect from reinfection. Still better, an effective vaccine given in early childhood would be required to afford long-term protection from the development of atherosclerosis, which starts at an early age. However, the final protective effect against acute myocardial infarctions could be seen only some 50 years after administration. The development of other chlamydial vaccines has led to disappointment, short-term/incomplete immunity and the risk of sensitising the recipient.

We should continue animal experiments and studies on pathogenetic mechanisms in order to understand what is going on in *C. pneumoniae* infections. We need to understand the pathogenesis at a subcellular level, in acute, sub-acute and chronic infection.

One should realise that nowadays cardiovascular diseases are the leading causes of death in both developed and developing countries. Any potential means of alleviating such massive global morbidity and mortality must be thoroughly and fastidiously evaluated.

REFERENCES

1. Saikku P, Leinonen M, Mattila K, *et al.* Serological evidence of an association of a novel Chlamydia, TWAR, with chronic coronary heart disease and acute myocardial infarction. *Lancet.* 1988 Oct 29; **2**(8618): 983–6.
2. Leinonen M, Linnanmaki E, Mattila K, *et al.* Circulating immune complexes containing chlamydial lipopolysaccharide in acute myocardial infarction. *Microb Pathog.* 1990 Jul; **9**(1): 67–73.
3. Arcari CM, Gaydos CA, Nieto FJ, *et al.* Association between *Chlamydia pneumoniae* and acute myocardial infarction in young men in the United States military: the importance of timing of exposure measurement. *Clin Infect Dis.* 2005 Apr 15; **40**(8): 1123–30.
4. Huittinen T, Leinonen M, Tenkanen L, *et al.* Synergistic effect of persistent *Chlamydia pneumoniae* infection, autoimmunity, and inflammation on coronary risk. *Circulation.* 2003 May 27; **107**(20): 2566–70.
5. Ieven MM, Hoymans VY. Involvement of *Chlamydia pneumoniae* in atherosclerosis: more evidence for lack of evidence. *J Clin Microbiol.* 2005 Jan; **43**(1): 19–24. Review.
6. Cochrane M, Pospischil A, Walker P, *et al.* Distribution of *Chlamydia pneumoniae* DNA in atherosclerotic carotid arteries: significance for sampling procedures. *J Clin Microbiol.* 2003 Apr; **41**(4): 1454–7.
7. Leinonen M, Saikku P. Evidence for infectious agents in cardiovascular disease and atherosclerosis. *Lancet Infect Dis.* 2002 Jan; **2**(1): 11–7. Review.
8. Hansson GK. Inflammation, atherosclerosis, and coronary artery disease. *N Engl J Med.* 2005 Apr 21; **352**(16): 1685–95. Review.

9. Belland RJ, Ouellette SP, Gieffers J, Byrne GI. *Chlamydia pneumoniae* and atherosclerosis. *Cell Microbiol.* 2004 Feb; **6**(2): 117–27. Review.

10. Wu L, Skinner SJ, Lambie N, *et al.* Immunohistochemical staining for *Chlamydia pneumoniae* is increased in lung tissue from subjects with chronic obstructive pulmonary disease. *Am J Respir Crit Care Med.* 2000 Sep; **162**(3 Pt 1): 1148–51.

11. Gieffers J, van Zandbergen G, Rupp J, *et al.* Phagocytes transmit *Chlamydia pneumoniae* from the lungs to the vasculature. *Eur Respir J.* 2004 Apr; **23**(4): 506–10.

12. Fong IW. Antibiotics effects in a rabbit model of *Chlamydia pneumoniae*-induced atherosclerosis. *J Infect Dis.* 2000 Jun; **181** Suppl 3: S514–8. Review.

13. de Kruif MD, van Gorp EC, Keller TT, *et al.* *Chlamydia pneumoniae* infections in mouse models: relevance for atherosclerosis research. *Cardiovasc Res.* 2005 Feb 1; **65**(2): 317–27. Review.

14. Andraws R, Berger JS, Brown DL. Effects of antibiotic therapy on outcomes of patients with coronary artery disease: a meta-analysis of randomized controlled trials. *JAMA.* 2005 Jun 1; **293**(21): 2641–7. Review.

15. Grayston JT, Kronmal RA, Jackson LA *et al.* Azithromycin for the secondary prevention of coronary events. *N Eng J Med* 2005; **352:** 1637–45.

16. Cannon CP, Braunwald E, McCabe CH *et al.* Antibiotic treatment of *Chlamydia pneumoniae* after acute coronary syndrome. *N Eng J Med* 2005; **352:** 1646–54.

17. Blessing E, Campbell LA, Rosenfeld ME, *et al.* A 6 week course of azithromycin treatment has no beneficial effect on atherosclerotic lesion development in apolipoprotein E-deficient mice chronically infected with *Chlamydia pneumoniae*. *J Antimicrob Chemother.* 2005 Jun; **55**(6): 1037–40.

18. Gieffers J, Fullgraf H, Jahn J, *et al.* *Chlamydia pneumoniae* infection in circulating human monocytes is refractory to antibiotic treatment. *Circulation.* 2001 Jan 23; **103**(3): 351–6.

19. Kutlin A, Roblin PM, Hammerschlag MR. Effect of prolonged treatment with azithromycin, clarithromycin, or levofloxacin on *Chlamydia pneumoniae* in a continuous-infection Model. *Antimicrob Agents Chemother.* 2002 Feb; **46**(2): 409–12.

20. Bin XX, Wolf K, Schaffner T, Malinverni R. Effect of azithromycin plus rifampin versus amoxicillin alone on eradication and inflammation in the chronic course of *Chlamydia pneumoniae* pneumonitis in mice. *Antimicrob Agents Chemother.* 2000 Jun; **44**(6): 1761–4.

21. Tiran A, Gruber HJ, Graier WF, *et al.* Aspirin inhibits *Chlamydia pneumoniae*-induced nuclear factor-kappa B activation, cytokine expression, and bacterial development in human endothelial cells. *Arterioscler Thromb Vasc Biol.* 2002 Jul 1; **22**(7): 1075–80.

22. Kothe H, Dalhoff K, Rupp J, *et al.* Hydroxymethylglutaryl coenzyme A reductase inhibitors modify the inflammatory response of human macrophages and endothelial cells infected with *Chlamydia pneumoniae*. *Circulation.* 2000 Apr 18; **101**(15):1760–3.

CHAPTER 14

Lymphogranuloma venereum

Claire Dewsnap and George Kinghorn
Department of Genito Urinary Medicine,
Royal Hallamshire Hospital, Sheffield, UK

INTRODUCTION

Lymphogranuloma venereum (LGV) is a sexually transmitted disease caused by serovars L1, L2 or L3 of *Chlamydia trachomatis*. Wallace originally described the disease in 1833. Durand, Nicolas, and Favre defined it as a clinical and pathological entity in 1913.[1]

LGV synonyms include lymphopathia venerea, tropical bubo, climatic bubo, strumous bubo, poradenitis inguinales, Durand-Nicolas-Favre disease, and lymphogranuloma inguinale.

Epidemiology

Until recently, it was uncommonly diagnosed in developed industrialised countries and then usually recognised as an imported infection from those tropical countries in Africa, South East Asia, South America and the Caribbean where it is endemic. However, recent outbreaks of LGV in homosexual men in several European countries are now challenging this traditional view.[1,2]

In 2003 a cluster of cases were reported in Rotterdam and the Netherlands.[3–5] Further outbreaks have been reported in Stockholm, Paris, Hamburg and now the UK.[6–9] The UK has reported 72 cases confirmed by the Health Protection Agency (HPA).[10]

All of these new cases occurring in Europe have been in men having sex with men (MSM). Co-infection with other sexually transmitted infection (STI) is common. HIV and Hepatitis C are strongly associated with these outbreaks.

In all cases presenting symptoms were predominantly anorectal with patients complaining of rectal pain, discharge, bleeding and diarrhoea. All reported cases across Europe have been confirmed L2 serovar.[10,11] Risk taking behaviour including unprotected anal intercourse and fisting have been commonly reported in these cases, mostly with multiple anonymous partners at saunas or 'sex parties'.[12]

PATHOGENESIS

The LGV serovars of *C. trachomatis* have a remarkable tropism for lymphoid cells and a special ability to cause systemic disease.The organism gains entry through skin breaks and abrasions, or may cross genital epithelial cells, to gain access to lymphatics. It travels to regional lymph nodes where it multiplies within mononuclear phagocytes.[1,13]

Transmission is predominately sexual. Non-sexual transmission by laboratory accidents or non-sexual personal contact or fomites has been recorded.

Replication within lymph nodes is characterised by painful lymphadenitis and associated constitutional symptoms. Early involvement causes fleshy lymph nodes that show reticulosis. Later, suppurative granulomatous lymphadenitis, perilymphadenitis with matting of nodes, and the formation of stellate abscesses occurs.

In later stages of LGV, hyperplasia of lymphatic tissue together with characteristic fibrosis and granulomas occur, which are associated with well-defined clinical appearances.

CLINICAL FEATURES

Historically LGV has been diagnosed 6 times more frequently in men than in women, however this sex difference is likely to relate to the increased difficulty in recognising the early stages of infection rather than to a biological difference in susceptibility. This statistic is still likely to ring true in tropical countries. Like other STIs, it most often occurs in younger sexually active adults in the 16-35 years old age group.[13]

The incubation period from the sexual exposure to the first symptoms usually varies between 3 days to 4 weeks.

PRIMARY LESION

The first lesion produced by LGV consists of a small, non-painful papule or erosion at the site of inoculation. There may be grouping of lesions that are herpetiform in appearance.[14] Such lesions are often transient and unnoticed. In some individuals, lymphangitis in the dorsal penis forming a cord-like structure may appear. This can persist to form a tender lymphoid nodule that may subsequently rupture to form sinuses or fistulas.

In women, and in homosexual men practising receptive anal intercourse, primary lesions occur internally and are often silent.

The oral cavity may also be a primary site of silent infection.

SECONDARY LESIONS

These are characterised by lymphoid proliferation. It first appears 10 to 30 days after post-infection.

Inguinal syndrome

Classically, there is tender unilateral or bilateral inguinal lymphadenopathy if the primary lesion affects the anterior vulva, penis or urethra. If there is also involvement of the femoral lymph nodes, a depression ("groove sign") is formed with the inguinal ligament separating the two groups of affected nodes. Two thirds of those individuals with inguinal lymphadenopathy develop unilateral bubo formation with erythema and oedema of the overlying skin. Stellate abscesses can develop and rupture occurs through single or multiple sinuses in around one third of individuals. This is usually associated with a reduction in pain.

Perirectal and pelvic lymphadenopathy occurs when the primary lesion affects the anus, posterior vulva, vagina, or cervix. Deep pelvic inflammation also frequently follows inguinal involvement. Abdominal or pelvic pain, worse when lying supine, may result. Submaxillary and cervical lymphadenopathy can occur with oral lesions. Rupture and sinus formation is unusual from these sites.

Anorectal syndrome

Proctocolitis may also be seen in secondary lesions, especially in women and receptive homosexual men. Gastrointestinal symptoms consisting of rectal pain, tenesmus, rectal bleeding, with mucous or purulent anal discharge occur and may be the presenting symptoms. Complications include rectal stricture, perirectal abscesses, and anal fistula formation. Perirectal outgrowths of lymphoid tissue can mimic haemorrhoids.

The features may be indistinguishable from those of inflammatory bowel disease. A strong index of suspicion and the taking of a sexual history will help in the investigation of such cases.

Erythema nodosum may also appear with these early lesions. Autoinoculation to the eyes may result in follicular conjunctivitis.

Late (Tertiary) Stage

Lesions may appear years after the primary infection and result from persistent lymphangitis, granuloma formation and fibrosis, and chronic tissue oedema.

There may be persistent genital ulcers, fistulas, urethral stricture, and genital elephantiasis.

Frozen pelvis, tubal infertility, perineal sinuses, and rectovaginal fistulae may occur.

Esthiomene results from sclerosing fibrosis of the subcutaneous tissues of the genitalia with chronic oedema, and structural distortion. Rectal stricture causes pencil-thin stools and may progress to intestinal obstruction.

DIAGNOSIS

The diagnosis is initially based on clinical findings and can be supported by laboratory tests (**Table 1**). Strains in the LGV biovar are characterized in the laboratory by their ability to grow in cell culture without the need for centrifuge-assisted infection or for pre-treatment of host cells with polycations. They also show faster and more vigorous growth in cell culture.

Genetic differences between *Chlamydia trachomatis* serovars, especially polymorphisms in the tryptophan synthase activity alpha-subunit, can explain variations in their pathogenesis.

Historically, the Frei intradermal test, based on hypersensitivity to a standardised antigen, was used. It became positive 2 to 8 weeks post-infection. Commercial production of the Frei antigen ceased in the 1970s and the test is no longer available.[1]

Diagnosis can be made by detection of *C. trachomatis* L1-3 strains from genital or rectal lesions or bubo aspirates. Cultural isolation is definitive, and can be established in 30% cases, but is no longer available in many laboratories[13]. In October 2004 the HPA began an enhanced surveillance program for LGV. This

Table 1. Differential diagnosis	
Primary lesions	syphilis chancroid genital herpes granuloma inguinale
Inguinal syndrome	syphilis chancroid genital herpes incarcerated inguinal hernia lymphadenitis secondary to other lower extremity infection tularaemia lymphoma plague cat-scratch disease
Anorectal syndrome	inflammatory bowel disease actinomycosis schistosomiasis
Rectal stricture	bowel malignancy trauma pelvic tuberculosis
Genital elephantiasis	filiariasis tuberculosis parasitic infection granuloma inguinale fungal infections

protocol recommends testing for chlamydia using in house nucleic acid amplification techniques (NAAT). If this is positive, confirmation of the diagnosis should be sought by reporting the case to HPA and providing the sexually transmitted bacterial reference laboratory (STBRL) with either a NAAT or dry swab. Further molecular tests will be performed to determine the serovar. These are specific DNA amplification of the *omp1* gene using nested PCR and restriction endonuclease digestion to identify specific serovars. Sequence diversity for the *omp1* gene has been used to further genotype strains in individual cases, for example a single strain known as AMSTLGVL2b was isolated in the Amsterdam cases and other variants have been isolated.[15]

NAAT tests are not licensed on rectal samples and the molecular tests used by STBRL are being validated. Enzyme immunoassay (EIA) tests are 75-80% sensitive and can be used as an alternative to NAAT in the HPA protocol.[12]

Serological tests can also be supportive of the diagnosis. The micro-immunofluorescence test is the most accurate serological test as it can distinguish between different chlamydial species. A microimmuno-fluorescence titre of 1:128 is strongly suggestive of LGV. A titre of >1:512 is typical during active infection. The disadvantage of the mirco-IF is that it is not widely available.

Complement fixation tests are less reliable because of greater cross-reactivity with other chlamydial species. The sensitivity is 80% for LGV. A titre of 1:16 is strongly suggestive and >1:64 typical in active LGV. A four-fold rise or fall is also indicative.[2,13]

Biopsy of lesions often fails to reveal pathognomonic features in LGV, even when special stains for intracellular *C. trachomatis* are used.

Other investigations
LGV often occurs with other STIs so comprehensive screening for other infections including HIV should be mandatory. In MSM particular attention should be paid to the sexual history and Hepatitis C testing should be included.[16]

Imaging studies, such as CT scan, may be useful if pelvic lymphadenitis or abscess is suspected. Barium studies can reveal the characteristic elongated stricture of rectal LGV.[1]

TREATMENT

Medical
Symptomatic treatment in terms of analgesia and the application of local heat to abscesses may be required to relieve acute symptoms

Table 2.
Recommended Regimen
Doxycycline 100 mg orally twice a day for 21 days.
Alternative Regimen
Erythromycin base 500 mg orally four times a day for 21 days.

Antibiotic treatment cures infection and prevents ongoing tissue damage, although tissue reaction can result in scarring. Doxycycline is the preferred treatment (**Table 2**).[17]

Azithromycin in multiple doses weekly for 3 weeks may also be effective, although clinical data are lacking.[13,17]

Surgical treatment

Buboes may require aspiration through intact skin or incision and drainage to prevent the formation of inguinal/femoral ulcerations.

Abscesses sometimes require surgical drainage. Other surgical intervention may be required for the consequences of the late stages of LGV.

Follow-Up

Patients should be followed clinically until signs and symptoms have resolved.

Management of Sex Partners

Persons who have had sexual contact with a patient who has LGV within the 3 to 6 weeks days before onset of the patient's symptoms should be examined, tested for urethral, cervical and rectal chlamydial infection, and treated.[15]

Pregnancy

Pregnant and lactating women should be treated with erythromycin. Azithromycin may prove useful for treatment of LGV in pregnancy, but no published data are available regarding its safety and efficacy. Doxycycline is contraindicated in pregnant women.

Coexisting HIV Infection

Persons with both LGV and HIV infection should receive the same regimens as those who are HIV-negative. Prolonged therapy may be required as delay in resolution of symptoms and reactivation may occur.[18]

REFERENCES

1. Perine PL, Stamm WE, Lymphogranuloma Venereum. In: Holmes KK *et al.* Sexually Transmitted Diseases. New York: McGraw-Hill 3rd Edition 1999. 423–32.
2. Mabey D, Peeling RW. Lymphogranuloma Venereum. *Sexually Transmitted Infections* 2002; **78:** 90–92.
3. Götz HM, Ossewaarde JM, Nieuwenhuis RF *et al.* Cluster van lymphogranuloma venereum onder homoseksuele mannen in Rotterdam met grensoverschrijdende gevolgen. *Ned Tijdschr Geneesk* 2004; **148:** 441–2.

4. Rutger F, Nieuwenhuis RF. Resurgence of Lymphogranuloma Venereum in Western Europe: An Outbreak of *Chlamydia trachomatis* Serovar L$_2$ Proctitis in The Netherlands among Men Who Have Sex with Men. *Clinical Infectious Diseases* 2004; **39**: 996–1003.

5. Nieuwenhuis RF, Ossewaarde JM, van der Meijden WI, Neumann HAM. Unusual presentation of early lymphogranuloma venereum in an HIV-1 infected patient: effective treatment with 1 g azithromycin. *Sex Transm Infect* 2003; **79**: 453–5.

6. Berglund T, Bratt G, Herrmann B, *et al*. Two cases of lymphogranuloma venereum (LGV) in homosexual men in Stockholm. *Eurosurveillance Weekly* 2005: **10**(3).

7. http://www.invs.sante.fr/presse/2004/le_point_sur/lgv_160604/

8. Plettenberg A, von Krosigk A, Stoehr A, Meyer T. Four cases of lymphogranuloma venereum in Hamburg, 2003. *Eurosurveillance Weekly* 2004: **8**(30). (http://www.eurosurveillance.org/ew/2004/040722.asp#4).

9. Macdonald N, Ison C, Martin I, *et al*. Initial results of enhanced surveillance for Lymphogranuloma venereum in England. *Eurosurveillance Weekly* Jan 2005: **10**(1)

10. Health Protection Agency. Lymphogranuloma Venereum in the UK- an update.*CDR weekly*. May 2005; **15**(20): 2.

11. CDC, Lymphogranuloma Venereum among Men Who Have Sex with Men - Netherlands, 2003-2004 *MMWR weekly*. October 29, 2004/**53**(42); 985-988. http://www.cdc.gov/mmwr/preview/mmwrhtml/mm5342a2.htm

12. Health Protection agency. Protocol for UK LGV enhanced surveillance. March 2005. http://www.hpa.org.uk/infections/topics_az/hiv_and_sti/LGV/publications/LGV_enhanced_surveillance_March_2005.pdf

13. BASHH guidelines. National guideline for the management of Lymphogranuloma Venereum 2001

14. Schachter J. Lymphogranuloma Venereum and other nonocular *Chlamydia Trachomatis* infections, in nongonococcal urethritis and related infections. *Washington, American Society for Microbiology*, 1977; 91–97.

15. Van der Laar M, Fenton K, Ison C. Update on the European lymphogranuloma venereum epidemic among men who have sex with men. *Eurosurveillance Weekly* June 2005; **10**(6)

16. Hannelore G *et al*. Preliminary report of an outbreak of lymphogranuloma venereum in homosexual men in the Netherlands, with implications for other countries in Western Europe. *Eurosurveillance Weekly* 2004; **8**(4).

17. CDC, 1998 Guidelines for Treatment of Sexually Transmitted Diseases. *MMWR* January 23, 1998; **47**(RR-1): 1–118

18. Van Dyke E, Piot P. Laboratory techniques in the investigation of chancroid, lymphogranuloma venereum and donovanosis. *Genitourinary medicine* 1992; **68**: 130-3.

CHAPTER 15

Chronic pelvic pain in young women
The importance of differential diagnosis

Richard Beard
Imperial College Medical School, London

Anusha Dias
Northwick Park and St Marks Hospital Trust, Harrow, UK

Women presenting with pelvic pain, are often diagnosed as having pelvic inflammatory disease (PID), particularly in departments of genito urinary medicine. Unless this diagnosis is supported by clinical, bacteriological and if in doubt, visual evidence at laparoscopy, some of these women will be unjustifiably labelled as PID and will become 'PID cripples'. When the pain recurs, they seek repeated courses of antibiotics from their general practitioners and are often seen by gynaecologists believing that they are infertile. Nevertheless, while it is essential to exclude PID as a cause of acute or chronic pain, it has to be admitted that an alternative diagnosis is sometimes difficult to make, particularly if laparoscopy is negative. This is well illustrated in the Guideline on the management of chronic pelvic pain (CPP) issued by the Royal College of Obstetricians and Gynaecologists in 2005[1].

CHRONIC PELVIC PAIN (CPP)

Chronic pelvic pain has been defined as a constant or intermittent pain in the lower abdomen or pelvis of at least six months duration, not occurring exclusively with menstruation or intercourse and not associated with pregnancy[1].

In Britain, the prevalence rate has been reported to be 21.5 per 1,000 women which is comparable to the rate of 21.5 for migraine and 41.5 for backache[2]. Mathias *et al.*[3] reported from a Gallup telephone survey of women between the ages of 18-50 years that 14.9 per cent had CPP of sufficient severity for 3 months or more to see their doctors[4]. Although our understanding of CPP has improved in recent years, it is important to remember that non-gynaecological causes eg abdominal wall pain and bowel pain, can simulate gynaecological pain. Also, CPP thought to be of gynaecological origin may, in reality, have causal pathology in organs such as the bladder or large bowel, or sometimes from sites outside the pelvis such as the duodenum, or abdominal wall. Thus it is essential to recognise that visceral pain is not a reliable guide as to the location of somatic pain.

DYSMENORRHOEA

Dysmenorrhoea is defined as lower abdominal pain occurring around the time of menstruation. It is usually described as a dull ache of variable intensity, and is influenced by various psychosocial and biological factors[5]. Strong positive associations can be demonstrated within families and with early menarche. However, no associations were found with parity and smoking. Several studies have demonstrated the importance of psychological factors. Skandhan *et al.*[6] showed that women with prior knowledge and understanding of menstruation resulted in them having higher rates of menstrual regularity and lower rates of dysmenorrhoea. Gath *et al.*[7] found a high index of neuroticism among dysmenorrhoea sufferers.

Diagnostically, it is important to recognise differences between the two classifications of dysmenorrhoea in current use. The first classification defines primary dysmenorrhoea as pain with no obvious cause, and secondary dysmenorrhoea as pain 'secondary' to identified pathology. The practical limitation of this definition is that it implies that the absence of visible pathology is evidence that the condition is physiological which we now know is not the case. Equally, it cannot be assumed from the term, secondary dysmenorrhoea, that visible pathology is necessarily the cause of the pain. A clinically more useful classification is one that distinguishes between pain occurring before the onset and often relieved by the menstrual flow (congestive dysmenorrhoea), and pain confined to the time of bleeding (spasmodic dysmenorrhoea). The advantage of this definition is that it locates the time in the cycle when the pain occurs without prejudging the cause and also that the underlying pathology is known to be different. Treatment of both congestive and spasmodic dysmenorrhoea is often initially in the form of the combined oral contraceptive pill. If this fails, ovarian steroids and prostaglandin synthetase inhibitors such as mefenamic acid (Ponstan) can be used. Psychological interventions are also helpful[8]. Relaxation training has been found to be effective with spasmodic dysmenorrhoea but not for congestive dysmenorrhoea.

ENDOMETRIOSIS

Endometriosis is an enigmatic disease associated with the presence of endometrium outside the uterine cavity. Its relationship to CPP has been well reviewed by Kennedy and Overton[9]. Roddick *et al.*[10] showed that it could present as dysmenorrhoea (45%), deep dysmenorrhoea (16%), rectal pain (8%), as a chronic non-cyclic pelvic ache or be asymptomatic. CPP may also involve other systems such as the gastrointestinal, urinary and pulmonary systems. Within the pelvis, the commonest sites for implantation of ectopic endometrium are the ovary (where it may form chocolate cysts), the peritoneum of the pouch of Douglas, the uterosacral ligaments and the pelvic peritoneum, particularly on the broad ligament and uterovesical folds.

However, there is little correlation between extent of endometriosis and severity of pain[11]. Theories have been postulated to explain why endometriosis causes pain. Bleeding from implantation sites occuring at the same time as from normally situated endometrium, is thought to cause the cyclical pain that women with endometriosis complain of. Some authors feel that retrograde menstruation which is the upward passage of menstrual blood through the fallopian tubes into the pelvic cavity may cause pain. Another theory suggests that reduced mobility of pelvic organs secondary to severe adhesions may be a cause. This could be a result of altered blood flow. The involvement of the autonomic nerves by endometrial tissue may be another possible mechanism. Vernon *et al.*[12] found that petechial or 'reddish implants' have a greater capacity for synthesising prostaglandin F while black implants have the least capacity. A theory, suggested by Schmidt[13] is based on the knowledge that women with endometriosis had more peritoneal fluid in the pouch of Douglas containing greater quantities of prostaglandin E2 and F2a. These compounds which are vasoactive, are likely to cause vascular stasis and hence pain.

The selection of treatments available for chronic pelvic pain thought to be caused by endometriosis has been well described by Wardle[14]. Options for medical treatment are drugs which suppress ovarian activity to a greater or lesser degree. These include Danazol – a derivative of 17a ethinyltestosterone, although this is not much favoured these days because of its known androgenising effects. Alternatively, while the GnRH analogues are expensive, they are more effective, better tolerated and without the risk of permanent side effects. If they are employed, 'add back' therapy with progesterone and oestrogen, should be used to relieve menopausal side-effects and to prevent bone loss[15]. Oral medroxyprogesterone acetate (Provera) is cheaper but less satisfactory for achieving ovarian down regulation. Surgery is the most commonly used treatment for endometriosis followed by a six month course of ovarian down regulation. For women who wish to conserve their fertility, this varies from local excision of deposits by open surgery to laparoscopic laser coagulation. For more severe cases, or when fertility is not an issue, total hysterectomy is an option, but this should be accompanied by a bilateral salpingoophorectomy as the growth of endometriotic tissue is driven by oestrogens. In young women removal of the ovaries should be a last resort and should be preceded by a diagnostic test of therapeutic efficacy by 3-4 month period of ovarian down-regulation to ensure that oophorectomy will be effective in curing the pelvic pain.

PELVIC CONGESTION

There is now good evidence to show that 84% of women with a visibly normal pelvis on laparoscopy, have pelvic congestion[16]. The name given to this condition describes the underlying pathophysiology. Inadequate clearance of venous blood results in the release of pain producing substances, the pain experienced being similar to the runner who develops cramp. Much of the study of the condition has been devoted to establishing its existence, so that, to date, the epidemiology of this condition has not been well characterised. However, it does seem likely that it is the cause of most cases that have been classified as 'chronic pelvic pain without obvious pathology' (CPPWOP). Stacey *et al.*[17] reporting on a consecutive series of women, referred to a genito urinary clinic and investigated laparoscopically for CPP, found that in 60 per cent of them there was no visible pathology. In an audit of clinical activity of a tertiary referral clinic devoted mainly to the investigation of women with CPPWOP over one year, the prevalence of pelvic congestion among 177 women with CPP was 77 per cent (Beard and Rogers unpublished). **Table 1** is a list of all diagnoses and their frequency, found in this audit.

Table 1. Distribution of diagnosis from audit of 177 women who attended a tertiary referral pelvic pain clinic (1997-98)

	n	%
Pelvic congestion	136	77
Ilioinguinal nerve damage	9	5
Trapped ovary(ies)	5	3
Ovarian remnant(s)	2	1
Others – endometriosis, no diagnosis, etc	25	14

DIAGNOSIS OF PELVIC CONGESTION

The most valuable diagnostic indicators of pelvic congestion are the history and clinical findings. **Table 2** is a comparison between symptoms in two groups of women with CPP – those with and without visible pathology at laparoscopy compared with a control group of women without CPP matched for age and parity. Typically, women with pelvic congestion present with a dull and aching pain interspersed occasionally with acute exacerbations. Pain is aggravated by standing, exercise, abdominal straining, intercourse and stress. It is relieved by lying down, relaxation, local heat and analgesics. Sexual problems are common. Of all women with pelvic congestion, 71 per cent complain of dyspareunia and 65 per cent of postcoital ache. This last symptom has a predictive value of 92 per cent for the diagnosis of pelvic congestion. Menstrual cycle defects are common (54%) particularly heavy bleeding in the first two days of menstruation, as is congestive dysmenorrhoea (69%). Women with the condition often complain of vaginal discharge, backache, headache and urinary symptoms and postdefaecation pain[18] (in contrast to the pain of the irritable bowel syndrome when pain is relieved by defaecation).

One of the most important physical signs in the diagnosis of pelvic congestion is ovarian point tenderness, at the junction of the upper and middle one third of a line drawn from umbilicus to anterior superior iliac spine, which is present in 77 per cent of women. Ovarian tenderness is also important, and can be elicited on bimanual examination in 86 per cent of these patients.

Table 2. Frequency of symptoms in two groups with chronic pelvic pain and a normal group of women (Beard et al.[18])

	Controls (36)	Pelvic Pathology (22)	Pelvic Congestion (35)
Activity-related Pain			
Standing	0%	18%	40%
Walking	0%	18%	49%
Bending/Lifting	0%	9%	60%
Postcoital ache	8%	9%	65%
Deep dyspareunia	11%	41%	71%
Associated Symptoms			
Menorrhagia	22%	27%	54%
Congestive dysmenorrhoea	14%	14%	69%
Spasmodic dysmenorrhoea	36%	59%	9%

INVESTIGATIONS

These should include a laparoscopy to exclude pelvic inflammatory disease and endometriosis and a vaginal ultrasound scan. Large dilated veins with a congested uterus and/or multicystic ovaries are often seen at laparoscopy and on scan. Adams et al.[19] and Farquhar et al.[20] showed with ultrasound scan that 50-56% of women with pelvic congestion have either multi- or polycystic ovaries.

The transcervical venogram was first described by Topolanski-Sierra in 1958[21]. Beard et al.[16] have subsequently developed a useful scoring system which quantifies the degree of venous dilation, severity of congestion and clearance of dye with 91 per cent diagnostic sensitivity and 89 per cent specificity. A needle is passed through the cervix to the fundus of the uterus and 20ml of radio-opaque dye is injected into the myometrium. The rate of passage of dye and its rate of clearance through the parauterine, paravesical and ovarian veins and the diameter of the vein, determines whether or not pelvic congestion is present. Pelvic venography should only be used as an investigative tool if there is any doubt about the cause of chronic pelvic pain – for example when pelvic congestion and endometriosis co-exist.

PSYCHOLOGICAL FACTORS IN CHRONIC PELVIC PAIN

Psychological factors such as specific attitudes to illness, emotional deprivation in childhood, and physical and sexual abuse are important antecedents for pelvic congestion1[1,22,23] which also make these individuals prone to the adverse effects of stress[24].

The influence of stress on the generation, maintenance, and exacerbation of CPP is shown in **Figure 1**. It illustrates the vicious circle of pain-stress-pain that is present in all individuals that suffer from chronic pain of any sort, but is of particular relevance in functional disorders such as the irritable bowel syndrome and pelvic congestion. The diagram is a valuable therapeutic tool

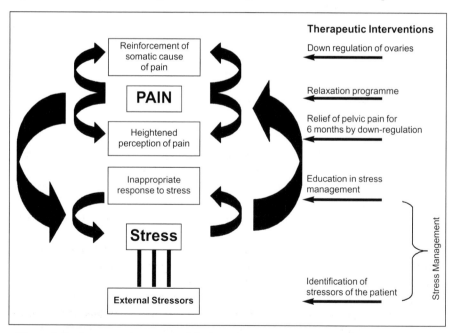

Figure 1. Explanatory scheme to explain the generation and maintenance of chronic pelvic pain and treatment

because it illustrates convincingly to patients how pain can rapidly become the major stressor leading to an increase in pain sensitivity and a disturbance of the pituitary-ovarian cycle and hence to ovarian dysfunction.

TREATMENT

The aim of treatment is to return women to an acceptable quality of life by teaching them that they are able to control and often to eliminate their pelvic pain. This is achieved by using medical therapy to induce a pain-free interval of approximately six months during which time, women, after psychological assessment, are taught stress and pain management. A variety of treatment programmes are described in the Textbook of Pain[25]. The place of specific interventions relative to psychological factors is shown graphically in **Figure 1**. It is important to reassure these women from the outset of treatment that a correct diagnosis has been made by inducing a relatively pain-free time in their lives by complete ovarian down regulation with one of the GnRH analogues. Experience has shown that down regulation most effectively suppresses CPP in women who become amenorrhoeic on this treatment. Severe menopausal symptoms, which may be quite disabling in some women, can be effectively prevented by the use of add-back HRT throughout the period of ovarian down regulation.

It is important to ensure that whilst the patient is on medical therapy, she is concurrently receiving formal stress and pain management counselling. Pearce et al.[24] showed an increase in the number of pain-free days in women who received counselling in the clinic setting who were taught relaxation techniques. Those patients who actively avoid the counselling, usually because they are not convinced that they need or can benefit from psychotherapy, are most likely to complain of continued CPP and breakthrough bleeding whilst on down regulation. Once they have completed treatment, these women are least likely to be able to control the CPP when their menses are resumed. When medical therapy comes to an end, the patient should be ready to apply the lessons she has learnt in the counselling sessions. Quite simply, this involves a progressive reduction in stressful activities such as emotionally or physically demanding jobs, applying techniques they have learnt on how to handle stress in a more appropriate manner, and the use of relaxation techniques they have learnt whenever an attack of pain is starting. In 75 per cent of patients the cause of their pain is understood and no longer dominates their lives. They find that they have learnt what brings on the pain and they can control it. In other words, they no longer fear the pain, and as the attacks of pain diminish in severity, so the quality of their lives improve. Most find, within a year of starting treatment that CPP is no longer a problem in their lives. The great value of this conservative approach to treatment is that young women become confident they can manage their pain when it inevitably recurs and that they are able to return to a normal life without having had to compromise ovarian function.

Hysterectomy combined with bilateral oophorectomy (TAH and BSO) remains a last resort for a few women. Beard *et al.*[26] found that of 778 women referred to the Pelvic Pain Clinic, only 36 of them required the operation. Most of these women were living in highly stressful situations and found that although they had become pain free on ovarian down-regulation, the CPP had returned with the same intensity after coming off treatment, which they could not manage. The operation is highly effective for relieving CPP. One year after surgery, 33 of the women were pain free, and all were well established on satisfactory HRT regimens. In summary, it is our experience that there is a small group of women of reproductive age, with CPP, whose quality of life is so poor that surgical removal of their ovaries is justified.

THE CASE FOR BILATERAL OOPHORECTOMY IN YOUNG WOMEN

Most gynaecologists believe that ovarian function should always be conserved in women under the age of 40, except when an ovary is malignant. This view has historical origins from the end of the nineteenth century when ovaries were increasingly being removed unnecessarily from young women. However, there is now an increasing body of evidence that conservation of the ovaries in women of reproductive age 'at all costs' is not always justified[27,28].

Ovaries, which are apparently histologically normal, may give rise to a number of symptoms such as chronic pelvic pain and/or severe cyclical premenstrual tension. If sufficiently severe, these symptoms may seriously interfere with the quality of life of women at a time in their lives when they are least likely to tolerate any impairment of their daily living. In a review of five women under the age of 35 years after they had had a bilateral oophorectomy for one of the above conditions by Carey[29], none of them regretted their decision. The only complaint two of them was that if only the operation had been done earlier, so much of their youth would not have been wasted. Mention has already been made of the study in which both ovaries were removed from 36 women with a mean age of 30 years as the only effective way of giving them relief from unremitting pelvic pain[26]. The point has to be made that the decision to undergo surgery was finally made by the patient and her partner and at no time was subsequently regretted. The benefit to 33 of the women was that they became pain free, resulting in a return to a normal quality of life that they had not believed possible. The authors stressed the need for careful selection and counselling of such women before undertaking such an operation, but the reality is that many sensible women in the same situation would have asked for the operation much earlier in their lives.

CHRONIC PELVIC INFLAMMATORY DISEASE

This is an important precursor of CPP because of the pelvic adhesions that may follow one or more acute attacks (see below). Detailed descriptions of the condition are given elsewhere in this book (see chapter 9).

RESIDUAL AND TRAPPED OVARIES

Peritoneal adhesions are usually asymptomatic but can cause pain if they are extensive particularly if they encapsulate an ovary, creating a 'trapped ovary'[30,31]. Surgical removal of the ovaries is the most effective way of relieving the CPP, but adhesiolysis is sometimes as effective but with the added risk of reformation of the adhesions with the return of the pain.

OVARIAN REMNANT SYNDROME

In this condition, fragments of ovary are left behind following what is frequently a difficult oophorectomy. These remnants may become active, often after 1-2 years of quiescence[30]. Typically women present with constant or cyclical pain on one or other side of the pelvis. Postcoital ache and pain after defaecation or micturition, is common. Localised tenderness can be elicited per abdomen even though there are no masses that can be felt on vaginal examination. Serum gonadotrophin concentrations are usually in the premenopausal range and are a useful diagnostic indicator. Ultrasound scanning to locate the ovarian remnant is helpful but the remnant cannot always be visualised even though it is found later at operation. Optimal treatment is by surgical removal of the ovarian remnant which requires a surgeon experienced in the procedure. Finding the remnant at laparotomy may be improved by pre-treatment of the women with clomiphene 50mg daily for ten days. The concomitant increase in pelvic pain which often follows this treatment is a further confirmation of the presence of an ovarian remnant.

VULVODYNIA

This is a severe intractable burning pain most commonly presenting in postmenopausal women which, contrary to pelvic congestion, is made worse by lying down and better by walking around. While the aetiology is unknown, it is likely to be due to a disturbance by control of the local circulation. History reveals the site of pain being more perineal than vaginal. Examination is unremarkable apart from some perineal or levator ani muscle tenderness. To date, no definitive treatment exists for this distressing condition, although pain modulation therapy may afford some relief.

ILIOINGUINAL NERVE ENTRAPMENT SYNDROME

This is a relatively common cause of chronic pelvic pain, presentation of which mimics pelvic congestion The ilioinguinal nerve originates from L1 and L2, runs forwards along the inner surface of the ilium from its dorsal origin to the ventral surface, passes through the abdominal muscle 1–2cm medial to the anterior superior iliac spine and emerges to supply the skin over the mons pubis, vulva, and front of the upper thigh. It can be compressed as it emerges through the muscles or more commonly damaged by operations in this region such as the Pfannenstiel and McBurney incisions. Typically the pain is aching and made worse by any whole body exercise, including sexual intercourse. Tenderness is increased by pressing on a point 1–2cm medial to the anterior superior iliac spine when the patient has been asked to tense her abdominal muscles. The diagnosis is confirmed by relief of the pain for 6–8 hours following injection of 10–20ml of 0.5% Bupivicaine around the course of the nerve. Division of the nerve transabdominally is an easy operation which is also the most effective way of relieving a pain that has often been present for many years[32].

IRRITABLE BOWEL SYNDROME (IBS)

This is a common non-gynaecological functional (stress linked) disturbance of the large bowel presenting with colicky abdominal pain with abdominal bloating and a bowel habit alternating between the passage of loose stools with mucus and constipation. Sufferers are polysymptomatic and have been found to be over anxious and highly sensitive[33]. Although IBS can simulate pelvic congestion, with pelvic pain, bloating and deep dyspareunia as shared symptoms, bowel dysfunction tends to predominate in the former[34]. A combination of debulking agents and psychotherapy has been shown by Svedlund et al.[35] to be the most effective treatment.

CONCLUSION

There are many conditions, both gynaecological and non-gynaecological, which can cause CPP. However, it cannot be overemphasised enough that in most cases the diagnosis can usually be made on a careful history and physical examination. One of the authors (RWB) has devised a structured questionnaire which the patient completes before coming to the clinic. This is a good way of obtaining most of the information required and for making the initial contact with the patient. Laparoscopy with good quality photographs and a vaginal ultrasound scan are also useful for providing patients with graphic evidence that helps them to understand the diagnosis. Diagnosis and treatment may be multidisciplinary particularly involving medical, surgical and psychological approaches combined with a ready resort to asking for advice from colleagues in relevant specialities.

REFERENCES

1. Kennedy SH, SJ Moore. The Initial Management of Chronic Pelvic Pain Guideline no. 41 of the Audit Committee, 2005; the Royal College of Obstetricians and Gynaecologists, London.
2. Zondervan KT, Yudkin PL, Vessey MP et al. Prevalence and incidence of chronic pelvic pain in primary care: evidence from a national general practice database Brit J Obstet Gynaecol 1999; **106:** 1149–1155.
3. Matthias SD, Kupperman M. Liberman R, et al. Chronic pelvic pain; prevalence, health related quality of life and economic correlates. Obstet Gyaecol 1996; **87:** 321–7.
4. Gillibrand P. The investigation of pelvic pain. 1981; Communication at the Scientific Meeting at the Royal College of Obstetrics and Gynaecology, London.
5. Andersch B, Milsom I. An epidemiologic study of young women with dysmenorrhoea. Am J Obstet Gynecol 1982; **44:** 655–660.
6. Skandham KP, Pandya AK, Skandhaus, et al. Menarche: prior knowledge and experience. Adolescence 1988; **23:** 149–154.
7. Gath D, Osbourn M, Burgany G et al. Psychiatric disorder and gynaecological symptoms in middle-aged women – a community survey. Brit Med J 1987; **294:** 213–218.
8. Chesney M, Tasto D. The effectiveness of behaviour modification with spasmodic and congestive dysmenorrhoea. Behaviour Research and Therapy 1975; **19:** 303–313.
9. Kennedy S, Overton C. Endometriosis and pelvic pain. Contemp Rev Obstet Gynaecol 1993; **5:** 94–97.

10. Roddick JW, Conkey G, Jacobs EJ. The hormonal response of endometrium in endometriotic implants and its relationship to symptomatology. *Am J Obstet Gynaecol* 1960; **79:** 1173–1177.

11. Ling FW. Randomized controlled trial of depot leuprolide in patients with chronic pelvic pain and clinically suspected endometriosis. *Obstet Gynecol* 1999; **93:** 51-58.

12. Vernon MW, Beard JS, Graves K, *et al.* Classification of endometriotic implants by morphological appearance and capacity to synthesize prostaglandin F. *Fertil Steril* 1986; **46:** 801–805.

13. Schmidt C. Endometrium: a reappraisal of pathogenesis and treatment. *Fertil Steril* 1985; **44:** 157–173.

14. Wardle P. In: Shaw RW ed. Conference Report: Intractable gynaecological pain – new management strategies. Royal College of Obstetricians and Gynaecologists, 1 April 1992. *Brit J Obstet Gynaecol* 1992; **12:** 355–359.

15. Royal College of Obstetricians and Gynaecologists, The investigation and management of endometriosis.Guidelines No. 24, July 2000.

16. Beard RW, Hyman JW, Pearce S, *et al.* Diagnosis of pelvic varicosities in women with chronic pelvic pain. *Lancet* 1984; **ii:** 946–949.

17. Stacey CM, Munday PE, Beard RW. Pelvic inflammatory disease, diagnosis and microbiology. 1989; Presented at Silver Jubilee Congress of Obstetrics & Gynaecology, London July 1989

18. Beard RW, Reginald PW, Wadsworth J. Clinical features of women with chronic lower abdominal pain and pelvic congestion. *Brit J Obstet Gynaecol* 1988; **95:** 153–161.

19. Adams J, Reginald PW, Franks S *et al.* Uterine size and endometrial thickness and the significance of cystic ovaries in women with pelvic pain due to congestion. *Br J of Obstet Gynaecol* 1990; **97:** 583–587.

20. Farquhar CM, Rogers V, Franks S, *et al.* A randomised controlled trial of medoxyprogesterone acetate and psychotherapy for the treatment of pelvic congestion. *Br J Obstet Gynaecol* 1989; **96:** 1153–1162.

21. Topolanski-Sierra R. Pelvic phlebotgraphy. *Am J Obstet Gynecol* 1958; **67:** 44–52.

22. Fry RPW, Beard RW,Crisp AH, *et al.* Sociopsychological factors in women with and without chronic pelvic venous congestion *J Psychosom Res* 1997; **42:** 71–85.

23. Reiter RC. A profile of women with chronic pelvic pain. *Clin Obstet Gynecol* 1990; **33:** 130–136.

24. Pearce S, Knight C, Beard RW. Pelvic pain – a common gynaecological problem. *J Psychosom Obstet Gynecol* 1982; **1:** 12–17.

25. Beard RW, Gangar KF, Pearce S. In. Wall PW, Melzack R editors. Gynaecological Pain. Textbook of Pain. 1994; Churchill Livingstone Edinburgh p. 597–814.

26. Beard RW, Kennedy RG, Gangar KF. Bilateral oophorectomy and hysterectomy in the treatment of intractable pelvic pain with pelvic congestion. *Br J Obstet Gynaecol* 1991; **98:** 988–992.

27. Reid BA, Gangar KF, Rogers V. *et al.* Long term results of bilateral oophorectomy for the treatment of chronic pelvic pain: relief of pain and special hormone replacement therapy requirements *J Obstet Gynaecol* 1996; **16:** 538–543.

28. Casson P, Hahn PM,Van Vugt DA, Reid RL. Lasting response to ovariectomy in severe intractable premenstrual syndrome. *Am J Obstet Gynecol* 1990; **162:** 99–105.

29. Carey A. *Proc Fed Int Gynec Obstet Congress,* 1997; Copenhagen.

30. Siddall-Allum J, Witherow R, Beard RW. Chronic pelvic pain caused by residual ovaries and ovarian remnants. *Br J Obstet Gynaecol* 1994; **101:** 979–985.

31. Christ JL, Lotze EC. The residual ovary syndrome. *Obstet Gynecol* 1975; **46:** 555–556.

32. Hahn L. Clinical findings and results of operative treatment in ilioinguinal nerve entrapment syndrome. *Br J Obstet Gynaecol.* 1989; **96:** 1080–1083.

33. Heaton KW. Irritable bowel syndrome: still in search of its identity. *Br Med J* 1983; **287:** 852–853.

34. Farquhar CM, Hoghton GBS, Beard RW. Pelvic pain – pelvic congestion or the irritable bowel syndrome? *Europ J Obstet Gynaecol and Reprod Biol* 1990; **37:** 71–75.

35. Svedlund J, Ottoson J-O, Sjodin I, *et al.* Controlled study of psychotherapy in irritable bowel syndrome. *Lancet* 1983; **ii:** 589–592.

CHAPTER 16

Chlamydial infections – an overview
Is it time for a wider hypothesis?

Robert S Morton
Sheffield, UK
with postscript by George Kinghorn
Royal Hallamshire Hospital, Sheffield, UK

INTRODUCTION

The genus Chlamydia may be listed as follows:

1. *C. trachomatis* with its serovars A, B, B1 and C, the cause of trachoma, the commonest cause of early blindness in the third world; its serovars D to K the cause of an increasingly common genito urinary infection with chronic and costly complications in perhaps 10 per cent; and its serovars L1, L2 and L3 the cause of lymphogranuloma venereum, now a relatively rare form of sexually transmitted disease with occasionally crippling complications.

2. *C. psittaci*, the cause of a rare form of chest infection in humans and birds particularly.

3. *C. pneumoniae*, the cause of acute pulmonary infections in humans in the western world. In some it has chronic, crippling and killing complications. Neither its prevalence nor morbidity rate have been adequately defined.

In the last half century it has become clear that while antibiotics effect clinical cure in these infections, they do not appear to eradicate the organism in many cases. In psitticosis, apparently cured humans and birds may continue to excrete organisms. In other chlamydial diseases relapses are regularly recognised. In all of the chlamydial infections listed asymptomatic periods of months or years may be followed by emergence of late overt disease.

Thus chlamydial infections can be viewed as having three stages – early, latent and late.

PATHOGENESIS OF CHLAMYDIAL INFECTIONS

Early chlamydial disease begins with serial infection of surface epithelial cells. This is effected by receptor-mediated endocytosis. Once inside a cell chlamydiae are contained within host derived endosomes. They coalesce within these cytoplasmic vacuoles. By utilising cellular material these ingested elementary bodies (EB) metamorphose into reticulate bodies (RB).

These undergo binary fission, mature and are released as EB on the natural death of the infected epithelial cell. The life cycle takes between 48 and 72 hours.

Dying epithelial cells also release cytokines[1] which prompt increased blood supply and increased permeability of basal membranes. Together these allow migration of lymph node cells, diapedesing from venules to reach the infected area and phagocytose invading and shed chlamydiae. In 1989 Shahmanesh[2] described the distinctive differential white cell count associated with acute chlamydial urethritis in men (**Table 1**). At the same time chlamydiae travel to the relevant lymph nodes. In some cases of urethritis they can be demonstrated by culture of lymph gland puncture material.

Table 1. Percentage of different inflammatory cells in urethral exudants from men with non-gonococcal urethritis (NGU) for the first time, presumed re-infections and recurrences without known sexual re-exposure.

Cells	First NGU (n = 18)	"Re-infections" (n = 19)	Other Recurrences (n= 19)
Macrophages	8.5 (5.4)*	2.0 (1.5)	2.3 (1.7)
Lymphocytes	2.6 (2.6)	1.6 (1.8)	1.6 (1.3)
Polymorphs	89.0 (7.0)	96.3 (2.3)	97.2 (2.3)

* n < 0.01 compared with both other groups.

Figures are mean (SD) obtained from May-Grünweld-Giemsa and Papanicolaou smears.

Complete phagocytosis is accomplished mainly by neutrophils. In addition to phagocytosis lymphocytes play a variety of roles, not least producing gamma interferons (IFN-gamma)[3] which amongst other functions improve the ability of monocytes and macrophages to ingest chlamydiae. There is some evidence that IFN-gamma, depending on concentration, may play a role in chlamydia persistence and reactivation.

Immune responses vary in degree between the chlamydial infections. Cellular responses predominate in trachoma and genito urinary disease. Serological responses are recognised only in *C. pneumoniae* disease and in lymphogranuloma venereum. Research on this aspect regarding responses to *C. trachomatis* serovars D-K continues.

In the late stages of chlamydial infections cellular immune responses are generally described as delayed hypersensitivity. It manifests leucocytes, lymphoid follicles, plasma cell infiltrations, fibroblasts and macrophages. In terms of clearing or containing antigenic material these responses are effective. But this occurs at a price. Extensive fibrosis produces paradoxical healing. Hence the blindness of trachoma, the pelvic scarring in lymphogranuloma venereum, the bone, joint, fascia and crippling scarring of fallopian tubes in genito urinary disease and of no less importance; the chronic, crippling and killing cardiovascular late forms of *C. pneumoniae* infections[4,5].

EARLY FORMS OF CHLAMYDIAL INFECTIONS

Trachoma presents as a persistent acute, bilateral conjunctivitis. Lymphogranuloma venereum, by contrast, presents as an evanescent genital sore lasting only a few days when the disease is then manifest in inguinal and pelvic glands. *C. psittaci* and *C. pneumoniae* both cause acute respiratory disease such as bronchopneumonia or pneumonia. Early genito urinary disease in men presents as acute anterior urethritis with discharge varying from the slight mucoid to the profuse purulent. In females, endocervicitis, with or without symptoms and a variable degree of discharge is usual. Urethritis may also occur in females. Proctitis may affect both sexes.

DIAGNOSIS

In the case of trachoma clinical diagnosis may be confirmed by culture or more modern tests. Nature's ability to clear antigenic material is thought to depend on the original organismal load and its duration. T. cell responses are depressed in persistent trachoma. Diagnosis of lymphogranuloma venereum generally calls for laboratory testing of inguinal lymph gland material and perhaps more than one lymphogranuloma venereum complement fixation test (LGVCFT).

The serological test for *C. pneumoniae* infection is commonly deployed in departments dealing with infectious diseases. So far as can be gathered it is more commonly used in cardiovascular departments in Scandinavia than elsewhere. In Finland *C. pneumoniae's* role in atheroma[6], in degenerative aortic stenosis[7] and in infra-renal aneurysms[8] has been defined.

It is in the genito urinary infections that laboratory tests for chlamydiae have been most thoroughly developed. From culture and monoclonal antibody testing, progress has been through polymerase and ligase chain reactions to a transcription mediated amplification test as the new gold standard. Thus reliable testing can now be applied to urine and self-taken genital swabs. In so-called first attacks of non-gonococcal urethritis *C. trachomatis* can be identified in around 70 per cent. These modern tests have revealed that some symptomless and signless patients may be carriers. There is in such cases, need for careful history taking and clinical examinations that aim to exclude asymptomatic complications such as prostatitis and salpingitis.

COMPLICATIONS OF TRACHOMA

Systemic complications of trachoma are virtually unknown. This contrasts with ophthalmia neonatorum due to *C. trachomatis* serovars D-K where pneumonia is recognised as an occasional complication. Joint and neurological complications are associated with serovars L1, L2 and L3. Application of the LGVCFT in a West Indian female with idiopathic multiple arthritis proved revealing. The persistent excretion of *C. psittaci* in "cured" humans and birds has led to destruction of exotic birds and closure of public aviaries.

In genito urinary disease, contiguous spread is common. In men, spread to the posterior urethra may be followed by chronic prostatitis or acute unilateral epididymitis. Only recently has *C. trachomatis* been found in prostatic material and then only in 4 of 135 cases[9]. In epididymitis the organism can be found in needle puncture specimens of the affected organ. Canalicular spread from the endocervix is common. As many as 10 per cent of infected women may suffer from endometritis followed by acute, subacute or chronic asymptomatic salpingitis. Recurrent acute and subacute attacks are recognised. Between 1 and 2 per cent of men with NGU develop Reiter's syndrome, partial or complete, with multiple arthritis, conjunctivitis or iritis and skin lesions. All of these have revealed *C. trachomatis* or its antigenic remnants[10,11]. Another[12,13] early complication is Fitz-Hugh Curtis syndrome which consists of acute peritonitis and peri-hepatitis with a variable degree of ascites. It can occur without evidence of pelvic infection. That the syndrome is due to *C. trachomatis* was described by Shanahan in 1990[14]. With the organisms he cultured in specimens from humans he gave mice peritonitis. He subsequently "cured" both humans and mice without surgery, that is, with antibiotics only. At follow-up Shanahan found chlamydiae in the spleens of both "cured" humans and mice.

TREATMENT OF EARLY CHLAMYDIAL INFECTIONS

Antibiotics have been effectively applied to all forms, generally for a week or longer in uncomplicated cases and up to three weeks or longer in complicated cases. The application of a wide variety of antibiotics has been well-documented in men with non-gonococcal urethritis. From the early 1950s to the late 1980s these effected high "cure" rates as estimated by clinical follow-up for three months. In the last decade a single dose treatment with azithromycin has become increasingly popular. Follow-up in these cases has been by laboratory testing after four weeks. One study found positive polymerase chain reaction tests in 5 of 98 females[15].

RECURRENT EARLY INFECTION

Early recurrence is well-recognised in all forms of chlamydial disease. It is seen as relapse and this applies to both treated humans and laboratory infected animals.

In lymphogranuloma venereum suspected relapses can generally be confirmed by rising titres of the LGVCFT. In recurrences of trachoma the relevant serovars are rarely detected. It is otherwise in suspected recurrences of chlamydial pneumonia. One report found the organism in 19 of 24 such cases[16].

Recurrence rates of NGU in the 1950s to 1980s were generally above 15 per cent at three months follow-up. Of 221 cases followed up by Munday for a year, recurrence occurred in 45 (20 per cent)[17], A three year follow-up of treated females showed a 38 per cent recurrence rate[18]. Little wonder then that one clinician who followed treated males for 5 years declared "Treatment helps – but not much." (Fowler, personal communication.)

In the last decade, after a single dose of azithromycin, application of the polymerase chain reaction to 98 females gave positive results in 5 (5.1 per cent)[15]. Three months clinical follow-up in similarly treated males gave a recurrence rate of 12 per cent[19]. One attempt to minimise recurrences of NGU compared results of triple tetracycline given for one and three weeks. The recurrence rate at three months was halved[20].

Hurst *et al.* treated groups of mice infected peritoneally with the organisms of lymphogranuloma venereum, psittacosis and trachoma for 200 consecutive days. This eliminated recurrences. At post mortem he found chlamydiae in spleens and livers[21-23].

THE NATURE OF RECURRENCES

Only in NGU is the nature of recurrences questioned. Some clinicians see such cases as re-infections even when re-exposure has been denied. That recurrences are more likely to be relapses is supported by a variety of clinical observations. Firstly, the sexual histories given by the men contrasts with those given by men with recurrence of gonorrhoea. Evans has given details[24]. Second, are the findings of Hurst *et al.* (*vide supra*) and thirdly, four out of six studies show that treatment of sex partners does not influence recurrence rates of NGU in men[25-30].

A persistent and striking feature of recurrences of NGU is that yields of positive diagnostic tests for *C. trachomatis* are usually half those found in initial attacks, for example, 35 per cent as against 70 per cent. Shamanesh *et al.* in 1996[31] reported the accompanying differential white cell counts in initial and recurrent episodes in both chlamydia positive and chlamydia negative cases. The lowest lymphocyte counts were in chlamydia negative recurrences. It is a well-established truism that re-infection with an organism previously subjected to primary immune responses is more assertively, more speedily and hence more effectively dealt with by a secondary immune response. This is attributed to the establishment of memory, helper and killer cells as part of the primary immune response. The poor yield of positive tests for *C. trachomatis* in recurrences can be seen as nature's success.

Does it matter whether recurrences originate exogenously or endogenously? This question is prompted by the observation that positive tests for *C. trachomatis* are more common in men with gonorrhoea than in men with NGU. Formerly, prompt treatment and cure of gonorrhoea was followed after some days by post-gonococcal NGU. This was clinically acceptable; it reflected differing incubation periods. In modern times, tests for both the gonococcus and the *C. trachomatis* are carried out at the initial attendance. Commonly both are found positive. Presumably some men have been carriers (*vide supra*) and others are incubating, one of two concomitantly acquired diseases. Could there be a third reason? Is it possible that the gonococcus has unmasked latent chlamydial infection? We know that any form of urethritis can reveal asymptomatic HIV infection, a condition in which some 80 per cent of the organismal load exists in the lymphatic system[32,33].

This explanation can be extended to explain why bacillary dysentery may precipitate Reiter's syndrome. It is noteworthy that dual infections are said to account for the observation that recurrences of PID respond better to combined treatment by an antibiotic and metronidazole. The same treatment approach has been useful in recurrent chlamydial chest infections[34].

There seems to be little doubt that a latent stage is a serious reality in some chlamydial infections. Before trying to define its nature let us look at the late overt stages.

LATE OVERT DISEASE

The course of late complications usually follows a long period of surreptitious and often symptomless and signless progress. Trachoma ends with blindness due to chronic low grade infection and scarring. In lymphogranuloma venereum the lower bowel is involved in the progressive scarring of lymph channels. "Pencil" stools result. In women progressive and recurrent episodes of pelvic infection due to serovars D-K commonly produce scarring that results in ectopic pregnancies and sterility. In men bone, joint and fascial deformities are common. Host genetics such as the Class 1 allele HLA-A31 and HLA-B27 may be associated in females and males respectively.

Late cardiovascular and pulmonary complications of *C. pneumoniae* infection have recently been described. The organism is frequently present in arthromatous plaques[4], in cases of degenerative aortic stenosis[7] and in infra-renal abdominal aortic aneurysms[8]. All such cases were also positive by the specific serological test for *C. pneumoniae* infection[4,7,8]. It is of interest to note that while antibiotics as well as immune responses may succeed in effecting some degree of clinical cure by reducing the organismal load in early overt disease, neither is as effective a feature in the late stages[35,36]. This is particularly so in *C. pneumoniae* infections. Even when antibiotics have been taken for a year there is little or no apparent benefit[37]. Chronic and continuous cardiovascular disease activity persists and proves to be both crippling and killing.

THE NATURE OF LATENT CHLAMYDIAL INFECTIONS

From what we know, the most likely siting for latent chlamydial infection is the lymphatic system, including the spleen. If this is true, how are chlamydiae held in a state of suspended animation for months or years? How do these organisms remain capable of maintaining continuous pathological activity elsewhere for long periods? How are chlamydiae transported to precipitate early and late overt complications?

It is suggested that the work of Shahmanesh *et al* in 1996 gives a clue[31]. They accorded a dominant role to macrophages in all forms of immune cellular responses to chlamydiae. Macrophages are descendants of monocytes which are capable of harbouring chlamydiae for 10 days. Macrophages are also capable of harbouring chlamydiae and they have a life cycle of a month. Macrophages also circulate freely, some taking up residence in spleen, lungs and serous cavities as well as lymph nodes. They are attracted to sites of inflammation. They are recognised as persisting in inguinal and pelvic glands in lymphogranuloma venereum. Their presence in abundance has been noted in early *C. pneumoniae* infections[38].

From the abundance of clinical observations now available it has recently been hypothesised that macrophages parasitise chlamydiae. This truncated state of phagocytosis appears to protect the organisms from both immune responses and antibiotics. The effect of both is confined to action only on the death of each macrophage and the shedding of EB and before they can be ingested by a new generation of macrophages. This serial process maintains latency and no less a low grade but progressive late disease process which ends in overt manifestations. The accompanying bio-chemical or molecular responses which support the hypothesis are detailed[39].

Thus all chlamydial diseases may be seen as having three stages – early, latent or late. In many, late manifestations result from years of persistent, low grade but progressive 'delayed hypersensitivity' ending with paradoxical healing causing chronic, crippling or in some, killing end results. There are memories here of syphilis.

THE FUTURE

Lymphogranuloma venereum and psittacosis are currently well controlled. Trachoma prevalence diminishes where running water and improved personal hygiene are made available. The World Health Organisation plans to eliminate trachoma by the year 2020. The plan will utilise a donation of azithromycin by Pfizer valued at £41 million.

In the UK we are about to introduce a nationwide screening programme to detect *C. trachomatis* serovars D-K. The emphasis is on prevention by early diagnosis and treatment of both index cases and their contacts. Consideration regarding which of the infected should be held in long term follow-up remains to be determined. Family histories may indicate those genetically predisposed to late overt disease: HLA studies should be considered. Those presenting with idiopathic iritis and found to have chronic prostatitis and/or sacro-ileitis should be considered as should all cases of salpingitis. Annual review of cases of Reiter's syndrome is already a standard procedure in some departments of genito urinary medicine.

While genito urinary chlamydial disease is believed to cost the UK £50 million per annum, no such estimate is available for *C. pneumoniae* infection. Its chronic, crippling and killing process is unlikely to cost less. Consideration of a preventive approach is indicated. There appears to be potential in the availability of a serological test for this chlamydial condition from an early stage. Its application to young people, that is, at a time when antibiotics may be effective, offers a chance to prevent cardiovascular complications. Widespread serological testing for syphilis in the 20th century was both health and wealth promoting.

POSTSCRIPT

Robbie Morton was a major figure in British venereology throughout the second half of the 20th century. Post-retirement, he developed a deep interest in chlamydial infections which was maintained until his death in 2003. He did not, like many, view Ct Dk infection as a simple acute condition always easily curable with antibiotics, but more as a potential chronic pathogen that could lie dormant and then be reactivated by a variety of stimuli including the acquisition of other acute STI.

Further evidence suggesting that chlamydia may develop latency has emerged recently. *In vitro* persistence is well established and is characterised by altered growth and common ultrastructural traits. It can be induced by exposure of cell cultures to antibiotics, including ampicilllin and erythromycin; by nutrient depletion, especially of glucose, amino acids, and iron; and by cytokines, especially gamma interferon[40].

In vivo persistence is less well established but there have been observations of altered morphological forms similar to those observed *in vitro*, of detection of chlamydial macromolecules, including m-RNA, in the absence of organism cultivability[41] and of clinical antibiotic resistance to fluoroquinolones[42]. Although it is difficult to rule out reinfection in sexually active adults, the repeated detection of the same genotypic strain of *C. trachomatis* from the same individual suggests the possibility of reactivation of latent infection. In tissue samples from individuals with chronic manifestations of chlamydial disease, the same pattern of protein expression has been found as occurs in *in vitro* models of chalmydial latency[43]. One such marker is high concentrations of heat shock protein-60 relative to MOMP[44].

The spontaneously occurring development of latency within cells of the monocyte-macrophage series supports the view expressed by Dr Morton of the potential for chlamydia to develop latency within lymphoid tissues. What is less clear is how easy and how often such latent infections may be reactivated to cause acute and chronic fibrosing manifestations of chlamydial infection.

Several authors have supported his view that the well-established biphasic development cycle unique to chlamydia now warrants the addition of a third persistent latency stage[45]. This represents a critical survival mechanism for the organism. Future research involving joint teams of clinicians and laboratory-based scientists using sophisticated molecular approaches will help to further elucidate the potential role of chlamydial latency in the pathogenesis of chronic disease manifestations within the genito urinary, respiratory, cardiovascular and other systems.

Of paramount concern to clinicians is whether current treatment regimes can always be relied upon to eradicate infection[46]. The fear is that, in at least some patients, especially where suboptimal antibiotic dosage and duration of treatment occur, latency rather than eradication may result. This may leave the individual susceptible to the future development of acute reactivation or ongoing chronicity, and transmissibility to new partners.

As yet, we have no definite answers from the national chlamydia-screening programme as to how often screening should be undertaken in the high-risk age group[47]. Whether or not the repeat finding of chlamydia positivity represents reinfection or relapse, an increasing number of clinicians recommend that further testing after treatment is desirable. Timing of retesting is uncertain, but clinicians on both sides of the Atlantic are suggesting that this might be best delayed until 3-6 months after initial treatment[48].

There remain many challenges to improved understanding of the natural history and pathogenesis of infections from the Chlamydiae genus and the most effective methods of combating their associated human and animal disease.

George Kinghorn

REFERENCES

1. Rasmussen SJ, Eckmann I, Quayle AJ, *et al.* Secretion of proinflammatory cytokines by epithelial cells in response to chlamydial infection suggests a central role for epithelial cells in chlamydial pathogenesis. *J Clin Invest* 1997; **99:** 77–87.
2. Shahmanesh M. Characteristics of inflammatory cells in urethral smears from men with non-gonococcal urethritis. *Genitourin Med* 1989; **65:** 18–21.
3. Lampe MF, Wilson CB, Bevan MJ and Starnbach MN. Gamma interferon production by cytotoxic T lymphocytes as required for resolution of *Chlamydia trachomatis* infection. *Infect Immun* 1998; **66:** 5457–61.
4. Mendall MA, Carrington D, Strachan D *et al. Chlamydia pneumoniae:* risk factors for seropositivity and association with coronary heart disease. *Infect* 1995; **30:** 121–8.
5. Saikku P, Matilla K, Nieminen MS, *et al.* Serological evidence of an association of a novel chlamydia TWAR with chronic coronary heart disease and acute myocardial infarction. *Lancet* 1988; **2:** 963-6.
6. Saikku P, Leinonen M, Tenkanen L, *et al.* Chronic *C. pneumoniae* disease in Helsinki Heart Study. *Ann Intern Med* 1992; **116:** 273–8.
7. Juvonen J, Juvonen T, Laurila A, *et al.* Can degenerative aortic valve stenosis be related to persistent *Chlamydia pneumoniae* infection? *Ann Intern Med* 1998; **128:** 741–4.
8. Petersen E, Boman J, Persson K, *et al. Chlamydia pneumoniae* in human abdominal aortic aneurysms. *Eur J Vascular Endovascular Surgery* 1998; **15:** 138–42.
9. Kreiger JN, Riley DE, Roberts MC, Bergen RE. Prokaryotic DNA sequences in patients with chronic idiopathic prostatitis. *J Clin Microbiol* 1996; **34:** 3120–8.
10. Gerard HC, Branigan PJ, Schumacher HR Jr, *et al.* Synovial *C. trachomatis* in patients with reactive Reiter's syndrome are viable but show aberrant gene expressions. *J Rheumatol* 1998; **25:** 734–42.
11. Morrison RP. Persistent *C. trachomatis* infection: *in vitro* phenomenon or *in vivo* trigger of reactive arthritis? (Editorial) *J Rheumatol* 1998; **25:** 610–12.
12. Muller-Schoob JW, Wana S-P, Murgine J, *et al. C. trachomatis* as possible cause of peritonitis, perihepatitis in young women. *Br Med J* 1978; **1:** 1022–4.
13. Eschenvach DA. Sexually Transmitted Diseases. New York: McGraw Hill, 1984; 633–8.
14. Shanahan D. Cloak and dagger – studies of chlamydial peritonitis in humans and mice. Paper read at meeting of the Medical Society for the Study of Venereal Disease, London. 30 November 1990.

15. Hillis SD, Coles FB, Lichfield B. *et al.* Doxycycline and azithromycin for prevention of chlamydial persistence or recurrence one month after treatment of women. A use-effectiveness study in public health. *Sex Trans Dis* 1998; **25;** 5–11.
16. Kaufpinen MJ, Saikku P, Kujala P. *et al.* Clinical picture of community acquired *Chlamydia pneumoniae* pneumonia requiring hospital treatment: a comparison between chlamydia and pneumococcal pneumonia. *Thorax* 1996; **51:** 185–90.
17. Munday PK. Persistent and recurrent NGU. In: Taylor-Robinson D. ed. *Clinical Problems in Sexually Transmitted Disease.* Dordrecht: Martinus Nijhof, 1985; 15–35.
18. Blythe MJ, Katz BP, Battergar BE *et al.* Recurrent genitourinary chlamydial infections in sexually active female adolescents. *J Pediatr* 1992; **121:** 487–93.
19. Dhar J, Arya OP, Timmins DJ. *et al.* The efficacy of azithromycin versus doxycycline in the treatment of non-gonococcal urethritis (abstract) *MSSVD Meeting,* Dublin 1992.
20. Bhattacharya MN, Morton RS. Long term triple tetracycline therapy in non-specific urethritis. *Br J Vener Dis* 1971; **147: 266**–9.
21. Hurst EW, Landquist JK, Melvin P. The therapy of experimental psittacosis and lymphogranuloma venereum. *Br J Pharm Chemother* 1950; **5:** 611–24.
22. Hurst EW, Landquist JK, Melvin P, *et al.* The therapy of experimental psittacosis and lymphogranuloma venereum. *Br J Pharm Chemother* 1953; **8:** 197–305.
23. Morton RS. A reappraisal of non-specific genital infection with reference to the work of the late Dr E Weston-Hurst. *Br J Vener Dis* 1983; **59:** 394–6.
24. Evans BA. The role of tetracyclines in the treatment of non-specific urethritis. *Br J Vener Dis* 1978; **54:** 107–11.
25. Woolley PD, Kinghorn GR, Talbot MD *et al.* Efficiency of combined metronidazole and triple tetracycline therapy in treatment of NGU. *Int J Sex Trans Dis AIDS* 1990; **1:** 35–7.
26. Evans BA. The role of tetracyclines in the treatment of non-specific urethritis. *Br J Vener Dis* 1977; **53:** 40–3.
27. Helmy N, Fowler W. Intensive and prolonged tetracycline therapy in non-specific urethritis. *Br J Vener Dis* 1975; **51:** 336–9.
28. Rosedale N. Female consorts of men with NGU. *Br J Vner Dis* 1959; **35:** 245–8.
29. Fitzgerald MR. Effect of epidemiological treatment of contacts in preventing recurrence of NGU. *Br J Vener Dis* 1984; **60:** 312–15.
30. Woolley PD, Wilson JD, Kinghorn GR. Epidemiological treatment of sexual contacts prevents recurrence of NGU. *Genitourin Med* 1987; **63:** 384–5.
31. Shahmanesh M, Pandit PG, Pound R. Urethral lymphocyte isolations in non-gonococcal urethritis. *Genitourin Med* 1996; **72:** 362–4.
32. Cohen MS, Hoffman JF, Royce RA *et al.* Reduction of concentration of HIV-1 in semen after treatment of urethritis: implications for prevention of sexual transmission of HIV-1. *Lancet* 1997; **349:** 1863–73.
33. Atkins Ml, Carlin EM, Emery VC, *et al.* Fluctuations of HIV load in semen of HIV positive patients with newly acquired sexually transmitted diseases. *Br Med J* 1996; **313:** 341–2.
34. Leiberman D, Schoeffer F, Dolder I, *et al.* Multiple pathogens in adult patients admitted with community-acquired pneumonia: a one-year prospective study of 346 consecutive patients. *Thorax* 1996; **51:** 179–84.
35. Jackson LA, Nicholas LS, Hickbert SR, *et al.* Lack of association between first myocardial infarction and past use of erythromycin, tetracycline, and doxycycline. *Emerg Infect Dis* 1999; **5:** 281–4.
36. Gupta S, Leathens EW. Carrington D, *et al.* Elevated *C. pneumoniae* antibodies cardiovascular events, and azithromycin in male survivors of myocardial infection.*Circulation* 1997; **96:** 404–7.
37. Sinisalo J, Mattila K. Nieminen MS *et al.* The effect of prolonged doxycyline therapy on *Chlamydia pneumoniae* serological markers, coronary heart disease risk, and forearm based nitric oxide production. *J Antimicrobiol Chemother* 1998; **41:** 85–92.

38. Johnson JD, Hand WL, Francis JB *et al.* Antibiotic uptake by alveolar macrophages. *J Lab Clin Med* 1980; **95:** 429–39.
39. Morton RS, Kinghorn GR. Genitourinary chlamydial infection: a reappraisal and hypothesis. *Int J STD & AIDS.* 1999; **10:** 765–775.
40. Harper A, Pogson CI, Jones ML, Pearce JH. Chlamydial development is adversely affected by minor changes in amino acid supply, blood plasma amino acid levels, and glucose deprivation. *Infect Immun.* 2000; **68:** 1457–1464.
41. Belland RJ, Zhong G, Crane DD, *et al.* Genomic transcriptional profiling of the developmental cycle of *Chlamydia trachomatis. Proc Natl Acad Sci. USA* 2003; **100:** 8478–8483.
42. Dreses-Werringloer U, Padubrin I, Jürgens-Saathoff B, *et al.* Persistence of *Chlamydia trachomatis* is induced by ciprofloxacin and ofloxacin *in vitro. Antimicrob Agents Chemother.* 2000; **44:** 3288–3297.
43. Dean D, Suchland RJ, Stamm WE. Evidence for Long-Term Cervical Persistence of *Chlamydia trachomatis* by *omp1* Genotyping. *J Infectious Diseases* 2000; **182:** 909–16.
44. Gérard HC, Whittum-Hudson JA, Schumacher HR, Hudson AP. Differential expression of three *Chlamydia trachomatis* hsp60-encoding genes in active vs. persistent infections. *Microb Pathog.* 2004; **36:** 35–39.
45. Hogan RJ, Mathews SA, Mukhopadhyay S, Summersgill JT, Timms P. Chlamydial Persistence: beyond the Biphasic Paradigm . *Infection and Immunity* 2004; **72:** 1843–1855.
46. Binet R, Maurelli AT. Frequency of Spontaneous Mutations That Confer Antibiotic Resistance in Chlamydia spp. *Antimicrob Agents Chemother.* 2005; **49:** 2865–2873.
47. LaMontagne DS, Baster K, Emmett L. Determinants of Chlamydia reinfection: The role of partner change and treatment. Abstract TO-405. 18th meeting of ISSTDR, Amsterdam. July 2005
48. Wright C, Middleton D. Subsequent Sexually Transmitted Infections in Women infected with *Chlamydia trachomatis* and *Neisseria gonorrhoeae.* Abstract TO-404. 18th meeting of ISSTDR, Amsterdam. July 2005